T0074119

Low Level X Window Programming

Ross J. Maloney

Low Level X Window Programming

An Introduction by Examples

 Springer

Dr. Ross J. Maloney
Yenolam Corporation
Booragoon, WA
Australia

ISBN 978-3-319-74249-6   ISBN 978-3-319-74250-2   (eBook)
https://doi.org/10.1007/978-3-319-74250-2

Library of Congress Control Number: 2018931452

Printed on acid-free paper

This Springer imprint is published by the registered company Springer International Publishing AG part of Springer Nature
The registered company address is: Gewerbestrasse 11, 6330 Cham, Switzerland

Preface

This book is the missing part of most X Window programming books, the part which others either neglect or skip over quickly. Those omissions are the subject material of this book.

Most books on X Window programming cover Xlib in passing. They pass on to use of toolkits for it is they which are most commonly used to write X Window programs. Such toolkits include Athena, Xt, Motif, GTK, Qt, among a number of others. Toolkits are used for they produce a finished graphics result in less time and can be used without entirely understanding what is going on behind the scenes. Low-level programming in X Window is analogous to assembly language programming. Whereas in assembler programming a knowledge of the computer hardware is required, in low-level X Window programming a knowledge of how the X Window System operated is required. From the perspective taken here, X toolkits are high-level languages and are not considered here. This contrasts to the standard X Window programming book.

With respect to these levels, brief consideration is given to the protocol underlying X Window. This is the equivalent of machine language. This is not a practical way of coding an X Window program but is covered as foundation material. An increased level of abstraction and removal from hardware detail is provided by Xlib which occupies most of this book. An overview of Xcb which has recently appeared as a replacement of Xlib is also included.

The philosophy in this book is to link the programming which produces outcomes for the program's user to the operation of X Window. The Xlib library functions have a direct connection to the messages passed between the client and server, the two main elements of an X Window system. This message connection means being able to write graphics programs which can perform the graphics operations the fastest possible under X. But to achieve such speed requires more knowledge. Without that knowledge, the required speed increase above that obtainable via a toolkit may not be obtained, let alone nothing appearing at all. More time is required in coding using Xlib than a toolkit. Whether a possible increase in execution speed balances out the longer coding time is a value judgement.

Knowledge is acquired here. Writing a program in Xlib is exercising knowledge of how the X Window system works; how the pieces are connected together to produce the total outcome. The aim of this book is to assist the reader in acquiring knowledge of using the Xlib library.

A *discuss and show me* style is used here. A discussion of the concepts is given, and then, those discussions are used to write a Xlib program. The output produced is shown together with the listing of the program. Exercises are then included to extend the discussion and to encourage the reader to reflect on the concepts just covered. Each program is written in a standard style and is as short in length as possible.

The aim is to equip the reader to produce Xlib programs to support many needs. X Window is present on computers ranging in performance from supercomputers to personal computers. The programmer engaged in different computing environments, application realms, and target end-users needs to bring knowledge specific to that environment, realm, and end-user type, to be successful. A toolbox (nor kit) of displaying colours, patterns, geometric shapes, text, and input control by mouse and keyboard each in an efficient and effective manner will help their adaptation. All these tasks can be done using a toolkit but done the way the toolkit is set up to do it. The reader will be exposed to handling all those tasks in this book to do them in an individual way.

Although all the programs contained in this book were developed on a laptop running Linux, they should carry over to all X Window environments.

Each chapter is designed to stand alone although there are some cross-references within the sections of a chapter and between chapters. The chapters are arranged in the order of increasing complexity.

This book does not provide a reference to the functions of the Xlib library, nor does it use all those functions. It shows how to combine those Xlib functions to produce functioning programs. References such as *Xlib Reference Manual* edited by Adrian Nye and published by O'Reilly & Associates, Inc. in 1993 provide detail of all Xlib functions together with their parameters, description of purpose and error returns. The reader should have access to such a source while reading and working through the examples contained here for obtaining a greater depth of knowledge. The book *Xlib Programming Manual* by Adrian Nye, published by O'Reilly & Associates, Inc. in 1995, could be used to advantage to put Xlib into the context of the overall X Window system's component parts. This book takes a subset of the components covered in the Xlib Programming Manual and puts them together into working programs. As with those references, this book considers release of the X Window software.

Thank You

The existence of this book is a result of the open source initiative. All text and programs were written using vim. The programs were converted from source code to executable code using the gcc compiler and associated libraries. The photo editor xv was used to obtain the screenshots which show the programs operating. All programs, text preparation and associated experimentation were done on a Linux system. The prepared text was typeset using LaTeX through many iterations. Without the X Window system and its associated libraries and utility programs, there would have been no subject matter and environment to elaborate upon.

To the countless people who brought those elements into existence, maintain them, and make them available, may I express my thanks.

Reader Background Assumed

This book is aimed at those readers interested in understanding how to program X Window at a low level. The majority of that level considered here is Xlib with the addition of Xcb and the X Window protocol itself.

It is assumed the reader knows the C language and has used X Windows to run application programs. A programming knowledge of one or more of the X toolkits available would be a further advantage so as to offer a contrast to using Xlib. Familiarity with the contents of, and access to a copy of *Xlib Programming Manual for Version 11* by Adrian Nye, published in 1995 by O'Reilly & Associates, Inc. ISBN 1-56592-002-3, and *Xlib Reference Manual* edited by Adrian Nye, published by O'Reilly & Associates, Inc. in 1993, ISBN 1-56592-006-6, is assumed. These volumes provide essential auxiliary information and detail.

The best advantage of this material is obtained by writing programs and debugging those programs. The examples and the exercises are starting points. The reader should have access to an X Window system which can be used for this practice.

Perth, Australia   Ross J. Maloney
November 2017

Contents

Chapter 1
Preliminaries

Armed with the knowledge gained from the examples in this book as a guide, and
a copy of Nye (1995), and particularly Nye (1993), useful programs can be written
using Xlib. The argument against doing so is the use of toolkits makes programming
easier and quicker, and the result is visually appealing. Although the programming
may be quicker to write using a toolkit due to the written application code being
shorter in length than when using by using Xlib, its execution time generally is slower.
Toolkits are the analogue of a compiler while Xlib is the analogue of an assembler,
and to squeeze the most out of hardware, an assembler is the better choice but at the
cost of programming effort. Xlib programs generally use fewer CPU instructions and
make more efficient use of the X Protocol than toolkit programs do. So if a program
is to have large usage, then the use of Xlib instead of a toolkit may be a better design
decision across the lifetime of the program.

Generally, the appearance on the screen of a toolkit implemented program is characteristic of the toolkit, with little opportunity to change it. Much thought goes into
that appearance during the design of the toolkit with the consequence that appearance
becomes desired. In the examples used in the following chapters, the appearance of
buttons, scrollbars, etc., may be thought of as bland. But what is demonstrated in
those examples is the basic scaffolding with complication associated with beautifi-
cation deliberately avoided. In those chapters, brief mention is made of complicating
factors which could be used to overcome such blandness if thought necessary.

This approach of augmenting a program using Xlib to obtain results readily available from a toolkit has disadvantages and advantages. The clear disadvantage is the
increase in complexity and length of the code which must be prepared. An advantage
is the desired *features* which might be available in one toolkit but not in another can
be implemented. In general terms, mixing of toolkits is not permitted: the features
in one toolkit are isolated to the environment of that toolkit.

The advantage of Xlib is it implements the *mechanism rather than policy* facet of
the X Window System design. To take good advantage of the design facet, Xlib needs
to be put into perspective of the larger X Window environment and to borrow from

© Springer International Publishing AG, part of Springer Nature 2017
R. J. Maloney, *Low Level X Window Programming*,
https://doi.org/10.1007/978-3-319-74250-2_1

it, which reverses the process whereby an environment has built upon Xlib. Much has been learnt on how to effectively use windows to make good human–computer communications since the 1987 introduction of X11. During this same time, Xlib has remained relatively static due to the low-level support it provides. On to this foundation, such advances can be grafted. To do this requires know-how.

But Xlib may not be the only approach to provide low-level graphics programming removed from the constraints of a toolkit. Xcb can offer an alternative. Xcb is a recent and evolving project aimed at replacing Xlib or to be used in combination with it. It is designed to give the programmer closer access to the X protocol than Xlib. By attempting to do such, it aims to make fuller access of the X Window communications and graphics capacity while removing some of the overhead it perceives at present in Xlib. Included here is a basic introduction to Xcb programming to contrast it to Xlib programming.

Since its roots in Project Athena as described in Champine (1991), the X Window system has evolved by being released as a number of versions. Each version has introduced different features. Version 11 is considered here.

1.1   The Place of the X Protocol

Xlib works directly on the X Protocol. The X Protocol is the information which is exchanged between the client and the server of the X Window system. It is the protocol which enables X to work. It is the existence of this protocol for information interchange which enables the client and the server of X Window to be on the same computer or separate computers connected by a network. The client program makes requests by exchanging protocol packets with the server program, using whatever connection path between the client and server programs involved. The more general this connection path software, the more general can be the distribution of the client and server programs. If the connection is through networking software supporting a local area network (LAN), then the X Window clients and servers involved in a particular X Window program must be within the computers linked by a LAN. If the networking software is capable of accessing the Internet, then the X Window clients and servers can be distributed across the Internet.

The association of the X Protocol and Xlib is analogous to the association between computer machine language and assembler language, and toolkits and compiler languages, as indicated by:

$$
\begin{array}{ccc}
\text{Toolkits} & \Longleftrightarrow & \text{compiler language} \\
\updownarrow & & \updownarrow \\
\text{Xlib} & \Longleftrightarrow & \text{assembler language} \\
\updownarrow & & \updownarrow \\
\text{X Protocol} & \Longleftrightarrow & \text{machine language}
\end{array}
$$

This arrangement shows an increasing complexity in progressing from top to bottom layer along each leg of this stack. Each layer embodies a level of removal from the detail of the implementation.

Knowing the X Protocol of X Window is analogous to knowing the combination of 0s and 1s which control the operation of the hardware of a particular computer (its machine language). Although this protocol is complex and difficult to understand, it's understanding leads to the most complete appreciation of way in which the required execution is performed. Xlib provides a means of obtaining a particular combination of 0s and 1s to produce a particular X Window function, just as an assembler language produces the combination of 0s and 1s which implements the instruction set of a particular computer. Just as a particular instruction given in an assembler language program generates the bytes corresponding to a particular instruction for a particular computer hardware, so a particular Xlib function produces the bytes which implement its correspondence in the X protocol. The toolkits, such as GTK, Athena, Motif, also use this protocol but use collections of protocol packets to perform their function. This corresponds to compiled languages such as C, Fortran, Ada in which they provide a higher-level of abstraction of the computing process. However, in both the toolkit and compiled language case, the written programs are converted by software to the lowest level elements of their particular leg of this stack.

This book is about programming to produce graphical interactions between a human user and the computer using the X Window protocol. It will be shown X Window produces not only drawings on a computer connected screen but enables control of keyboard input to a program and also *point-and-click* services to direct choice selection of the user. These services are available through the X Window protocol under the control of the program which uses this protocol. X Window toolkit distances the program coding from this underlying protocol. The protocol could be called directly as will be shown in the final chapter although this is of little practical use. Xlib is a level just above this protocol. The majority of this book concerns Xlib. Xcb which is an alternative to Xlib but at the same level from the protocol is addressed in Chap. 8.

Xlib is the C language binding to the X Protocol. Xlib is used in combination with programs written in the C programming language. When writing C programs, the functions of Xlib are used in the same manner as is used with inline assembler. Xlib is a library of functions.

Although it is possible to create an X protocol packet *by hand*, as is shown in Chap. 9, for practical programming purposes that is not a good idea. The disadvantage of using the *by hand* approach includes:

- non-standard, or unusual, approach making program maintenance more difficult;
- most programmers are not interested in, nor understand, the protocol to the level required.

This approach must have been used when the initial Xlib library was being developed. Today it would be more of academic, research, or teaching interest.

1.2   X Window Programming Gotchas

When programming with X Window in general and Xlib in particular, the following is need to be kept in mind:

1. All windows are contained within the root window;
2. A sub-window must be contained within its parent or be truncated;
3. A parent window alone has a title bar;
4. Menus, buttons, and dialogue boxes are all treated as windows;
5. All length measurements are in screen pixels;
6. Each window contains and carries its own coordinate system

The display screen of the X Window server is the root window. Every window created under X Window is contained within it. The server does not attempt to change the dimensions of a window or change its position so as a window is contained within the root window. The server if requested to show a window will do as requested, but parts of the window exceeding the expanse of the root window will be cut off.

All sub-windows must be displayed within the confines of the window which is its parent. An example of such a sub-window is a menu. If a sub-window exceeds the screen presence of its parent window, then the part or parts of the sub-window in excess will be removed by the X Window screen manager.

When a window is created with the root window as its parent, then this window will have a title. The contents of this title can be explicitly assigned in the programming which sets up the window. However, the window manager in use on the server may or may not show this title. This behaviour is dependent on the set-up of the window manager.

In X Window, everything is a window. There are no such special entities as menus, buttons, dialogue boxes, slider bars, highlights, or 3D effects, or anything else. However, there are a few exceptions. One is the cursor used to mark the mouse pointer's position on the screen. Also, neither a line, a character in a font, nor an icon is a window. However, in all those exception cases, each must be drawn in a window.

Dimensions of windows and their position on the screen are always in the dimension of screen pixels. The physical appearance on the screen of a window is determined by the pixel distribution on the screen being used. So, it is possible for the appearance of a window to change when viewed on different screens.

Each window carries its own coordinate system. The origin of that coordinate system is in the top left-hand corner of the window. The x-coordinate increases from left to right. The y-coordinate increases from top to bottom of the window. There are no negative coordinates. All coordinates are in screen pixels.

The approach taken in this book is to discuss and show. In this regard, although error checking is important it can hide the basics which are more important here than in creating robust application programs. Error checking is an addition onto the scope of this book.

1.3   Programming in X Window

Programming in the X Window System is centred on a window. In the creation of a final displayed image, many windows can be involved with the final effect being influenced by the overlapping, appearance, disappearance, and adjacency of a number of such windows, and their contents. Therefore, mastery of X Windows programming starts by mastering the programming of a single window. All X Window programming consists of four principal parts:

1. Creation of a window;
2. Making that window visible;
3. Drawing into that window; and
4. Handling input on that window.

Each of these parts will be discussed and demonstrated by examples in the following chapters. Each of these window parts has a number of sub-parts. The complexity, and the resulting power and flexibility, of X Window programming results from imparting interactions between those principal parts, and their sub-parts.

The X Window System is defined by its protocol, and Xlib is the part which operates close to this protocol. X Window is a client and server system. The protocol is a series of messages passed between the client and the server. The *client* is the program, such as those which will be written in this book, which contains the Xlib function calls. Those function calls generate the protocol messages which are sent to the server. The *server* is a provided piece of X Window code which acts upon the requests sent to it via the client's protocol messages. For example, the client program gives the details of how a window is to appear and requests it to appear on the display. The server actually drives the hardware to produce the window on the display.

The Xlib function calls are part of a library that provides a programmer access to the protocol messages. As such, they might be considered as the *assembly language* of the X Window System. As in programming in general, higher order languages exist. In the context of the X Window System, these are known as *toolkits*. The use of toolkits distances the programmer from much (but not all) of the detail involved in programming the X Window System protocol. In a lot of cases, this is done by providing *a policy*, which becomes characteristic of the toolkit, for interlinking the underlying protocol requests. But as stated in Scheifler et al. (1988) (page xxii), an aim in creating the X Window System was to *provide mechanism rather than policy*. As a result, Xlib provides the most practical means of exploring what can be achieved by using the X Window System. A cost of that understanding is that more is required from the programmer. The source programs become longer than those using toolkits and the chance of oversights increase. A means of assisting the programmer in using Xlib is provided in the following by the use of complete, working examples.

Chapter 2
Getting Something to Show

This chapter is concerned with the basics of Xlib programming. The purpose of a Xlib program is to produce one, or more windows. So all Xlib programs produce at least a single window. Or do they? It is better to say Xlib is windows orientated. A Xlib program may not produce a window, instead use its input/output system for other purposes. In this chapter, the sounding of the bell on the X Window server is used as an example.

Production of a window is not easy under Xlib, but a logical approach yields the required result. This is true not only for a single window but also for the general construction of such programs. The basic approach outlined in this chapter which will be used throughout this book. To demonstrate the approach, a program to construct a simple single window is produced. A Xlib program will generally contain more than a single window as will also be demonstrated in this chapter. However, the basic done on a single window can be done on many. The following chapters will expand on this basic. Having more than one window being displayed also requires consideration of the relation of one window with respect to the others. This chapter starts such considerations.

2.1 Basic Xlib Programming Code Blocks

The approach to Xlib programming proposed here is to follow a series of code blocks. In some instances, all these steps are not required as will be shown in the examples in this book. The proposed nine steps to produce a Xlib application program using Xlib are:

Electronic supplementary material The online version of this chapter
(https://doi.org/10.1007/978-3-319-74250-2_2) contains supplementary material, which is
available to authorized users.

1. open connection to the server
2. create a top-level window
3. give the Window Manager hints
4. establish window resources
5. create all the other windows needed
6. select events for each windows
7. map the windows
8. enter the event loop
9. clean up before exiting

2.2   Creating a Single Window

One of the difficulties with X Window programming is a lot has to be done before
anything appears on the display screen. If all those pieces are not in place correctly,
nothing appears, even though it is nearly correct. Here, a simple example is used
to demonstrate the programming steps that are necessary to produce a visible result
from X Window.

The first example is trivial, but it demonstrates the basic processes which need to
be followed in programming using Xlib. The example produces a blank window of
a given size in the default colour on the default display screen. Figure 2.1 shows the
output produced. Although this example is trivial in its result, it shows the blocks
of code involved in producing a functioning Xlib program. It will be seen these
code blocks are not trivial in themselves. Because those blocks are repeated with
all the Xlib programs in this book, first a template for writing Xlib programs will
be introduced before applying it to the specific example. As a result, this chapter is
important as it sets the tone for the approach used throughout this book.

Figure 2.1, as with all the display outputs given in this book, is a screenshot. The
grey-dotted surround is the background produced by the window manager used to

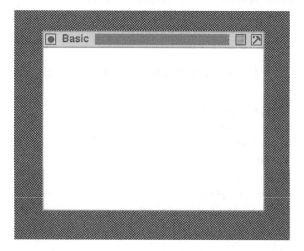

Fig. 2.1 The window
produced by the Xlib code of
Fig. 2.2

execute the Xlib program. It is shown to indicate the limit of the window produced by the Xlib program example. The top-coloured header bar is also produced by the window manager. Some window manager produces no such header bar, while other managers produce more elaborate headers to assist the user of the display to iconify the window, hold the window in place on the screen, to have the window manager convert the window so if occupies the full screen, plus other controls over the default screen manager's behaviour. The border around the window can be controlled via Xlib together with the size of the window. These controls will be considered further in examples following.

2.2.1 Open Connection to the Server

As described on page 126 of Mansfield (1993), each X client application contains a part of Xlib built into it at compile time. This is code of the Xlib function called in the application. The purpose of this code is to convert the Xlib function calls contained in the application program into X protocol requests for sending across the connection path to the server. A management component is also installed. This management part buffers the X protocol requests so as to make most efficient use of the connection path between this client and the required server. The Xlib component also provides data structures to represent locally each remote server with which the client requires access. The application can then use this local representation to obtain information about a server without making requests across the connection to the server itself. It also buffers X events pertaining to the application received from all servers. Each X application contains an individual copy of the description of each server to which it is connected.

The structures Display, Screen, and Visual are established in the Xlib portion on a X11 client's code when the connection to the server is made. The Visual structure contains information about how colours are represented for a screen. The Screen structure contains information both of the physical nature (such as its height, width, black and white pixel patterns, bits per pixel (depth)) and how that physical screen falls in the X11 model (i.e. its root window, default colour map, GC for the root). The Display structure contains information relating to the formation of X protocol packets that are to be transmitted and received between the client and the server. Examples of such information includes the maximum number of 32-bit words in a request, screen byte order, host:display string used, default screen number, and number of screens on the server. These three structures are defined in the Xlib.h header file.

The members of the Display, Screen, and Visual structures are not accessed directly by application codes. In the instances where default values are requested for these structures by the application codes, X11 makes eleven XDefault* functions available for setting such values. These functions are also available as Default* macros for explicit calling.

To use X Window, a client program first requests a connection to be made to a server. This will establish in the client's Xlib component a representation of the

server in the form of a Display structure. To do this, the function XOpenDisplay()
is used. It returns a pointer to the application of the Display structure stored in the
Xlib component of the client program. This structure describes detail configuration
information of the server. The XOpenDisplay() is implemented by a CreateGC protocol request (STRANGE). Information contained in these structures are accessed
by the client application via Default macros.

2.2.2 Top-Level Window

An X Window application is composed only of windows. X Window only provides
one type of window, but it can be fitted out differently for different uses. There are
no specialised buttons, scroll bars, text entry fields, etc. like exist in other windowing
systems. Each of these auxiliary elements must be created from a window or a
combination of more than one window, in X Window. X Window provides freedom
of combination within the restriction of hierarchical relationship among the windows.
By so doing, X Window is said to provide *mechanism without imposing policy*. It is
this generality which gives X Window both powerful, but also presents difficult for
the programmer in there being a large number of options available for use. These
options are explored throughout this book.

All windows in X Window form a hierarchy. A parent window can contain sub-
windows, and those sub-windows can contain sub-windows, and so on. This hierarchical relationship forms with the parent at the root of its hierarchical tree. The screen
surface occupied by such sub-windows must fall inside the surface area defined for
its parent. These parents can result from independently or inter-dependent running
programs, and their screen surface area allocation could be separated or overlapping,
overlapping fully or partially. Consistent with the window hierarchy, those parent
windows are themselves sub-windows of a master window, called the *root window*.
This root window is controlled by the Window Manager on the server.

When a window is initialised, it needs to specify its parent. In the case of a top-level
window, this parent is the root window. As described in Sect. 2.2.1, the first action
a client program performs is to call XOpenDisplay() to create a Display, Screen,
and Visual data structures in the Xlib portion of the client's executable code. These
structures support the hierarchical window structure which the client program then
builds up, and subsequently uses.

The calls XCreateSimpleWindow() and XCreateWindow() are available
in Xlib for creating a window. The XCreateWindow() call has greater generality
and is used here.

Say the code of Fig. 2.2 is contained in a file called basic.c. On a Linux system
using gcc version 4.1.1 and X11 version 7.1.0, this code was compiled and linked
with the shell command:

```
gcc −o basic −I /usr/include/X11 −L /usr/X11R6/lib −lX11 basic.c
```

where the X11 system header files are stored in directory /usr/include/X11
and the X libraries to be linked with are in directory /usr/X11R6/lib. In most

```
/*   This program creates and displays a basic window.   The window
 *   has a default white background.
 *
 *   Coded by:   Ross Maloney
 *   Date:       August 2006
 */

#include   <X11/Xlib.h>
#include   <X11/Xutil.h>

int main(int argc, char *argv[])
{
   Display            *mydisplay;
   XSetWindowAttributes   myat;
   Window             mywindow;
   XSizeHints         wmsize;
   XWMHints           wmhints;
   XTextProperty      windowName, iconName;
   XEvent             myevent;
   char *window_name = "Basic";
   char *icon_name   = "Ba";
   int                screen_num, done;
   unsigned long      valuemask;


                     /* 1. open connection to the server */
   mydisplay = XOpenDisplay("");

                     /* 2. create a top-level window */
   screen_num = DefaultScreen(mydisplay);
   myat.background_pixel = WhitePixel(mydisplay, screen_num);
   myat.border_pixel = BlackPixel(mydisplay, screen_num);
   myat.event_mask = ButtonPressMask;
   valuemask = CWBackPixel | CWBorderPixel | CWEventMask;
   mywindow = XCreateWindow(mydisplay,
                     RootWindow(mydisplay, screen_num),
                     200, 200, 350, 250, 2,
                     DefaultDepth(mydisplay, screen_num),
                     InputOutput,
                     DefaultVisual(mydisplay, screen_num),
                     valuemask, &myat);

                     /* 3. give the Window Manager hints */
   wmsize.flags = USPosition | USSize;
   XSetWMNormalHints(mydisplay, mywindow, &wmsize);
   wmhints.initial_state = NormalState;
   wmhints.flags = StateHint;
   XSetWMHints(mydisplay, mywindow, &wmhints);
   XStringListToTextProperty(&window_name, 1, &windowName);
   XSetWMName(mydisplay, mywindow, &windowName);
```

Fig. 2.2 Placing a basic window onto the screen

```
XStringListToTextProperty(&icon_name, 1, &iconName);
XSetWMIconName(mydisplay, mywindow, &iconName);

                    /* 4. establish window resources */
                    /* 5. create all the other windows needed */
                    /* 6. select events for each window */
                    /* 7. map the windows */
XMapWindow(mydisplay, mywindow);

                    /* 8. enter the event loop */
done = 0;
while ( done == 0 )  {
  XNextEvent(mydisplay, &myevent);
  switch (myevent.type) {
  case ButtonPress:
    break;
  }
}

                    /* 9. clean up before exiting */
XUnmapWindow(mydisplay, mywindow);
XDestroyWindow(mydisplay, mywindow);
XCloseDisplay(mydisplay);
}
```

Fig. 2.2 (continued)

instances, the path to these resources has been established by the computer system administrator, in which case this command could be simplified to:

gcc −o basic −lX11 basic.c

The resulting executable basic is then executed via a shell command:

./basic &

With respect to, the X Window example of Fig. 2.2, the following should be noted:

- It is possibly the simplest example possible;
- The example has no way in it of terminating its execution. This on a Unix system would be done via using ps from the shell to find the process ID of the executing code, and using that ID in a kill command from the shell to terminate this process.
- The nine steps are shown as comments, but only five are used;
- Because of the manner in which the program has to be terminated, step 9 is not necessary because it is never going to be executed;
- The use of the maximum number of defaults has been used to reduce the size of the example to a minimum;
- The event loop of step 8 is necessary, otherwise no window will appear on the server's screen. Try removing that loop to verify this statement. The loop is required to provide event processing which is necessary to make Xlib function.
- **Important**. The same variable of type XEvent must be used in the XNextEvent() function call and all subsequent processing of that event. In this example that only occurs in the switch statement.

Figure 2.1 shows what appears on the screen when the program of Fig. 2.2 is executed. This example only creates a single window and places it on the screen. The window is blank. Notice: **When creating a window, there is no graphic context (GC) involved** (see later). A graphic context is only involved when drawing done on the window–the graphic context is associated with drawing operations.

Figure 2.1 shows some additions. These includes window decoration and surrounding black and white stipple pattern of the root window used on the computer from where the screenshot was taken. These will appear in all screenshots on the following pages. They are a property of the X11 Window Manager, which is a subject beyond the scope of this current work.

Note: X Window applications can start out as a *wire frame* attached to the pointer on a screen, or mapped directly to the screen at the position given in the application code. Which approach is used in nominated in the application code. In the wire frame approach when a mouse button is pressed, the Window Manager draws the window generated in the coded at the current position of the mouse pointer on the screen. This does not occur with the code of Fig. 2.2, or any of the other programs contained in this work. Instead, the initial window is drawn on the screen at the position nominated in the XCreateWindow() call. The behaviour required is set using a XSetWMNormalHints() call. This call supplies the Window Manager on the computer executing the code, additional information without which the user is asked to supply via the mouse pointer.

2.2.3 Exercises

1. Modify the code of Fig. 2.2 so error checking is implemented.
2. What simple change can be introduced into the code of Fig. 2.2 so clicking the mouse anywhere in the limits of the white window will cause the program to terminate?
3. What simple change can be made in the code of Fig. 2.2 so clicking the mouse inside the limits of the white window will give a bell sound every time the mouse is clicked?
4. Change the code of Fig. 2.2 so the white window is coloured yellow.
5. Find several X11 Window Managers where the XSetWMNormalHints() call does, and does not, have the effect indicated above. For example, the hints have an effect in twm but not in dwm. Why does this occur and how does it influence use of code implemented in X Window?

2.3 Smallest Xlib Program to Produce a Window

The code of Fig. 2.2 includes all of the parts recommended for inclusion when writing an Xlib program. This approach will be used in all subsequent examples. But it also implements *policy* in providing support for the underlying window

```
/*   The simplest Xlib program possible which produces a window.
 *   A Window coloured white is placed on the screen.
 *
 *   Coded by:   Ross Maloney
 *   Date:       April 2012
 */

#include <X11/Xlib.h>
#include <X11/Xutil.h>

int main(int argc, char *argv)
{
   Display          *mydisplay;
   XSetWindowAttributes   myat;
   Window           mywindow;
   XEvent           myevent;
   int              screen_num, done;
   unsigned long    valuemask;

                    /* 1.  open connection to the server */
   mydisplay = XOpenDisplay("");

                    /* 2.  create a top-level window */
   screen_num = DefaultScreen(mydisplay);
   myat.background_pixel = WhitePixel(mydisplay, screen_num);
   valuemask = CWBackPixel;
   mywindow = XCreateWindow(mydisplay,
                            RootWindow(mydisplay, screen_num),
                            200, 200, 350, 250, 2,
                            DefaultDepth(mydisplay, screen_num),
                            InputOutput,
                            DefaultVisual(mydisplay, screen_num),
                            valuemask, &myat);

                    /* 3.  give the Window Manager hints */
                    /* 4.  establish window resources */
                    /* 5.  create all the other windows needed */
                    /* 6.  select events for each window */
                    /* 7.  map the windows */
   XMapWindow(mydisplay, mywindow);

                    /* 8.  enter the event loop */
   XNextEvent(mydisplay, &myevent);

                    /* 9.  clean up before exiting */
}
```

Fig. 2.3 Small Xlib program which yields a window

manager. However, X Window was designed to *provide mechanism rather than policy*. So, what is the smallest amount of Xlib code required to produce a window on the screen? The code in Fig. 2.3 is an answer.

When executed, the code of Fig. 2.3 produces a window on the screen the same as shown in Fig. 2.1. In this code, a number of parameters were left unspecified, for example, the colour of the window's border. Default values are supplied to these parameters either by the X server or the window manager in use. Because the code does not provide a title, the window is titled Untitled by the window manager. No *hints* are given to the window manager to assist it in displaying the window, but the window manager does its job. In the program, there are four basic Xlib calls used with four auxiliary calls. Although no events are linked to the window, the Xlib call XNextEvent() is required for the window to appear. Because no events are specified in the myevent variable, the XNextEvent() call generates an indefinite wait. Without this call nothing appears on the screen.

2.3.1   Exercises

1. List the Xlib and auxiliary call in the program of Fig. 2.3.
2. Change the code of Fig. 2.3 so the window is coloured green.
3. What parts of the code in Fig. 2.2 which are not included in Fig. 2.3 implement X Window *policy*?
4. What is the purpose of the XNextEvent() call in the program of Fig. 2.3? What happens when this call is removed?

2.4   A Simple but Useful Xlib Program

The program of Fig. 2.4 is offered as a counter to the argument Xlib programs are complex and lengthy. It would be a plus if such a program could actually do something. The program here sounds the computer's bell. No window is created nor displayed. The program needs to open a connection with a display, and in this program, the default display of the system is used. The bell is associated with the display.

The bell is one of a number of services made available by the server. The client program sends X protocol requests to the server, which then initiates the requested function. For the majority of such requests, the server uses the kernel of the underlying computer's operating system to fulfil the request. Aside from the bell, other examples of such requests are drawing on the display, mouse handling, and keyboard operations. Each of these request types are considered in the following chapters. The size of the client program using such requests increases as the complexity of such requests increase.

```
/*   An elementary X Window program.  A display is linked to this
 *   program, the keyboard bell is then sounded, then the program
 *   terminates.
 *
 *   Coded by:   Ross Maloney
 *   Date:       January 2012
 */

#include   <X11/Xlib.h>
#include   <X11/Xutil.h>

int   main(int argc, char *argv[])
{
   Display            *mydisplay;

                      /* 1.   open connection to the server */
   mydisplay = XOpenDisplay("");

                      /* 2.   create a top-level window */
                      /* 3.   give the Window Manager hints */
                      /* 4.   establish window resources */
                      /* 5.   create all the other windows needed */
                      /* 6.   select events for each window */
                      /* 7.   map the windows */
                      /* 8.   enter the event loop */
   XBell(mydisplay, 0);
                      /* 9.   clean up before exiting */
   XCloseDisplay(mydisplay);
}
```

Fig. 2.4 A program to ring the system's bell

2.4.1 Exercises

1. Modify the program of Fig. 2.4 so the loudest bell ring is produced by the program.
2. Add to the program of Fig. 2.4 so the user gives the level of loudness of the bell ring.
3. List five instances where the program of Fig. 2.4 could be applied.

2.5   A Moving Window

The following will show, a graphical user interface (GUI) is composed of many parts and those parts are implemented as separate, but related, windows. This window base is more apparent when using Xlib than with toolkits such as Xt, Motif, and Gtk which also use the X Window System, and the application programming interface (API) of Microsoft Windows. So if a program contains a GUI, then there are multiple windows in use. But a program can contain multiple windows without those windows configured to implement a GUI.

As an example of multiple windows in this section, a second window is added to the window created by the program of Fig. 2.2. This additional window required additional programming effort but less than what was needed to form the first/background window, although the background window was also required. A similar amount of effort would be required for each subsequent window added to form the collective of a GUI. In this example, the second window is remapped in different positions on the first window giving an apparent movement. Figure 2.5 shows two instances from the result produced.

For this example, a window named `rover` of 50 pixels horizontal by 70 pixels vertical and black in colour is created. This window is a child of the background window named `mywindow` which is white in colour. The child window is made to walk

Fig. 2.5 A black window moving across a white window

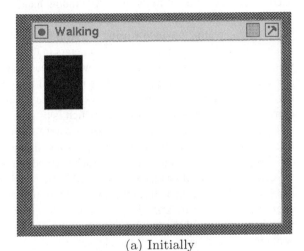

(a) Initially

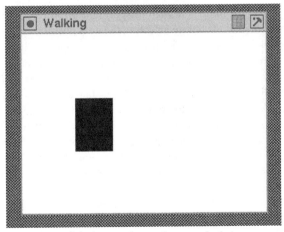

(b) A number of seconds later

across the parent window. This is done by changing the position where the child window is to be displayed. When a window is created using the XCreateWindow() (or the XCreateSimpleWindow()) Xlib call, a position for displaying the window must be given. This position is relative to a coordinate system (in units of screen pixels) attached to the parent of the window being created. This coordinate system is fixed once the window is created. However, a XWindowChanges structure which is handled by the XConfigureWindow() Xlib call can be used to change this position. The new position is where the window will appear on the screen the next time it is displayed. But a window can only appear on the screen once. So, if after a call to XMapWindow() has been made to display a window at the original position, a subsequent call to XMapWindow() unmaps (delete) the window from the screen and display it at the new position. An intervening call to XUnmapWindow() is **not** needed. This is different to the way X Window handles bitmap patterns, which. is discussed in Sect. 4.2

As when creating a window using the Xlib function call XCreateWindow(), a value mask is used to indicate the parameters in the XWindowChanges structure which XConfigureWindow() is allowed to change. In this case, both the position coordinates are to be changed which is indicated by logically ORing the CWX and CWY bit specifiers. The required values of those coordinates are assigned in the corresponding records of the variable which is of type XWindowChanges before using it in the call to XConfigureWindow(). This is seen in the program in Fig. 2.6 which produced the screen display show in Fig. 2.5.

This program is driven by events which the code in the program creates. Events are central to X Window and are discussed in Sect. 3.3. Most X Window programs use events. To indicate a change in the configuration (in this case, position) of the window, a StructureNotifyMask is inserted in the event mask used when the two windows of the program were created. The event loop of the program contains a ConfigureNotify clause to perform processing when the call to XConfigureWindow makes a change to the window's position. The processing performed there is to map (display) the window with its new coordinates, and then wait 3 seconds before selecting the next position of the window. The delay of 3 seconds is to enable individual position changes of the window to be observed on the screen. The delay is created by the sleep() general system call which requires the unistd.h header file. The exposure event used in the program of Fig. 2.6 is not really necessary in this particular instance.

X Window tries to optimize sending of messages between the client program and the server these messages being responsible for handling window activity, events, etc. A client message request queue is provided by Xlib as part of the client program, and the server maintains a received request queue. When an event occurs, the server immediately (except when grabs are involved) sends an event message to an event queue maintained by Xlib within the client program. A XNextEvent() call in the event loop of the client program processes the next event on that client event queue. If the queue is empty, the client flushes its request queue and waits for an event message from the server. So an XNextEvent() call will only immediately sent a request to the server if the client event queue is empty. To force an immediate server

```
/*   First a basic window with a white background is created.
 *   Then another window, a child of the first is created with
 *   a black background.  This second window is repeatedly
 *   mapped onto its parent window and then removed after 3
 *   seconds.  Each mapping is at different location.
 *
 *   Coded by:   Ross Maloney
 *   Date:       March 2011
 */

#include  <X11/Xlib.h>
#include  <X11/Xutil.h>
#include  <unistd.h>

int main(int argc, char *argv[])
{
    Display          *mydisplay;
    XSetWindowAttributes   myat;
    Window           mywindow, rover;
    XWindowChanges   alter;
    XSizeHints       wmsize;
    XWMHints         wmhints;
    XTextProperty    windowName, iconName;
    XEvent           myevent;
    char *window_name = "Walking";
    char *icon_name = "Wk";
    int              screen_num, done;
    unsigned long    valuemask;
    int              x, y;

                   /* 1.  open connection to the server */
    mydisplay = XOpenDisplay("");

                   /* 2.  create a top-level window */
    screen_num = DefaultScreen(mydisplay);
    myat.background_pixel = WhitePixel(mydisplay, screen_num);
    myat.border_pixel = BlackPixel(mydisplay, screen_num);
    myat.event_mask = ExposureMask | StructureNotifyMask;
    valuemask = CWBackPixel | CWBorderPixel | CWEventMask;
    mywindow = XCreateWindow(mydisplay,
                        RootWindow(mydisplay, screen_num),
                        200, 300, 350, 250, 2,
                        DefaultDepth(mydisplay, screen_num),
                        InputOutput,
                        DefaultVisual(mydisplay, screen_num),
                        valuemask, &myat);

                   /* 3.  give the Window Manager hints */
    wmsize.flags = USPosition | USSize;
    XSetWMNormalHints(mydisplay, mywindow, &wmsize);
    wmhints.initial_state = NormalState;
    wmhints.flags = StateHint;
```

Fig. 2.6 To walk one window across another

```
XSetWMHints(mydisplay, mywindow, &wmhints);
XStringListToTextProperty(&window_name, 1, &windowName);
XSetWMName(mydisplay, mywindow, &windowName);
XStringListToTextProperty(&icon_name, 1, &iconName);
XSetWMIconName(mydisplay, mywindow, &iconName);

                /* 4.  establish window resources */
myat.background_pixel = BlackPixel(mydisplay, screen_num);

                /* 5.  create all the other windows needed */
rover = XCreateWindow(mydisplay, mywindow,
                      100, 30, 50, 70, 2,
                      DefaultDepth(mydisplay, screen_num),
                      InputOutput,
                      DefaultVisual(mydisplay, screen_num),
                      valuemask, &myat);

                /* 6.  select events for each window */
valuemask = CWX | CWY;

                /* 7.  map the windows */
XMapWindow(mydisplay, mywindow);

                /* 8.  enter the event loop */
done = 0;
x = 11;  y = 12;
while ( done == 0 )  {
   alter.x = x;
   alter.y = y;
   XConfigureWindow(mydisplay, rover, valuemask, &alter);
   XFlush(mydisplay);
   XNextEvent(mydisplay, &myevent);
   switch (myevent.type) {
   case  Expose:
     break;
   case  ConfigureNotify:
     XMapWindow(mydisplay, rover);
     sleep(3);
     x += 5;  y += 6;
   }
}

                /* 9.  clean up before exiting */
XUnmapWindow(mydisplay, mywindow);
XDestroyWindow(mydisplay, mywindow);
XCloseDisplay(mydisplay);
}
```

Fig. 2.6 (continued)

request to be sent, a `XFlush()` call can be used. This is done in the code of Fig. 2.6 to ensure the server acts immediately upon the window position change contained in the `XConfigureWindow()` call. Any events the server may sent to the client program's event queue as a result of the flushed request are processed after events already on the client's event queue.

2.5.1   Exercises

1. Insert additional code into the program of Fig. 2.6 to check for errors.
2. What parameters in creating a window can be changed other than the position where it is to be displayed?
3. When `StructureNotifyMask` is include in the event mask during the creation of a window, what events are brought into consideration for the window?
4. Give three instances of exposure events detectable by the X Window server which would require processing by the client program.
5. The black window produced by the program of Fig. 2.6 eventually disappears from the screen. Why does this happen? Describe the X Window System mechanism involved.

2.6   Parts of Windows Can Disappear from View

A window is the building block from which all X Window applications are made. Each window is a rectangular area on a screen. These windows have the property of forming a hierarchy such that all windows are related to one another by a repeating *parent/child* pairing in which one parent can have one or more children. On the screen, the window of a child is clipped by the X Window server so it is contained withing the window of its parent. This family grouping makes it highly likely two or more windows will occupy the same location on a screen. In operation, the X Window server places all window on the screen one after another. So, if two or more windows occupy the same screen location, a window, or part of a window, could be obscured from view by another window on the screen. The art of X Window programming is to ensure relevant information for the human user is simultaneously available on the screen given the constraints on the X Window System in regard to handling of different windows.

What happens when a window obscuring one or more other windows, or parts of windows, is removed from the screen? To address this question requires knowing the component parts of X, together with how they interact. This question is a consequence of having more than one window on a screen. Most graphical user interfaces (GUIs) are built from multiple windows. As a result, the answer is of practical importance. The greater the number of windows present on screen, the more likely will be the need to deal with the consequences of the answer.

Each window is rectangular in shape, has a border, and a foreground, and background. All drawing on to a window is down using that window's foreground. Drawing on a window's foreground is done using a `Graphics Context` (GC) which has a number of parameters itself, including a foreground and a background. The background of a window can be set to contain a visual pattern without using a GC. Memory for Xlib structures declared in a client program does not (in most cases) become part of the client program but is part of the server. Such server memory is referenced by the protocol requests which result from Xlib calls contained in the code of the client program.

When a window is created by the client program, the window's size, the position it is to occupy on the screen, appearance of its border, and contents of its background are stored as a structure in the memory of the server. The client program can then request the server to display (map) this structure onto the screen. The client program can also request the server to remove (unmap) this structure from the screen. Unmapping a window does not necessarily destroy the window structure on the server.

It is natural to expect when a window is unmapped, any windows it partial obscured will become fully visible. After all, the information about all windows is already in the server. The natural expectation is the server should look after restoration. However, what is done depends on what has been asked to happen. A window can request in the `XCreateWindow()` (or `XCreateSimpleWindow()`) call in the client program for creation of a window for the server to provide such service. There are two such services: `save under` and `backing store`. A program showing how such service requests are made will be given shortly. Although requested, the server may not provide such services. This is particularly true of servers from later releases of the X Window System. If a client program requires such services and they are not available, the performance quality of the client program can be adversely affected.

In an introductory chapter on Xlib programming, it might appear inappropriate to consider server behaviour, particularly associated with recovery from overlaying of windows. But server and client program interaction are at the heart of X. Simplistically, the client requests the server to perform operations. The server has functions it can perform, but they may not align completely with what the client program expects. All Xlib programs need to be performed withing the client–server environment which X provides. The following starts consideration of such constraints. Further constraints will appear later.

2.6.1 Testing Overlay Services Available from an X Server

No X server is guaranteed to provide *save under* or *backing store* services. So any particular X server either will or will not provide such services. The program of Fig. 2.7 checks whether such services are provided. The results of the checking are sent to standard output.

```
/*  A  program  to  check  whether  the  X  server  provides  Backing  store
 *  and  Save  under.
 *
 *  Writtem  by:    Ross  Maloney
 *  Date:           February  2011
 */

#include   <X11/Xlib.h>
#include   <stdio.h>

int   main(int  argc,  char  *argv)
{
   Display        *e6display;
   Screen         *screenptr;
   int            screen_num;

   e6display  =  XOpenDisplay("");
   screen_num  =  DefaultScreen(e6display);
   screenptr  =  ScreenOfDisplay(e6display,  screen_num);

   printf("Macro_=_%d\n",  DoesSaveUnders(screenptr));
   if  (  DoesSaveUnders(screenptr)  )
     printf("Does_screen_unders\n");
   else
     printf("Does_NOT_provide_screen_unders\n");

   switch  (  DoesBackingStore(screenptr)  )  {
   case  WhenMapped:
     printf("Backing_store_provided_when_window_is_mapped\n");
     break;
   case  Always:
     printf("Backing_store_is_always_provided\n");
     break;
   case  NotUseful:
     printf("Does_NOT_provide_backing_store\n");
     break;
   default:
     printf("Something_wrong_with_DoesBackingStore()_call\n");
   }

   XCloseDisplay(e6display);
}
```

Fig. 2.7 Program to check which overlay services a server provides

The *save under* and *backing store* services differ slightly. In *save under*, the contents of the screen onto which a window is mapped is save by the server at the instance before the window is mapped, using the memory of the server. When a window is unmapped, the server moves its copy of the original contents of the screen before the window was mapped back onto the screen. These changes are generally small areas of screen, say those resulting from a window forming a menu item. However, the restored content may be from more than one window. With *backing store*, the contents of a whole window is saved in the server's memory. The server detects a window is going to be totally or partially obscured, and knowing which window has *backing store* enabled, the total contents of the window, or windows, involved are saved. When the window which caused the saving to occur is unmapped, the total contents of the window having the backing store is redrawn by the server to the screen. The client program, after defining which windows are to have *save under* and *backing store* attributes is not be involved in the implementation of these services. The client program can, however, request the server to notify it when such actions are performed.

2.6.2 Consequences of No Server Overlay Services

To demonstrate overlaying windows and what can follow when one or more are removed from the screen, a program controlling four windows is used. The program is in Fig. 2.8. Four windows (mywindow, win1, win2 and ontop are created using the window attributes of the myat structure with the valuemask variable indicating which window attributes have been requested. Windows win1, win2 and ontop are children of the mywindow window. The program considers the foreground and background of each window separately.

The background of windows mywindow, win1, and win2 is set to be white in colour. The background of the fourth window, ontop is set to be coloured black.

The background of the base window (mywindow) is tiled with a black and white checker-board pattern which had been created externally, using the utility program bitmap. This pattern is stored as a bitmap in the array backing_bit, which has variables backing_width and backing_height associated with it. The tiling property of a window repeats this 16×16 pixel across the 350×250 pixel background of the mywindow window. First, the bitmap is converted into a Pixmap named back by the Xlib function call XCreatePixmapFromBitmapData(). This Pixmap is inserted into the background of mywindow by the XSetWindow BackgroundPixmap() Xlib function call.

The foreground of windows win1, win2, and ontop is to be coloured black. Such colouring is performed as a specific case of drawing on the foreground. X Window requires a graphics context (GC) to be used when performing any drawing operations on a window's foreground. A GC itself has both a foreground, and a background the colouring of both is required to be specified. This is done in the program of Fig. 2.8 using the Xlib functions XSetForeground() and XSetBackground(), respectively.

```
/*  First a window with a black and white checker-board pattern is
 *  drawn.  Two rectangles are then drawn on that window.  The
 *  background of each of these two windows is white in colour.
 *  A GC is then created having a foreground colour of black.
 *  This GC is used to paint the foreground of the two windows
 *  black in colour.  A third is created with a black background
 *  and is displayed overlaying the two windows.  This overlaying
 *  window is then removed.  This process is event driven with a 2
 *  second delay in the event loop.
 *
 *  Coded by:    Ross Maloney
 *  Date:        March 2011
 */

#include  <X11/Xlib.h>
#include  <X11/Xutil.h>
#include  <unistd.h>

#define backing_width 16
#define backing_height 16
static unsigned char backing_bits [] = {
    0xff,  0x00,  0xff,  0x00,  0xff,  0x00,  0xff,  0x00,  0xff,  0x00,
    0xff,  0x00,  0xff,  0x00,  0xff,  0x00,  0x00,  0xff,  0x00,  0xff,
    0x00,  0xff,  0x00,  0xff,  0x00,  0xff,  0x00,  0xff,  0x00,  0xff,
    0x00,  0xff };

int main(int argc,  char *argv [])
{
    Display          *mydisplay;
    XSetWindowAttributes   myat;
    Window           mywindow,  win1,  win2,  ontop;
    XWindowChanges   alter;
    XSizeHints       wmsize;
    XWMHints         wmhints;
    XTextProperty    windowName,  iconName;
    XEvent           myevent;
    GC               gc;
    char *window_name = "Uncover";
    char *icon_name = "Uc";
    int              screen_num,  done;
    unsigned long    valuemask;
    Pixmap           back;
    int              count;

                    /* 1.  open connection to the server */
    mydisplay = XOpenDisplay ("");

                    /* 2.  create a top-level window */
    screen_num = DefaultScreen (mydisplay);
    myat.background_pixel = WhitePixel (mydisplay,  screen_num);
    myat.border_pixel = BlackPixel (mydisplay,  screen_num);
```

Fig. 2.8 Creating four windows then removing two

```
myat.event_mask = ExposureMask;
myat.save_under = True;
valuemask = CWBackPixel | CWBorderPixel | CWEventMask
            | CWSaveUnder;
mywindow = XCreateWindow(mydisplay,
                         RootWindow(mydisplay, screen_num),
                         200, 300, 350, 250, 2,
                         DefaultDepth(mydisplay, screen_num),
                         InputOutput,
                         DefaultVisual(mydisplay, screen_num),
                         valuemask, &myat);
back = XCreatePixmapFromBitmapData(mydisplay, mywindow,
                         backing_bits, backing_width,
                         backing_height,
                         BlackPixel(mydisplay, screen_num),
                         WhitePixel(mydisplay, screen_num),
                         DefaultDepth(mydisplay, screen_num));
XSetWindowBackgroundPixmap(mydisplay, mywindow, back);

                /* 3.   give the Window Manager hints */
wmsize.flags = USPosition | USSize;
XSetWMNormalHints(mydisplay, mywindow, &wmsize);
wmhints.initial_state = NormalState;
wmhints.flags = StateHint;
XSetWMHints(mydisplay, mywindow, &wmhints);
XStringListToTextProperty(&window_name, 1, &windowName);
XSetWMName(mydisplay, mywindow, &windowName);
XStringListToTextProperty(&icon_name, 1, &iconName);
XSetWMIconName(mydisplay, mywindow, &iconName);

                /* 4.   establish window resources */
gc = XCreateGC(mydisplay, mywindow, 0, NULL);
XSetForeground(mydisplay, gc, BlackPixel(mydisplay, screen_num));
XSetBackground(mydisplay, gc, WhitePixel(mydisplay, screen_num));

                /* 5.   create all the other windows needed */
win1 = XCreateWindow(mydisplay, mywindow,
                         100, 30, 50, 70, 2,
                         DefaultDepth(mydisplay, screen_num),
                         InputOutput,
                         DefaultVisual(mydisplay, screen_num),
                         valuemask, &myat);
win2 = XCreateWindow(mydisplay, mywindow,
                         100, 150, 150, 30, 2,
                         DefaultDepth(mydisplay, screen_num),
                         InputOutput,
                         DefaultVisual(mydisplay, screen_num),
                         valuemask, &myat);
myat.background_pixel = BlackPixel(mydisplay, screen_num);
```

Fig. 2.8 (continued)

```
ontop = XCreateWindow(mydisplay, mywindow,
                      120, 40, 80, 130, 2,
                      DefaultDepth(mydisplay, screen_num),
                      InputOutput,
                      DefaultVisual(mydisplay, screen_num),
                      valuemask, &myat);

                /* 6.  select events for each window */
                /* 7.  map the windows */
XMapWindow(mydisplay, mywindow);
XMapWindow(mydisplay, win1);
XMapWindow(mydisplay, win2);

                /* 8.  enter the event loop */
done = 0;
count = 0;
while ( done == 0 )  {
  XFlush(mydisplay);
  XNextEvent(mydisplay, &myevent);
  sleep(2);
  switch (myevent.type) {
  case  Expose:
    count++;
    switch (count)  {
    case 1:
      XFillRectangle(mydisplay, win1, gc, 0, 0, 50, 70);
      XFillRectangle(mydisplay, win2, gc, 0, 0, 150, 30);
      break;
    case 3:
      XMapWindow(mydisplay, ontop);
      break;
    case 6:
      XUnmapWindow(mydisplay, ontop);
      break;
    case 9:
      XUnmapWindow(mydisplay, win2);
      break;
    default:
      break;
    }
    break;
  }
}

                /* 9.  clean up before exiting */
XUnmapWindow(mydisplay, mywindow);
XDestroyWindow(mydisplay, mywindow);
XCloseDisplay(mydisplay);
}
```

Fig. 2.8 (continued)

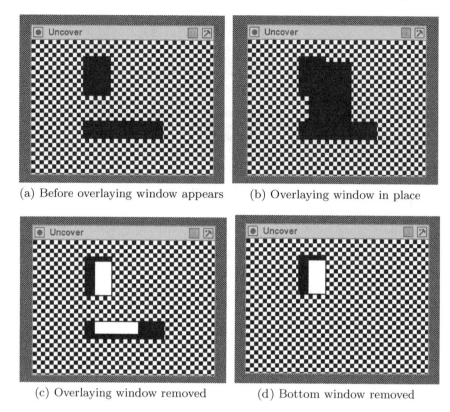

(a) Before overlaying window appears   (b) Overlaying window in place

(c) Overlaying window removed   (d) Bottom window removed

Fig. 2.9 Effect of removing an overlaying window

Once the windows have been created, they are shown (mapped) onto the screen using the XMapWindow() Xlib function. Figure 2.9 shows four snapshots of the actions of the program of Fig. 2.8. Initially, the parent window mywindow and two of its children win1 and win2 are on screen as shown in Fig. 2.9a. The checker-board Pixmap on the background of the parent window is a dominate feature.

When a window becomes visible, the server will issue an *exposure* event notification and the window of the client will be notified if such an event type has been set into the attribute structure of the window. In the program of Fig. 2.8, this is done with the myat.event_mask = ExposureMask statement and the inclusion of myat in all the XCreateWindow() Xlib functions used to set up the four windows. A property of X Window System is only after the server has issued the first exposure event for a X program can any drawing occur on the foreground of any window of that program. In most X programs, this first exposure will result from the program's parent window. In the program of Fig. 2.8, the parent window is mywindow.

As with all X programs, the event loop controls the operation of the program after initialisation and creation of windows and other resources such as GCs, etc. In this loop of the program in Fig. 2.8, a 2-second delay has been introduced by the `sleep()` system call to enable the sequence of changes on the screen to be observed. After the occurrence of the first exposure event, the foreground of windows `win1` and `win2` is coloured black using the Xlib function `XFillRectangle()`. When these windows first appear on the screen, they are coloured white (that is not shown in Fig. 2.9. When the third exposure event is processed, window `ontop` is mapped to the screen as shown in Fig. 2.9b. On the sixth exposure event, this most recently displayed window (`ontop`) is removed from the screen. The effect is shown in Fig. 2.9c. Finally, the bottom window (`win2` is removed from the screen with the result shown in Fig. 2.9d.

Although this program requested the server to use `save under` on all windows, it was not provided. Figure 2.9c, d show this not happening. In these figures, the white areas are the backgrounds of windows `win1` and `win2`. These window portions were overlayed by window `ontop` in Fig. 2.9b. Removing this window, destroyed the portion of the foreground of the other windows covered. The background of those windows then become visible. This is shown in Fig. 2.9 where window `win2` is removed but the checker-board background pattern of the parent window is undisturbed.

If the requested `save under` service had been available, then Fig. 2.9c would have been the same as (a). The white portion in Fig. 2.9 would be black.

The principle here is window foreground content is lost when the foreground is overlayed by another window. The background content of a window is not changed.

In the program of Fig. 2.8, exposure events were only counted to perform different operations of the program. However, exposure event notifications contain a lot of information about the cause of the event. This information can be used by a program to *manually* redraw all, or part, of a window which has become uncovered.

2.6.3 Exercises

1. Implement checking for errors in the code of Fig. 2.8.
2. Extend the program of Fig. 2.8 to check whether the server being used provides all standard server services.
3. Execute the program of Fig. 2.8 on a server which does have *save under* support and note the difference in behaviour to that depicted in Fig. 2.9.
4. How can the occurrence of exposure events be monitored (as a debugging aid) in programs such as in Fig. 2.8?
5. If the contents of a window's foreground can be lost by overlaying, how can information being shown in a window be protected from occurrence of such events?
6. Modify the program of Fig. 2.8 so the server is at one fixed address on a network and the client is at another.
7. Use the `bitmap` utility program to create two additional bitmaps then modify the program of Fig. 2.8 so one bitmap is tiled on the background of window `win1` and the other on the background of `win2`. How does this modification affect the mapping and unmapping of those respective windows?

8. Rewrite the program of Fig. 2.8 in a X Window toolkit of your choice. All facets of the program must be implemented. What is the difference in length of the original and toolkit versions of the program?

9. Modify the program of Fig. 2.8 such the windows win1, win2, and ontop overlay each other. Then remove each of these windows in several different operations. Does the same foreground/background retention by the server apply in all such removal operations?

10. Rewrite the code of Fig. 2.8 using XSetWindowBackgroundPixmap() and XClearWindow() Xlib function calls. What advantages are derived by such a approach (Hint: Consider the exposure event which are generated)? Where would this approach be advantageous?

11. Implement the operation of the program of Fig. 2.8 using something else than the event mechanism used in this program.

12. Using Fig. 2.8 as a model, write a program which generates 10 windows of different size and position on screen produced by an algorithm of your choice. Your program should then map all those windows onto a parent window, and then remove (unmap) each window in a different order to which they were initially mapped to the screen.

2.7 Changing a Window's Properties

When a window is created by the XCreateWindow() or XCreateSimple-Window() xlib calls, properties are associated with the window brought into existence. Such properties can be explicitly assigned by parameters passed in the creation statement or implicitly, mainly due to inheritance from the window's parent. As stated above, most practical X Window programs consist of multiple windows. It is not unreasonable to expect windows created for each of the multiple tasks to which each can be applied will need to change their properties after they are created. Changes in a window's circumstances in the overall execution of the program can warrant changing the window's properties.

A selection of functions available to change window properties after the window has been created is shown in Table 2.1. This table also indicates the type of properties each window possesses.

Once a window is displayed on the screen, its properties are fixed. Changed properties will take effect when the window is next mapped to the screen using a XMapWindow() call. So additional comments on some of those property changing library calls follow.

The XReparentWindow() statement is useful to reuse a window. For example, if a window has been set up as a *cancel* button, it can be used on different windows to serve the function. First, this button is created with one window as its parent as required with the XCreateWindow() statement. When use in this

Table 2.1 Xlib functions available to change an existing window's properties

Xlib function	Description
XSetWindowBackground()	set background colour of a window
XResizeWindow()	set horizontal and vertical size of window
XReparentWindow()	re-link a window to a different parent
XMoveWindow()	move a window relative to its parent
XSetWindowBorder()	change the colour of a window's border
XSetWindowAttributes()	reset a window's attributes
XWarpPointer()	moving the pointer to a different window

window combination is no longer required, the button can be reused with a different window, which involves linking this button window to the new parent window by using XReparentWindow(). In re-linking a window, it automatically destroys the previous parent–child relationship for a window can only have one parent at a time. An advantage of re-parenting is unmapping the parent also removes any of its child windows currently mapped to the screen.

The user of a X Window program can only interact with one window at a time. This window is the one on which the mouse pointer lies. For example, keyboard entry can only be directed to the window on which the pointer lies. If the program requires windows to be accessed in a sequence in response to keyboard entry, then the XWarpPointer() call can be used to position the pointer to the next window in response to characters typed into the current window.

Situations occur when a window is too small in some situations. It is also inappropriate to size a window for the largest possible size when it is created. The XResizeWindow() call can be used to change the size of a window as a program detects appropriate.

XSetWindowBackground() can be used to change the single colour of a window's background. There is no corresponding function to change the foreground colour. If a Pixmap has previously been applied to the window's background, it is overwritten by a single colour as a consequence of this call. There is also a XSetWindowBackgroundPixmap() call to apply a Pixmap to the background of a window thus changing what was previously on the window's background. Such a Pixmap is *tiled* onto the background, repeating itself so as to completely cover the window's background if the Pixmap is of smaller dimension than the window's background. The foreground and background of a Pixmap cannot be changed once the Pixmap is created.

Sometimes it is convenient to re-position a window on the screen under program control. This done using the XMoveWindow() call. The position is specified in coordinates defined relative to the parent of the window being moved. All windows have a parent. The root window, which covers a whole screen, is the parent for at least the first window in any X Window program.

`XSetWindowAttributes()` can be used to change the attributes of a window which are allowed to be changed. When a window is created, the attributes allowed to be changed are set. This call changes the selection for the window. Those attributes not mentioned in this call are set to default values. An example where this call could be used is to cancel generating an exposure event when this window is mapped to the screen after the first. The window would be created with the exposure event enabled. When the window exposure event occurs the `XSetWindowAttributes()` call would be used to remove this event from occurring again for this window.

Xlib provides other window property changing functions. Xlib also provides functions to change the characteristics of a Graphic Context (GC) after it is created.

2.8 Summary

This chapter lay the foundations for programming with Xlib by putting Xlib into the X Window framework. It showed the basics of creation and display one, two, and four windows. All X11 programs have a base window. The chapter also established a framework for the steps which can be used to build a Xlib program. Both of these aspects will be continually used through the remainder of this work. The previous section gave a quick summary of some Xlib functions available to change properties of a window after it is created.

The examples in this chapter give rise to the important principles:

- Server memory stores Xlib data structures associated with windows, GCs, Pixmaps, etc.;
- The background of a window is not lost when another window overlays it;
- The foreground of a window is lost when a window is overlayed.
- The name of Xlib functions calls commence with an X and all significant subwords in the name commence with a capital.
- A window has both a foreground and a background.
- A Graphics Context has both a foreground and a background.
- A drawing operations on the foreground of a window has to be done using a Graphics Context.
- Nothing can be drawn into the foreground of any window before the first occurrence of an *exposure* event of the containing program.
- The server is separate from the client program and the two pass messages to perform their cooperation and that message passing can be across a network.

These points will be expanded upon in subsequent chapters.

Since Xlib became available there has been a number of additions to its capabilities and a few revisions to existing approaches. Most of those revisions relate to creation of the environment in which the X11 program operates. Window manager hint functions are examples. This chapter used those latest revisions. Those revisions lengthen this creation process but add flexibility. As with the examples here, most X11 program contain at least a base window but as shown in this chapter is not always the case.

As will be show in subsequent chapters, X11 programs generally consist of multiple windows which build upon the created base. As has been indicated here, the use of additional windows does not proportional lengthening the source code of the program containing multiple windows. X Window toolkits generally work in reduced length of source code but do so by imposing their look and feel which inhibits flexibility of choice by the programmer of the resulting program.

Chapter 3
Windows and Events Produce Menus

This chapter shows how to program to produce a menu. A menu is a way of presenting selection options to a program user. A so-called *pull down menu* will be used here whereby such a menu drops down, or appears on the screen below a selection window, called a *button*. A button is a particular case of a window. Implementing a *pop up* menu whereby a menu appears at the mouse pointer which is positioned anywhere on the screen, after a mouse button is pressed, follows the same development considered here.

Menus are driven by events. In the X Window context, an event is produced when something happens in the program. The programming of the program specifies what such occurrences are to be and links such consequences to processing options. Such events are asynchronous in they can occur at anytime and, if there are more can one event type specified in the program, in any sequence. The X Window System stores each such event in a list in the order of their occurrence. The program then takes the events present and processes them one after the other. This mechanism enables the events to occur at a frequency which greater than what the program can handle. This arrangement simplifies the programming of event handling. In the context of menus, the events of interest are those associated with pressing of a mouse button.

Events are central to the operation of a X program. They have already been used in the program of Fig. 2.2. This chapter will show how to extend their use.

Menu events are inter-related to windows, the windows which form the menu. The purpose of each window component follows from the decoration on the window. The decorations considered in this chapter are colour and patterns of colour with lettered labels being a type of pattern. Those colours and patterns can be used to label menu components.

Electronic supplementary material The online version of this chapter (https://doi.org/10.1007/978-3-319-74250-2_3) contains supplementary material, which is available to authorized users.

The ideas presented in this chapter are fundamental to X programming. Here, only simple instances of buttons and events will be demonstrated in the context of creating and manipulation of menus. These concepts are also be used in following chapters.

3.1 Colour

Use of colour in graphics increases the quality of their appearance and hopefully their utility. X Window supports colour in both a simple and more complex manner.

In its simplest form, an X Window program presents a series of bits which are passed to the graphics hardware to generate colour. Today, a *True Colour* model is commonly used on basic hardware. It consists of using 8 bits, or two hexadecimal digits, to represent each individual primary colour. Those primary colours are red, green, and blue. On a screen, they are applied in an additive manner. For example, the colour white is produced by giving each of red, green, and blue their maximum value of `ff` (hex). Black would be produced by assigning each of red, green, and blue their minimum values of 0. In X Window, the value of the colour is passed as a single variable composed of the red, green, and blue values concatenated together. For example, the value `f4c016` contains the value `f4` for red, `c0` for green, and `16` for blue.

In more complex colour system called *Color Characterisation Convention* or *CCS*, the *X Color Management System* or *Xcms* is used to represent colour in a colour space. This representation can be in a device-dependent or a device-independent form. The device-independent form complies with the international standard on colour and takes the properties of the human visual system into consideration. Several such models exist, such as *CIEXYZ, CIExyY,* and *CIELab,* but the *TekHVC* model developed by Tektronix is popular. In the Tektronix model, colour is described in terms of hue (or colour), value (or intensity), and chroma (or saturation) and is denoted as such in the *TekHVC* model. No matter which of the device-independent models are used to denote a colour, the description has to be converted to red, green, and blue values for representation on a screen.

The `XcmsLookupColor()` function is part of the *Xcms* services provided by Xlib. This function enables a colour definition in one colour space to be converted to another. The program in Fig. 3.1 shows conversion of a RGB colour definition (the device-dependent definition) to a TekHVC definition, and then performing the conversion the other way. In the TekHVC model, hue (H) has the range 0–360°, while value (V) and chroma (C) have the range 0–100 percent. Each of hue, value, and chroma are stored as double length floating point quantities while red, green, and blue are stored as short integers by the `XcmsColor` structure used by `XcmsLookupColor()`. This structure is defined in the `X11/Xcms.h` header file. In the program of Fig. 3.1, the results of the conversions are printed on the terminal with no window appearing on the screen.

```
/*   This program converts colours between different Xcms colour
 *   spaces.   First a RGB colour is converted to its
 *   representation in the TekHVC colour space.   Then a colour
 *   defined in the TekHVC colour space is converted to RGB.
 *   The results of each conversion are printed on the terminal.
 *
 *   Coded by:   Ross Maloney
 *   Date:       13 September 2012
 */

#include   <X11/Xlib.h>
#include   <X11/Xutil.h>
#include   <X11/Xcms.h>
#include   <stdio.h>

int main(int argc, char *argv[])
{
    Display          *mydisplay;
    XcmsColor        *exact, *available;
    Status           status;
    int              screen_num;
    int              red, green, blue;
    char             rgb[10], tekcolour[40];
    XcmsFloat        h, v, c;

                    /* 1.  open connection to the server */
    mydisplay = XOpenDisplay("");

                    /* 2.  create a top-level window */
    screen_num = DefaultScreen(mydisplay);
    exact = malloc(sizeof(XcmsColor));
    available = malloc(sizeof(XcmsColor));

                    /* 3.  give the Window Manager hints */
                    /* 4.  establish window resources */
                    /* 5.  create all the other windows needed */
                    /* 6.  select events for each window */
                    /* 7.  map the windows */

                    /* 8.  enter the event loop */
    printf("default_white_=_%x\n", WhitePixel(mydisplay, screen_num));
    red = 0xc4;
    green = 0xde;
    blue = 0x12;
    sprintf(rgb, "#%02x%02x%02x", red, green, blue);
    printf("rgb_=_%s\n", rgb);
    status = XcmsLookupColor(mydisplay,
                          XDefaultColormap(mydisplay, screen_num),
                          rgb, exact, available, XcmsTekHVCFormat);
    h = exact->spec.TekHVC.H;
    v = exact->spec.TekHVC.V;
    c = exact->spec.TekHVC.C;
```

Fig. 3.1 A program to convert between Xcms colour spaces

```
switch ( status )  {
case XcmsSuccess :
   printf ( "Success : ⌴h⌴=⌴%lf ⌴⌴v⌴=⌴%lf ⌴⌴c⌴=⌴%lf \n" , h , v , v );
   break ;
case XcmsSuccessWithCompression :
   printf ( "Compressed : ⌴h⌴=⌴%lf ⌴⌴v⌴=⌴%lf ⌴⌴c⌴=⌴%lf \n" , h , v , v );
   break ;
case XcmsFailure :
   printf ( "Xcms⌴ failure \n" );
   break ;
default :
   printf ( " This ⌴should ⌴never ⌴happen\n" );
}
h = 192.4;
v = 82.6;
c = 56.1;
sprintf ( tekcolour , "TekHVC: %5.1 f / %4.2 f / %4.2 f" , h , v , c );
printf ( "tekcolour ⌴=⌴%s \n" , tekcolour );
status = XcmsLookupColor ( mydisplay ,
                           XDefaultColormap ( mydisplay , screen_num ) ,
                           rgb , exact , available , XcmsTekHVCFormat );
red = exact ->spec .RGB. red ;
green = exact ->spec .RGB. green ;
blue = exact ->spec .RGB. blue ;
switch ( status )  {
case XcmsSuccess :
   printf ( " Success : ⌴red ⌴=⌴%x ⌴⌴green ⌴=⌴%x ⌴⌴blue ⌴=⌴%x \n" ,
            red , green , blue );
   break ;
case XcmsSuccessWithCompression :
   printf ( "Compressed : ⌴red ⌴=⌴%x ⌴⌴green ⌴=⌴%x ⌴⌴blue ⌴=⌴%x\n" ,
            red , green , blue );
   break ;
case XcmsFailure :
   printf ( "Xcms⌴ failure \n" );
   break ;
default :
   printf ( " This ⌴should ⌴never ⌴happen\n" );
}

            /* 9.   clean up before exiting */
   XCloseDisplay ( mydisplay );
}
```

Fig. 3.1 (continued)

Xcms allowance RGB values of 16 bits in contrast to the 8 bits used with *True Colour*. For use in *True Colour*, the high-order two hex digits of the 16-bit red, green, and blue values are used. For backward compatibility, the XcmsLookupColor () function can use the #rrggbb manner of specifying an RGB value for conversion. In most cases, the default colourmap for the computer can be used with access provided through the DefaultColormap () function.

As shown in Fig. 3.1, calls to `XcmsLookuoColor()` can have three outcomes. A `XcmsSuccess` is returned if the conversion was successful, while `XcmsFailure` is returned if unsuccessful. With `XcmsSuccessWithCompression`, the converted colour was outside of the colours which the current computer could display but a colour of *closest fit* was returned for display.

The printing out of the value returned by the `WhitePixel()` call gives an indication of the number of bits being used on the colour graphics hardware of the computer which executed the call. This follows as white is generated by having red, green, and blue at their maximum values, and `WhitePixel()` returns the maximum value.

The use of RGB values to colour different parts of windows, standard graphics, and text will be demonstrated in a number of the example program which follow from here.

3.1.1   Exercises

1. Modify the program of Fig. 3.1 so the given RGB values are converted to their corresponding representation in the CIEXYZ, CIExyY, CIEuvY, CIEuv, and CIELab colour spaces.
2. Modify the program of Fig. 3.1 so the RGB values result in a `XcmsFailure` status being returned.
3. Change the program of Fig. 3.1 so the RGB values specified result in a `XcmsSuccessWithCompression` status being returned.
4. Although the program of Fig. 3.1 does not generate a window on the screen, the X11 header files `Xlib.h` and `Xutil.h` are required. Why?

3.2   A Button to Click

In this example, the simple window of Fig. 2.2 is extended to contain a button as shown in Fig. 3.2. The button has a background colour of red and contains the labelling *quit* in a yellow font. Clicking a mouse button while the pointer is on this window button will terminate the program.

This example creates a sub-window to the main window and then links it to the mouse button click for this window alone. This event is then processed in an *event loop* to quit the program. Also, the foreground and background of the window are changed from their default colours of black and white, respectively. Figure 3.2 shows what appears on the screen.

Because the button window has the main window specified as its parent in the XCreateWindow() call which generates the button window, the location of this window specified by the third and fourth parameters of the call is relative to the parent window.

Fig. 3.2 A window with a quit button

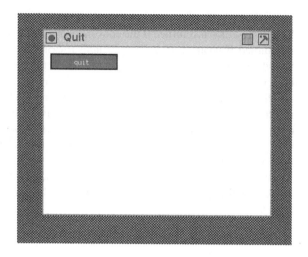

There are two means of controlling the colour used for a window. Foreground and background pixel values can be used. They are available in the window attribute data structure XSetWindowAttributes which is used with the XCreateWindow() call. The colours can also be given in the XGCValues data structure which is used with the XCreateGC() call to create a Graphics Context (GC). In both cases, the foreground and background members are of type long which indicates they are 32-bit values. In both cases, the values set in the data structures have different effects. In the case of the XSetWindowAttributes data structure, the values set there remain on the screen for the duration of existence of the window created using them. Since a GC is used with each drawing operation on a window, and there can be many drawing operations on a window (as will be shown subsequently here), values set into a XGCValues data structure tend to be localised in their affect. The rule is, once the values in either data structure are used, they remain in effect until the values are changed and the data structure is referenced in a screen operation.

Any number of GCs can be created. However, since they are stored in the server, care should be exercised to not overload the server's capacity. Only one GC can be used at any one time with a window. But the GC associated with any window at the time of any drawing operation can be changed prior to the drawing operation. Manipulation of GCs will be considered in a following example. In the present example (Fig. 3.3), the foreground and background members of the XSetWindowAttributes are used.

In the example in Fig. 2.1, the BlackPixel() and WhitePixel() macros are used to set contrasting values for the foreground and background, respectively. These macros (being linked to the screen in use) are guaranteed to give contrast between the foreground and background. But in this example, the background is set to red. The 32 bits of the background pixel value are divided into 8 bits to represent the respective red, green, and blue components of the required colour. As opposed to using these red, green, and blue values directly, X Window favours the use of indices to a *colourmap* for the screen to be used.

X Window favours the use of a colour-name database to obtain the red, green, and blue values for any colour to be shown on a screen. Those values are accessed by naming the colour. On UNIX systems, the file which shows all the available colour names and their red, green, and blue component colours is /usr/X11R6/lib/X11/rgb. txt. For fast access, this information is compiled into a X Window server. It is a two-step process to obtain the value for use as the foreground or background of a window or GC. First, the red, green, and blue values corresponding to the colour name are extracted, together with the corresponding values of the nearest colour that the server can provide. This can be done using a XLookupColor() call to obtain the red, green, and blue component colours, then using a XAllocColor() call to form the required value to assign to the foreground or background pixel value. Alternatively, both steps can be done using a XAllocNamedColor() call. This latter approach is used in the example in Fig. 3.3.

This example calls for the button to contain the label *quit*. The text for this label will be drawn into the button window. Text is drawn in the currently loaded font in the foreground of a window. A GC is necessary for all drawing, and text is drawn on to a window. A default GC could be used. By default contrasting foreground and background colours (usually black and white, respectively) are provided by a default GC. But members of a default GC must not be changed. Since the text is to be in a yellow colour, it is necessary to create a specific GC for drawing this text. In creating a GC, it is important both the foreground and background remembers of the GC should always be set.

A GC is created from a XGCValues data structure. When a GC is created, members in the XGCValues data structure which are not assignment explicit values are given default values. One member of this data structure is the font to be used when text operations are performed using the corresponding GC. There is a default font which is implementation dependent. For simplicity, this default font is used in this example.

Operations using a GC, such as drawing lines or displaying text, are event driven. The event used in this example is the exposure event which occurs when a window becomes visible. This event, plus one for a mouse click, must be associated with the button window when it is created as is expressed via the event mask applied. These assignments enable the event loop of the code in Fig. 3.3 to use the Exposure case of the switch statement to draw the text into the button when it first appears. The ButtonPress case clause is executed when a mouse button is clicked. Figure 3.2 shows the result of this program on the screen.

Clicking of any mouse button on the button causes the program to exit. This is a result of the button event being set for the button window when it was created. A more specific left-, middle-, or right-hand mouse button event is available under Xlib, but a general case was used in this instance. The same mouse button click, outside of the button window but inside the main window, does not to have any effect. Thus, the button click event is included in the XSetWindowAttributes data structure (member event_mask) of the button window, but not for the main window. The main window has no events associated with it so no events are set in its

```
/*   This  program  creates  a  button,  labelled  'quit'  located  in  a
 *   window.   Clicking  the  mouse  on  this  button  terminates  the
 *   execution  of  this  program.   The  button  has  a  red  background
 *   and  the  labelling  is  in  a  yellow  font.   The  window  itself  has
 *   a  default  white  background.
 *
 *   Coded  by:   Ross  Maloney
 *   Date:         June  2008
 */

#include   <X11/Xlib.h>
#include   <X11/Xutil.h>

int  main(int  argc,  char  *argv[])
{
  Display            *mydisplay;
  XSetWindowAttributes   myat,  buttonat;
  Window             mywindow,  button;
  XSizeHints         wmsize;
  XWMHints           wmhints;
  XTextProperty      windowName,  iconName;
  XEvent             myevent;
  XColor             exact,  closest;
  GC                 mygc;
  XGCValues          myvalues;
  char *window_name = "Quit";
  char *icon_name    = "Qt";
  int                screen_num,  done;
  unsigned long      valuemask;


                    /* 1. open connection to the server */
  mydisplay = XOpenDisplay("");

                    /* 2. create a top-level window */
  screen_num = DefaultScreen(mydisplay);
  myat.background_pixel = WhitePixel(mydisplay, screen_num);
  myat.border_pixel = BlackPixel(mydisplay, screen_num);
  valuemask = CWBackPixel | CWBorderPixel;
  mywindow = XCreateWindow(mydisplay,
                           RootWindow(mydisplay, screen_num),
                           200, 200, 350, 250, 2,
                           DefaultDepth(mydisplay, screen_num),
                           InputOutput,
                           DefaultVisual(mydisplay, screen_num),
                           valuemask, &myat);

                    /* 3. give the Window Manager hints */
  wmsize.flags = USPosition | USSize;
  XSetWMNormalHints(mydisplay, mywindow, &wmsize);
  wmhints.initial_state = NormalState;
```

Fig. 3.3 Code which creates a window with a coloured button for quitting

```
wmhints.flags = StateHint;
XSetWMHints(mydisplay, mywindow, &wmhints);
XStringListToTextProperty(&window_name, 1, &windowName);
XSetWMName(mydisplay, mywindow, &windowName);
XStringListToTextProperty(&icon_name, 1, &iconName);
XSetWMIconName(mydisplay, mywindow, &iconName);

                    /* 4. establish window resources */
XAllocNamedColor(mydisplay,
            XDefaultColormap(mydisplay, screen_num),
            "yellow", &exact, &closest);
myvalues.foreground = exact.pixel;
XAllocNamedColor(mydisplay,
            XDefaultColormap(mydisplay, screen_num),
            "red", &exact, &closest);
myvalues.background = exact.pixel;
valuemask = GCForeground | GCBackground;
mygc = XCreateGC(mydisplay, mywindow, valuemask, &myvalues);

                    /* 5. create all the other windows needed */
valuemask = CWBackPixel | CWBorderPixel | CWEventMask;
buttonat.border_pixel = BlackPixel(mydisplay, screen_num);
buttonat.background_pixel = myvalues.background;
buttonat.event_mask = ButtonPressMask | ExposureMask;
button = XCreateWindow(mydisplay, mywindow,
                    10, 10, 100, 20, 2,
                    DefaultDepth(mydisplay, screen_num),
                    InputOutput,
                    DefaultVisual(mydisplay, screen_num),
                    valuemask, &buttonat);

                    /* 6. select events for each windows */
                    /* 7. map the windows */
XMapWindow(mydisplay, mywindow);
XMapWindow(mydisplay, button);

                    /* 8. enter the event loop */
done = 0;
while ( done == 0 ) {
  XNextEvent(mydisplay, &myevent);
  switch (myevent.type) {
  case Expose:
    XDrawImageString(mydisplay, button, mygc, 35, 15, "quit",
                    strlen("quit"));
    break;
  case ButtonPress:
    XBell(mydisplay, 100);
    done = 1;
    break;
  }
}
```

Fig. 3.3 (continued)

```
                        /* 9. clean up before exiting */
        XUnmapWindow(mydisplay, mywindow);
        XDestroyWindow(mydisplay, mywindow);
        XCloseDisplay(mydisplay);
}
```

Fig. 3.3 (continued)

XSetWindowAttributes data structure. As a result, a mouse click on this main
window but outside of the button has no effect. The XMapWindow() calls for the
main and button windows result in both windows appearing when the program starts
with an Exposure event.

3.3 Events

Events occur as a result of X Window activity. The aim of X programming is to
take advantage of events as a means of human interaction with the program. For
example, moving the mouse pointer above a button which appears on a window
and then physically pressing a button on the mouse, an event is sent in to the
X Window System. Determining what the event is and how to process its occurrence is performed by the X Window application, i.e. by client computer code.

When an event occurs, a notification message is sent to the client program by the
X Window System. There are six overall things to remember about events. They are:

- events are centrally captured by the X Window System;
- X then notifies the program which has been associated with the event;
- a single event results in a single notification message;
- the event notification message indicates what type of event it is;
- depending on what type of event, different additional information is passed in the
  notification message;
- the window in which the event occurred is identified in the notification message.

Appendix E of Nye (1993) is the reference on all events which can occur and the
information that is contained in each notification message.

An example to demonstrate processing of a mouse click event is given in Fig. 3.4
with the screen output shown in Fig. 3.5. A mouse click is a very common event used
for communication between a human and the windows-based program. This might be
selecting an item from a menu list through a mouse click. In the example in Fig. 3.4,
the program starts by showing a yellow window. When a mouse click occurs, the
coordinates of the position of the mouse pointer are printed on the console display
and a red window containing a green window inside it is displayed on this point.
This happens no matter what mouse button is clicked. However, when the left-hand
mouse button is pressed, the computer also rings the bell. If the right-hand button is
used and the mouse pointer is over the green window contained in the red window,

```
/*   This program consists of a base window coloured yellow.  When
 *   the mouse * pointer is over this window and a mouse button is
 *   pressed, the coordinates * of the pointer relative to the
 *   window is printed on the console window and a * red window
 *   containing a green window is drawn at that point.  If the
 *   mouse button pressed is the left-hand mouse button, then the
 *   beep of the computer is also sounded.
 *   If the right-hand mouse
 *   button is clicked over the green window, the text 'ouch!' is
 *   also printed on the display console window.
 *
 *   Coded by:   Ross Maloney
 *   Date:       June 2008
 */

#include <X11/Xlib.h>
#include <X11/Xutil.h>
#include <stdio.h>

int  main(int  argc,  char  *argv)
{
    Display             *mydisplay;
    XSetWindowAttributes  baseat,  redat,  greenat;
    Window              baseW,  redW,  greenW;
    XSizeHints          wmsize;
    XWMHints            wmhints;
    XTextProperty       windowName,  iconName;
    XEvent              abc,  myevent;
    XColor              exact,  closest;
    GC                  baseGC;
    XGCValues           myGCValues;
    char  *window_name  =  "Events";
    char  *icon_name    =  "Ev";
    int                 screen_num,  done;
    int                 x,  y;
    unsigned long       valuemask,  red,  green;

                        /* 1.   open connection to the server */
    mydisplay  =  XOpenDisplay("");

                        /* 2.   create a top-level window */
    screen_num  =  DefaultScreen(mydisplay);
    XAllocNamedColor(mydisplay,
                     XDefaultColormap(mydisplay,  screen_num),
                     "yellow",  &exact,  &closest);
    baseat.background_pixel  =  closest.pixel;
    baseat.border_pixel  =  BlackPixel(mydisplay,  screen_num);
    baseat.event_mask  =  ButtonPressMask;
    valuemask  =  CWBackPixel  |  CWBorderPixel  |  CWEventMask;
```

Fig. 3.4 A program processing mouse button click events

```
baseW = XCreateWindow(mydisplay,
                        RootWindow(mydisplay, screen_num),
                        300, 300, 350, 400, 3,
                        DefaultDepth(mydisplay, screen_num),
                        InputOutput,
                        DefaultVisual(mydisplay, screen_num),
                        valuemask, &baseat);

                /* 3.  give the Window Manager hints */
wmsize.flags = USPosition | USSize;
XSetWMNormalHints(mydisplay, baseW, &wmsize);
wmhints.initial_state = NormalState;
wmhints.flags = StateHint;
XSetWMHints(mydisplay, baseW, &wmhints);
XStringListToTextProperty(&window_name, 1, &windowName);
XSetWMName(mydisplay, baseW, &windowName);
XStringListToTextProperty(&icon_name, 1, &iconName);
XSetWMIconName(mydisplay, baseW, &iconName);

                /* 4.  establish window resources */
XAllocNamedColor(mydisplay,
                  XDefaultColormap(mydisplay, screen_num),
                  "red", &exact, &closest);
red = closest.pixel;
XAllocNamedColor(mydisplay,
                  XDefaultColormap(mydisplay, screen_num),
                  "green", &exact, &closest);
green = closest.pixel;

                /* 5.  create all the other windows needed */
                /* 6.  select events for each window */
                /* 7.  map the windows */
XMapWindow(mydisplay, baseW);

                /* 8.  enter the event loop */
done = 0;
while ( done == 0 ) {
  XNextEvent(mydisplay, &abc);
  switch(abc.type) {
  case ButtonPress:
    if (abc.xbutton.button == Button1) XBell(mydisplay, 100);
    if (abc.xbutton.button == Button3
        && abc.xbutton.window == greenW) printf("ouch!\n");
    x = abc.xbutton.x;
    y = abc.xbutton.y;
    if (abc.xbutton.window == baseW)
printf("Yellow_window:_");
    if (abc.xbutton.window == redW)  printf("Red_window:_");
    if (abc.xbutton.window == greenW)
printf("Green_window:_");
      printf("x_=_%d__y_=_%d\n", x, y);
```

Fig. 3.4 (continued)

```
redW = XCreateSimpleWindow(mydisplay, baseW, x, y,
                100, 50, 1,
                BlackPixel(mydisplay, screen_num), red);
XMapWindow(mydisplay, redW);
XSelectInput(mydisplay, redW, ButtonPressMask);
greenW = XCreateSimpleWindow(mydisplay, redW, 10, 20,
                40, 20, 1,
                BlackPixel(mydisplay, screen_num), green);
XMapWindow(mydisplay, greenW);
XSelectInput(mydisplay, greenW, ButtonPressMask);
break;
    }
}


            /* 9.   clean up before exiting */
XUnmapWindow(mydisplay, baseW);
XDestroyWindow(mydisplay, baseW);
XCloseDisplay(mydisplay);
}
```

Fig. 3.4 (continued)

the text ouch! is typed on the control console window from which the program as launched. The program is terminated by means outside of this particular program.

In this program, the XCreateSimpleWindow() function is used to create the red and green windows. This is a simpler call to setup a window in comparison to the XCreateWindow() which is used for the yellow window, and most of the other examples in this book. But associated with such simplification comes restrictions. A window created using XCreateSimpleWindow() inherits its depth, class, visual, and its cursor from its parent, and all its properties are undefined including events. It is wise to know how to use both forms for setting up a window so the appropriate selection can be made for each situation which may occur. Notice that the placement of the red and green windows are relative to their respective parents. Because the red window is dynamically placed on the yellow window, the x and y coordinates for the pointer at the moment the mouse button is pressed is used for that positioning. The coordinates of a mouse position are relative to the window over which the mouse pointer is located. In the case of the green window, its position is fixed relative to its red window parent.

The program of Fig. 3.4 also prints the window (yellow, red, or green) in which the mouse pointer was located when its button was pressed. This was implemented using three if statements as opposed to a single switch statements which would not work as required. Can you think of the reason why the switch statement is inappropriate in this situation?

The XAllocNamedColor() function is used to generate the hardware bit patterns which produce the required colours. These are stored in variables of type XColor. The pixel field of such a structure is then used in the function call which invoke the colour.

Fig. 3.5 Dynamic window
placement following a
mouse click

The base window requires certain properties to be set. In the program example, the
colour of the window's background, the colour of the window's border, and which
events the window is interested are specified. Only events which are specified in the
properties of the window are notified by the X Window System as occurring in this
window. In the example, events are defined for the base (yellow) window but not the
red and green windows. The XSelectInput() function performs this linkage.

All events are captured and queued by the X Window System for processing by
the application program. The program takes the next event from the queue by using
the XNextEvent() call as shown in the code of Fig. 3.4. Since events are added
at the opposite end of the queue from where they are taken for processing by the
application program, events do not get lost if the application does not process them
faster than the arrival time of successive events.

Figure 3.5 shows what appears on the screen when the program of Fig. 3.4 is
operating. Notice the red window is contained entirely within the yellow window
and is truncated if it otherwise extends outside the yellow window. This results from
the dynamic placement of the red window. The coordinates printed on a terminal by
this program are relative to the window over which the mouse pointer is located. In
this particular example with three windows, there are three coordinate systems, each
with the same unit, a unit of pixels. The program of Fig. 3.4 takes those coordinates
and then uses them as the position for locating the red/green window combination
on the yellow window. So mouse button clicks on red or green windows, give small
numbers (as the coordinates) in comparison to yellow window which is larger in

size. Remember, the origin of the coordinate system of each window is at the top left-hand corner of the window. No graphics context (GC) is needed in any of the three windows.

Printing the name (colour) of the window in which the mouse button was clicked while operating the program showed windows loose their name. When the mouse is first clicked on the yellow window, the coordinates printed are given as relating to the yellow window. A red/green window is then displayed at this point. If the mouse is moved over the red or green window and clicked, the coordinates printed are identified (by the printf statements in the program) as belonging to the red or green window. If the mouse is then moved to the red or green window and the button pressed, the correct window is identified. However, if the mouse button is not clicked over the last red/green window which last appeared, then the coordinates are printed correctly, but the identification of the window does not appear. The X Window System event mechanism appears only to have a single depth of window identification tracking. Is this a bug in the X Window System, or a feature? Despite this apparent lost of identification, the coordinates are still relative to the window which is visibly under the mouse pointer when the button is pressed.

3.3.1 Exercises

1. Modify the program of Fig. 3.4 so a different mouse pointer Pixmap is used when the mouse is in the yellow, red, and green windows.
2. Modify the program of Fig. 3.4 to include the label `Cancel` centrally located in black characters on the green window (now acting as a button)
3. Remove the `XSelectInput()` function calls in the program of Fig. 3.4 and explain the resulting behaviour of the program.
4. Using the program of Fig. 3.4 as a model, write a program with the same yellow, red, and green windows which prints on the terminal the x and y coordinates of the position of the mouse pointer when the left-hand mouse button is clicked. What do you notice about those coordinates in each window?

3.4 Menus

Menus are a means of enabling a program user to control the operation of the program. This is done by presenting the user with a list of buttons as a selection, which the user clicks the mouse button while the pointer is on the required button. Such buttons are collected together, and selection of one button from a menu can lead to another menu which provides further selections. By using such nesting of menu selections, a tree of decisions can be presented to the program's user, successive selections (menus) being presented through selections previously made. The programmer is responsible for creation of such decision trees, collecting together appropriate decisions, linking one decision to the next, and presenting each to the program user.

Because menus are composed of buttons, they present a source of binary input to the program. A particular selection is made or it is not made.

Menus are handled well in toolkits. By contrast, Xlib has no menus. But Xlib has the resources to create menus. When toolkits (such as Xt) are used to create a menu, they impose certain *characteristics* which the programmer works with, and which are visible in the final program. For example, the appearance of the menu buttons, how they are decorated individually and collectively, how they pop-up on the screen, etc., are determined by the toolkit with limitation on programmer control. The programmer accepts these constraints as a trade-off against ease of creating a menu structure for the program. By using Xlib directly to create menus, the freedom of Xlib can be used to generate the menu which has exactly the characteristics desired by the programmer.

In the following two examples, the use of Xlib to create simple menus is demonstrated. Each example uses different techniques. Although each example is complete, each could be extended to encompass more complex selection situations. Each starts with a single button and builds upon this button as in the example of Fig. 3.3.

3.4.1 *Text Labelled Menu Buttons*

The program output shown in Fig. 3.7 consists of a main window and a selection button. The selection button is green in colour with the label *selection* in pink characters. By clicking the left-hand mouse button on this selection button, an option menu of *flowers, pets*, and *quit* appears, each option labelled in *blue* with a *pink* background. On moving the mouse pointer to each option, the background changes to *red*. Clicking the right-hand mouse button on the *quit* option terminates the program. The implementation code is in Fig. 3.6.

Page 528 of Nye (1995) discusses three manners of creating menus. The approach adopted here is to form a single pop-up window to contain all the selections which are to be made available. The individual selections are them inserted into this window using the XDrawImageString() call. A property of the XDrawImage String() call is the characters contained in the string are written into a window using the foreground colour of the specified GC. A bounding box for such a string is written to the window in the background colour specified in the GC. By appropriate placement of those strings, the foreground colour of the containing window can be used to separate each option. When the mouse pointer is in proximity to a string (and hence the option), the string can be re-drawn using a GC with contrasting background (and foreground) colour assignments. From the coordinates of the mouse pointer within the option containment window, the option being selected can be determined by a simple calculation.

```
/*  This program consists of a main window on which is placed a
 *  selection button. The selection button is green in colour
 *  with the label 'selection' in pink characters. By clicking
 *  the left mouse button on this selection button an option menu
 *  of 'flowers', 'pets', and 'quit' appears, each option
 *  labelled in blue with a pink background. On moving the mouse
 *  pointer to each option, the pink background of the option
 *  changes to red. Clicking the right mouse button on the 'quit'
 *  option terminates the program.
 *
 *  Coded by: Ross Maloney
 *  Date:     July 2006
 */

#include <X11/Xlib.h>
#include <X11/Xutil.h>
#include <string.h>

static char *labels[] = {"Selection", "flowers", "pets", "quit"};

static char *colours[] = {"green", "pink", "blue", "red"};

int main(int argc, char *argv)
{
    Display            *mydisplay;
    XSetWindowAttributes   myat, buttonat, popat;
    Window             mywindow, button, optA1, panes[3];
    XSizeHints         wmsize;
    XWMHints           wmhints;
    XTextProperty      windowName, iconName;
    XEvent             myevent;
    XColor             exact, closest;
    GC                 myGC1, myGC2, myGC3;
    XGCValues          myGCvalues;
    char  *window_name = "Select";
    char  *icon_name   = "Sel";
    int                screen_num, done, i;
    unsigned long      valuemask;
    int                labelLength[4], currentWindow;
    unsigned long      colourBits[6];

                    /* 1.  open connection to the server */
    mydisplay = XOpenDisplay("");

                    /* 2.  create a top-level window */
    screen_num = DefaultScreen(mydisplay);
    for (i=0; i<4; i++)  labelLength[i] = strlen(labels[i]);
    colourBits[0] = WhitePixel(mydisplay, screen_num);
    colourBits[1] = BlackPixel(mydisplay, screen_num);
    myat.background_pixel = colourBits[0];
    myat.border_pixel = colourBits[1];
    valuemask = CWBackPixel | CWBorderPixel;
```

Fig. 3.6 A window with a coloured button with a menu option for quitting

```
mywindow = XCreateWindow(mydisplay,
                         RootWindow(mydisplay, screen_num),
                         300, 300, 350, 400, 3,
                         DefaultDepth(mydisplay, screen_num),
                         InputOutput,
                         DefaultVisual(mydisplay, screen_num),
                         valuemask, &myat);

            /* 3.give the Window Manager hints */
wmsize.flags = USPosition | USSize;
XSetWMNormalHints(mydisplay, mywindow, &wmsize);
wmhints.initial_state = NormalState;
wmhints.flags = StateHint;
XSetWMHints(mydisplay, mywindow, &wmhints);
XStringListToTextProperty(&window_name, 1, &windowName);
XSetWMName(mydisplay, mywindow, &windowName);
XStringListToTextProperty(&icon_name, 1, &iconName);
XSetWMIconName(mydisplay, mywindow, &iconName);

            /* 4.  establish window resources */
for (i=0; i<4; i++) {
        XAllocNamedColor(mydisplay,
                         XDefaultColormap(mydisplay, screen_num),
                         colours[i], &exact, &closest);
        colourBits[i+2] = exact.pixel;
}
myGCvalues.background = colourBits[2];  /* green */
myGCvalues.foreground = colourBits[3];  /* pink */
valuemask = GCForeground | GCBackground;
myGC1 = XCreateGC(mydisplay, mywindow, valuemask, &myGCvalues);
myGCvalues.background = colourBits[3];  /* pink */
myGCvalues.foreground = colourBits[4];  /* blue */
myGC2 = XCreateGC(mydisplay, mywindow, valuemask, &myGCvalues);
myGCvalues.background = colourBits[5];  /* red */
myGC3 = XCreateGC(mydisplay, mywindow, valuemask, &myGCvalues);

            /* 5.  create all the other windows needed */
valuemask = CWBackPixel | CWBorderPixel | CWEventMask;
buttonat.background_pixel = colourBits[2];  /* green */
buttonat.border_pixel = colourBits[1];
buttonat.event_mask = ButtonPressMask | ExposureMask
                      | Button1MotionMask;
button = XCreateWindow(mydisplay, mywindow,
                       20, 50, 70, 30, 2,
                       DefaultDepth(mydisplay, screen_num),
                       InputOutput,
                       DefaultVisual(mydisplay, screen_num),
                       valuemask, &buttonat);
popat.border_pixel = colourBits[1];
popat.background_pixel = colourBits[3];  /* pink */
popat.event_mask = 0;
```

Fig. 3.6 (continued)

```
optA1 = XCreateWindow ( mydisplay , mywindow ,
                        50 , 60 , 100 , 150 , 2 ,
                        DefaultDepth ( mydisplay , screen_num ) ,
                        InputOutput ,
                        DefaultVisual ( mydisplay , screen_num ) ,
                        valuemask , &popat ) ;
popat . event_mask = ButtonPressMask | EnterWindowMask
                     | LeaveWindowMask | ExposureMask ;
for ( i =0; i <3; i++)
  panes [ i ] = XCreateWindow ( mydisplay , optA1 ,
                        0 , i *50 , 100 , 50 , 2 ,
                        DefaultDepth ( mydisplay , screen_num ) ,
                        InputOutput ,
                        DefaultVisual ( mydisplay , screen_num ) ,
                        valuemask , &popat ) ;

             /* 6.  select events for each window */
             /* 7.  map the windows */
XMapWindow ( mydisplay , mywindow ) ;
XMapWindow ( mydisplay , button ) ;

             /* 8.  enter the event loop */
done = 0 ;
while ( done == 0 )  {
  XNextEvent ( mydisplay , &myevent ) ;
  switch ( myevent . type )  {
  case Expose :
    XDrawImageString ( mydisplay , button , myGC1 , 10 , 17 , labels [ 0 ] ,
                       labelLength [ 0 ] ) ;

    break ;
  case ButtonPress :
    XMapWindow ( mydisplay , optA1 ) ;
    currentWindow = 0 ;
    for ( i =0; i <3; i++)  {
      XMapWindow ( mydisplay , panes [ i ] ) ;
      XDrawImageString ( mydisplay , panes [ i ] ,
                 myGC2 , 0 , 10 , labels [ i +1], labelLength [ i +1]) ;
    }
    if ( myevent . xbutton . window == panes [ 2 ] )  done = 1 ;
    break ;
  case EnterNotify :
    XSetWindowBackground ( mydisplay , panes [ currentWindow ] ,
                           colourBits [ 3 ]) ;
    XClearWindow ( mydisplay , panes [ currentWindow ] ) ;
    XDrawImageString ( mydisplay , panes [ currentWindow ] ,
                 myGC2 , 0 , 10 , labels [ currentWindow +1],
                 labelLength [ currentWindow +1]) ;
    for ( i =0; i <3; i++)
      if ( panes [ i ] == myevent . xcrossing . window )  {
        currentWindow = i ;
        break ;
    }
```

Fig. 3.6 (continued)

```
      XSetWindowBackground(mydisplay , myevent . xcrossing . window ,
                          colourBits [5]) ;
      XClearWindow(mydisplay , myevent . xcrossing . window ) ;
      XDrawImageString(mydisplay , panes [currentWindow] ,
                       myGC3, 0, 10, labels [currentWindow +1] ,
                       labelLength [currentWindow +1]) ;
      break ;
    }
  }
}

                    /* 9.  clean up before exiting */
  XUnmapWindow(mydisplay , mywindow ) ;
  XDestroyWindow(mydisplay , mywindow ) ;
  XCloseDisplay (mydisplay ) ;
}
```

Fig. 3.6 (continued)

The mouse gives the user control of the operation of this program. The mouse
generates events. It is the events which control this program. Some of those events
are generated by the mouse. Another event, an exposure event, is also used. The
design of the program must consider how these events are to be generated to provide
the required level of user control.

Fig. 3.7 A selection menu

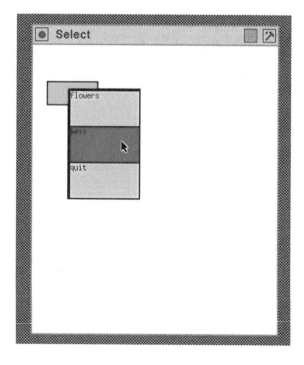

In this example, three GCs are used; one for the selection button, another for each option, and the third for when the mouse pointer is over a menu option. Three windows are to be created. One window is the top-level window in which the selection button is to be positioned. Another is the window which forms the button itself, and the third is the window to contain the selection options available. Although a separate XSetWindowAttributes structure could be used for each of the three windows which compose this example, only one is used here for efficiency in writing the program and for subsequent memory usage when the program is executing.

This program starts with the top-level window and the selection button on screen. An Expose event is used to provide a label on this button. By clicking the left-hand button of the mouse when the mouse pointer is above the button, the selection menu appears on screen. Using a button click means the button window will need to respond to a ButtonPress event. The selection window with its three options should then appear on screen. But this window is not permanent; it should be present while a selection is being made, and up to the time when a selection is made. This can be achieved by having the selection window accept a ButtonRelease event. In the program, upon receiving this button release event, the selection window would be unmapped (from the screen). This selection menu would appear on screen when the left mouse button is pressed over the selection window, the mouse would be moved over the selection menu while holding down this left mouse button, and the mouse button released when the pointer is over the required selection option.

How should the program be constructed so as to accept the selection option? A MotionNotify event could be assigned to the selection window. Then, with each movement of the mouse while the mouse button is depressed, an event is transmitted from the server to the client. This event is transmitted together with its x and y coordinate of occurrence, relative to a window, which in this case is the selection window. If the selection options were arranged as lines of text saying *flowers, pets*, and *quit*, the program could calculate which line of text (option) the mouse pointer was over. The ButtonRelease event is also transmitted with the x and y coordinate of the mouse pointer when the mouse button is released. From this position information, the line of text (option) over which the mouse pointer was positioned at the time of the release is calculated, thus determining the option selected, and the selection window then be unmapped. But the MotionNotify and the ButtonRelease both give the same coordinate information. The reason for considering these two events is the MotionNotify event indicates the currently proposed option, and the problem state this option (text) should be shown on a red-coloured background as opposed to the unselected background of pink. The ButtonRelease is necessary to indicate a selection has finally been made.

There are two approaches to the selection determination. One approach is to have different options as lines on a selection window when it appears. The problem with this approach is the need for the MotionNotify event. This event floods the connection (network) between the client and the server with MotionNotify event packets with each movement of the mouse pointer. For each of these events, the program has to determine over which selection option the mouse pointer is positioned. If this occurrence is different from the previous MotionNotify event, then the current option needs to have its background coloured red, and the previous option needs to be coloured pink. Requiring such determinations and network activity make this option unattractive for this particular visual selection process.

An alternative approach is to create a window for each of the three selection options together with a window to contain those three component windows. The three selection option windows are positioned to be contained inside of the containing window. In place of the MotionNotify event for the single selection window, each of the three selection windows of this approach is given a EntryNotify and a LeaveNotify event. Only when the mouse pointer moves out-from, or in-to an option window, will an event be transmitted. This reduces event activity. Further, the out-from, or the in-to, selection window is identified in the event message making the program's task of setting the background colour of the corresponding option straightforward. However, this approach uses four windows instead of the one used in the above approach. But X Window excels in using multiple windows.

The identification of the window which is currently under the mouse pointer in the selection pane, and thus should have its background colour set to red, is included in the EnterNotify event packet. Similarly, the mouse pointer has just left the window identified in the LeaveNotify event packet, should have its background set to pink. The setting of background colours is by using call to XSetWindowBackground(). However, changing the background of a window structure does not immediately change the background of the window on the screen. This is important as it is a general principle: **Any change to a window definition or a GC content only effects subsequent usage**. To make the change visible, a XClearWindow() call can be used. One problem with XClearWindow() is it removes everything inside of the window. In the case of a window used as a button, the button label would be removed, and this has to be replaced.

In using different combinations of the same colours and repeated need to access the labelling of buttons, it is advantageous in a program to store information related to these objects once. Then these stored values can be used repeatedly. This is done in the listing of Fig. 3.6 by the use of the array labels, the lengths of those label strings in the array labelLength, and the array colours to store the pixel values for each of the four colours use in this example. The three windows which form the selection menu are held in the array panes. Care must be exercised in the programming to select the appropriate combination of the stored values.

X Window generates a separate event when a mouse pointer enters or leaves a window. Both these entry and exit events can be used in the event loop of an Xlib program. However, in the program listed in Fig. 3.6 only the window entry event is used in relation to selection from the pop-up menu. The program keeps track of the menu item (window) which was previously under the mouse pointer. When the mouse pointer enters a window corresponding to a menu item, the statement of the problem requires this window to change colour to a red background. Correspondingly, the menu item which the pointer has left needs to be changed back to a pink background. Not only the background of the windows corresponding to the menu items need to be changed, but also the background of the labels of those windows need to be changed.

Figure 3.6 performs those requirements. A button press event is used both to activate the selection menu and also to obtain that selection.

Notice how this approach, although lengthy, enables a Xlib program to be written using whatever policy is thought appropriate. Compare the colouring technique for button selection used in the example as in Fig. 3.6 to what is available using the button widgets of toolkits such at Athena, Motif (LessTif), Gtk, Qt, etc. This approach adheres closer to the design philosophy of X Window of providing *mechanism without imposing policy*.

3.4.2 Exercises

1. Change the single button of Fig. 3.6 to a menu bar composed of three buttons, arranged horizontally across the top of the top-level window. Label those buttons *left*, *centre*, and *right*. Each of those buttons is to activate the selection menu of Fig. 3.6.
2. Change the font used in labelling the buttons and the selections in Fig. 3.6. Use the same font for the three selection options and a different font for labelling the first button.
3. Rewrite the program of Fig. 3.6 such the selection under the mouse pointer does not change colour.
4. Change the background colour of the selection windows to a colour with RGB values of 50:205:50. Hint: Look at the file rgb.txt which is included in all UNIX-like systems which run X Window.
5. Rewrite the example of Fig. 3.6 without using storage such as arrays labels, labelLength, and colours. Compare the length of this program with the line count of Fig. 3.6.
6. Rewrite the example of Fig. 3.6 replacing the XDrawImageString() calls with XDrawString() calls. What effect does this have on the program and its performance? (The program will be shorter since XDrawString() does not change that background around the string it draws. One fewer GC is necessary. This reduces the size and complexity of this program.)

3.5 Further Consideration of Mouse Events

A mouse is an event-generating device which the user can control. It can be moved to positions on the screen, and its buttons can be clicked. This section extends previous considerations of events triggered by a pressing a mouse button, releasing of that mouse button, and when the mouse pointer enters and leaves a window.

Handling of patterns is an important part of X Window and consequently Xlib programming. They are an alternative to plain colour decoration of a window. Here, they are used as decorations of targets for event handling.

The program of Fig. 3.8 was written to explore mouse-generated events. It consists of a 200x200 pixel window (called `baseW`) into which two 100x100 pixel windows (called `fileW` and `editW`) are placed. Bitmaps are useful in this application. Further information on handling and use of bitmaps is given in Sect. 4.1. Here, they are used as a means to display patterns in a window. The `fileW` window is filled with a bitmap of the character `F` using an image format where the pattern has a black foreground and a white background. The `editW` window is filled with a bitmap of the character `E` held in image format. This is character has a white foreground and a black background. The same `F` and `E` images are displayed in an overlapping configuration on the `base` window but now using opposite foreground and background colour assignments of grey and white. This combination of letters is partially obscured by the contents of the `fileW` and `editW` windows. Each of the three windows is initialised to generate button press events, exposure events, an event when the mouse pointer enters the window, and when the mouse pointer leaves the window.

The bitmaps here are handled using the X11 image format. This is different to standard bitmap format. One advantage of image format is the data are held in the client program allowing the data to be manipulated by the client program without the need of communication via the X Protocol between the client and the server. To display the contents of the image, a `XPutImage()` call is used. Another advantage is storage on a server can be more limited than what is available for the client program. By appropriate design of the client program, the same server Pixmap storage could be shared by multiple images, using it to display different bitmaps. No matter whether image or bitmap format is used, the pattern of bits which produce the picture on the screen has to be transmitted from client to server. In the program in Fig. 3.8, these advantages of image format are used in a limited manner through the `pattern` variable of type `Pixmap`. This variable is used to create each of the Pixmaps used from the bitmap data by `XCreatePixmapFromBitmapData()` calls. Image format is useful for this purpose and in displaying general pictures as shown in Sect. 6.5.

The `F` and `E` character bitmaps used in the program were generated via a Encapsulated Postscript program. The program used to create the `E` character was:

```
%!PS−Adobe−2.0 EPSF−1.3
%%BoundingBox: 5 0 105 100

/Times−Bold findfont
130 scalefont
setfont
15 15 moveto
(E) show

showpage
```

This small Postscript program was then processed by the `convert` program, which is part of the `ImageMagick` open source package. It produced an X-bitmap (xbm) file which was then included in the program's source code. Before such inclusion, the upper-case characters in the X-bitmap were converted to their lower-case equivalents using the standard utility `tr`. These X-bitmaps (structures `f_bits` and `e_bits`)

```
/*   This program examines the use of mouse generated events in
 *   relation to windows.  A 100x100 pixel window contains two
 *   50x50 pixel windows side by side.  The left of those
 *   windows is labelled File and the right window is labelled
 *   Edit.  Each of the three windows is enabled to generate an
 *   event when the mouse pointer enters or leaves the window,
 *   and also if the left-hand button on the mouse is clicked or
 *   released.  Each of the File and Edit windows change their
 *   combination of foreground and background grey colouring
 *   when each of these four events occur in them.
 *
 *   Coded by:   Ross Maloney
 *   Date:       August 2008
 */

#include <X11/Xlib.h>
#include <X11/Xutil.h>
#include <stdio.h>

/* The big F bitmap */
#define f_width 100
#define f_height 100
static char f_bits [] = {
  0x00, 0x00, 0x00, 0x00, 0x00, 0x00, 0x00, 0x00, 0x00, 0x00,
  0x00, 0x00, 0x00, 0x00, 0x00, 0x00, 0x00, 0x00, 0x00, 0x00,
  0x00, 0x00, 0x00, 0x00, 0x00, 0x00, 0x00, 0x00, 0x00, 0x00,
  0x00, 0x00, 0x00, 0x00, 0x00, 0x00, 0x00, 0x00, 0x00, 0x00,
  0x00, 0x00, 0x00, 0x00, 0x00, 0x00, 0x00, 0x00, 0x00, 0x00,
  0x00, 0x00, 0x00, 0x00, 0x00, 0x00, 0x00, 0x00, 0x00, 0x00,
  0x00, 0x00, 0x00, 0x00, 0x00, 0x00, 0x00, 0x00, 0x00, 0x00,
  0x00, 0x00, 0x00, 0x00, 0x00, 0x00, 0x00, 0x00, 0x00, 0x00,
  0x00, 0x00, 0x00, 0x00, 0x00, 0x00, 0x00, 0x00, 0x00, 0x00,
  0x00, 0x00, 0xf0, 0xff, 0xff, 0xff, 0xff, 0xff, 0xff, 0xff,
  0xff, 0x3f, 0x00, 0x00, 0x00, 0xf0, 0xff, 0xff, 0xff, 0xff,
  0xff, 0xff, 0xff, 0xff, 0x3f, 0x00, 0x00, 0x00, 0xf0, 0xff,

         .
         .
         .

  0x00, 0x00, 0x00, 0x00, 0x00, 0x00, 0x00, 0x00, 0x00, 0x00,
  0x00, 0x00, 0x00, 0x00, 0x00, 0x00, 0x00, 0x00, 0x00, 0x00,
  0x00, 0x00, 0x00, 0x00, 0x00, 0x00, 0x00, 0x00 };

/* The big E bitmap */
#define e_width 100
#define e_height 100
static char e_bits [] = {
  0x00, 0x00, 0x00, 0x00, 0x00, 0x00, 0x00, 0x00, 0x00, 0x00,
  0x00, 0x00, 0x00, 0x00, 0x00, 0x00, 0x00, 0x00, 0x00, 0x00,
  0x00, 0x00, 0x00, 0x00, 0x00, 0x00, 0x00, 0x00, 0x00, 0x00,
  0x00, 0x00, 0x00, 0x00, 0x00, 0x00, 0x00, 0x00, 0x00, 0x00,
```

Fig. 3.8 A program for tracing the occurrence of mouse events

```
0x00 ,   0x00 ,   0x00 ,   0x00 ,   0x00 ,   0x00 ,   0x00 ,   0x00 ,   0x00 ,   0x00 ,
0x00 ,   0x00 ,   0x00 ,   0x00 ,   0x00 ,   0x00 ,   0x00 ,   0x00 ,   0x00 ,   0x00 ,
0xf0 ,   0xff ,   0xff ,   0xff ,   0xff ,   0xff ,   0xff ,   0xff ,   0xff ,   0x7f ,
0x00 ,   0x00 ,   0x00 ,   0xf0 ,   0xff ,   0xff ,   0xff ,   0xff ,   0xff ,   0xff ,
0xff ,   0xff ,   0x7f ,   0x00 ,   0x00 ,   0x00 ,   0xf0 ,   0xff ,   0xff ,   0xff ,
0xff ,   0xff ,   0xff ,   0xff ,   0xff ,   0x7f ,   0x00 ,   0x00 ,   0x00 ,   0xf0 ,
0xff ,   0xff ,   0xff ,   0xff ,   0xff ,   0xff ,   0xff ,   0xff ,   0x7f ,   0x00 ,

              .
              .
              .
              .

0x00 ,   0x00 ,   0x00 ,   0x00 ,   0x00 ,   0x00 ,   0x00 ,   0x00 ,   0x00 ,   0x00 ,
0x00 ,   0x00 ,   0x00 ,   0x00 ,   0x00 ,   0x00 ,   0x00 ,   0x00 ,   0x00 ,   0x00 ,
0x00 ,   0x00 ,   0x00 ,   0x00 ,   0x00 ,   0x00 ,   0x00 ,   0x00 };

Window                baseW ,  fileW ,  editW ;

int  main ( int  argc ,  char  *argv )
{
    Display            *mydisplay ;
    XSetWindowAttributes   baseat ;
    XSizeHints         wmsize ;
    XWMHints           wmhints ;
    XTextProperty      windowName , iconName ;
    XEvent             myevent ;
    GC                 GC1, GC2, GC3, GC4 ;
    Pixmap             pattern ;
    XImage             *f , *e ;
    char *window_name = "Triggering" ;
    char *icon_name    = "Trig" ;
    int                screen_num , done , count ;
    unsigned long      valuemask ;

                  /* 1.   open connection to the server */
    mydisplay = XOpenDisplay ( "" ) ;

                  /* 2.   create a top-level window */
    screen_num = DefaultScreen ( mydisplay ) ;
    baseat . background_pixel = WhitePixel ( mydisplay ,  screen_num ) ;
    baseat . border_pixel = BlackPixel ( mydisplay ,  screen_num ) ;
    baseat . event_mask = ButtonPressMask  |  EnterWindowMask
          |  LeaveWindowMask  |  ExposureMask  |  ButtonReleaseMask ;
    valuemask = CWBackPixel  |  CWBorderPixel  |  CWEventMask ;
    baseW = XCreateWindow ( mydisplay ,
                            RootWindow ( mydisplay ,  screen_num ) ,
                            300,  300,  204,  200,  2,
                            DefaultDepth ( mydisplay ,  screen_num ) ,
                            InputOutput ,
                            DefaultVisual ( mydisplay ,  screen_num ) ,
                            valuemask ,  &baseat ) ;
```

Fig. 3.8 (continued)

```
                    /* 3.   give the Window Manager hints */
wmsize.flags = USPosition | USSize;
XSetWMNormalHints(mydisplay, baseW, &wmsize);
wmhints.initial_state = NormalState;
wmhints.flags = StateHint;
XSetWMHints(mydisplay, baseW, &wmhints);
XStringListToTextProperty(&window_name, 1, &windowName);
XSetWMName(mydisplay, baseW, &windowName);
XStringListToTextProperty(&icon_name, 1, &iconName);
XSetWMIconName(mydisplay, baseW, &iconName);


                    /* 4.   establish window resources */
GC1 = XCreateGC(mydisplay, baseW, 0, NULL);   /* white - black*/
XSetForeground(mydisplay, GC1,
                    BlackPixel(mydisplay, screen_num));
XSetBackground(mydisplay, GC1,
                    WhitePixel(mydisplay, screen_num));
GC2 = XCreateGC(mydisplay, baseW, 0, NULL);   /* black - white*/
XSetForeground(mydisplay, GC2,
                    WhitePixel(mydisplay, screen_num));
XSetBackground(mydisplay, GC2,
                    BlackPixel(mydisplay, screen_num));
GC3 = XCreateGC(mydisplay, baseW, 0, NULL);   /* white - grey*/
XSetForeground(mydisplay, GC3, 0x9e9e93);
XSetBackground(mydisplay, GC3,
                    WhitePixel(mydisplay, screen_num));
GC4 = XCreateGC(mydisplay, baseW, 0, NULL);   /* grey - white*/
XSetForeground(mydisplay, GC4,
                    WhitePixel(mydisplay, screen_num));
XSetBackground(mydisplay, GC4, 0x9e9e93);
pattern = XCreateBitmapFromData(mydisplay, baseW, f_bits,
                                    f_width, f_height);
f = XGetImage(mydisplay, pattern, 0, 0, f_width, f_height, 1,
                XYPixmap);
f->format = XYBitmap;
pattern = XCreateBitmapFromData(mydisplay, baseW, e_bits,
                                    e_width, e_height);
e = XGetImage(mydisplay, pattern, 0, 0, e_width, e_height, 1,
                XYPixmap);
e->format = XYBitmap;


                    /* 5.   create all the other windows needed */
fileW = XCreateWindow(mydisplay, baseW,
                    0, 0, 100, 100, 2,
                    DefaultDepth(mydisplay, screen_num),
                    InputOutput,
                    DefaultVisual(mydisplay, screen_num),
                    valuemask, &baseat);
```

Fig. 3.8 (continued)

```
editW  =  XCreateWindow( mydisplay ,  baseW ,
                         100 ,  0 ,  100 ,  100 ,  2 ,
                         DefaultDepth ( mydisplay ,  screen_num ) ,
                         InputOutput ,
                         DefaultVisual ( mydisplay ,  screen_num ) ,
                         valuemask ,  &baseat );

                   /* 6.   select events for each window */
                   /* 7.   map the windows */
XMapWindow( mydisplay ,  baseW );
XMapWindow( mydisplay ,  fileW );
XMapWindow( mydisplay ,  editW );

                   /* 8.   enter the event loop */
done  =  0;
count  =  0;
while  (  done  ==  0  )   {
  XNextEvent ( mydisplay ,  &myevent );
  count++;
  switch  ( myevent . type )   {
  case   Expose :
    printf ( "%2d_" ,  count );
    printf ( "+++Exposure_of_Window_" );
    name_window ( myevent . xbutton . window );
    printf ( "_occurred\n" );
    if  ( myevent . xbutton . window  ==  fileW  )
      XPutImage ( mydisplay ,  fileW ,  GC1 ,  f ,  0 ,  0 ,  0 ,  0 ,  f_width ,
                  f_height );
    if  ( myevent . xbutton . window  ==  editW  )
      XPutImage ( mydisplay ,  editW ,  GC2 ,  e ,  0 ,  0 ,  0 ,  0 ,  e_width ,
                  e_height );
    if  ( myevent . xbutton . window  ==  baseW  )   {
      XPutImage ( mydisplay ,  baseW ,  GC3 ,  e ,  0 ,  0 ,  25 ,  75 ,  e_width ,
                  e_height );
      XPutImage ( mydisplay ,  baseW ,  GC4 ,  f ,  0 ,  0 ,  75 ,  85 ,  f_width ,
                  f_height );
    }
    break ;
  case   EnterNotify :
    printf ( "%2d_" ,  count );
    printf ( "+++Window_" );   name_window ( myevent . xbutton . window );
    printf ( "_entered\n" );
    if  ( myevent . xbutton . window  ==  fileW  )
      XPutImage ( mydisplay ,  fileW ,  GC3 ,  f ,  0 ,  0 ,  0 ,  0 ,  f_width ,
                  f_height );
    if  ( myevent . xbutton . window  ==  editW  )
      XPutImage ( mydisplay ,  editW ,  GC3 ,  e ,  0 ,  0 ,  0 ,  0 ,  e_width ,
                  e_height );
    break ;
```

Fig. 3.8 (continued)

```
    case   LeaveNotify :
      printf ("%2d_" , count );
      printf ("——Leaving_Window_" );
      name_window ( myevent . xbutton . window );
      printf (" \n" );
      if ( myevent . xbutton . window == fileW  )
        XPutImage ( mydisplay ,  fileW ,  GC1 ,  f ,  0 ,  0 ,  0 ,  0 ,  f_width ,
        f_height );
      if ( myevent . xbutton . window == editW  )
        XPutImage ( mydisplay ,  editW ,  GC2 ,  e ,  0 ,  0 ,  0 ,  0 ,  e_width ,
        e_height );
      break ;
    case   ButtonPress :
      printf ("%2d_" , count );
      printf (" Button_pressed _in _Window_" );
      name_window ( myevent . xbutton . window );
      printf (" \n" );
      break ;
    case   ButtonRelease :
      printf ("%2d_" , count );
      printf (" Button_released _in _Window_" );
      name_window ( myevent . xbutton . window );
      printf (" \n" );
      break ;
    }
  }

                 /* 9.   clean  up  before  exiting */
  XUnmapWindow ( mydisplay ,  baseW );
  XDestroyWindow ( mydisplay ,  baseW );
  XCloseDisplay ( mydisplay );
}

name_window ( int  window )
{
  extern   Window baseW ,  fileW ,  editW ;

  if  ( window == baseW  )   printf ("baseW" );
  if  ( window == fileW  )   printf (" fileW" );
  if  ( window == editW  )   printf (" editW" );
  return ;
}
```

Fig. 3.8 (continued)

in the source code of Fig. 3.8 are reasonably large in the space their definitions take up in the code and have been reduced. This space consumption is made worse as a consequence of using an X-bitmap representation for a reasonably large character. This contrasts to the size of the Postscript program which generated each of these characters. Despite this, bitmaps are the standard means of drawing pattern in X. The resulting screen display is shown in Fig. 3.9.

Fig. 3.9 Initial window
colouring of event
experimentation program

Notification of entry and leaving a window, as well as the window where the
mouse button is pressed or released, is done by printing a message to a terminal. The
printing of a counter (count) is used to track events which are collected by the Xlib
function XNextEvent(). As expected from the arrangement of the three windows,
leaving and entry of windows occur in pairs. Also, when the mouse pointer enters
either the fileW or editW windows, the letter shown in the window is changed so
as the foreground is grey and the background is white.

Figure 3.9 shows the initial displayed image before the mouse pointer enters the
displayed windows. This program was run five times. In each run, the mouse was
moved in a *circuit* which was composed of the following. After the program was
started, the mouse pointer enters the editW window from the right edge. It then
moved into the fileW window on the left, then moved to the baseW window which
extended across the total width of the image, then up through the bottom edge of the
editW window. What differed in the three situations was the occurrence of button
press and release.

In the first trial, the mouse pointer moved about the *circuit* without a button press.
The follow trace of those events was generated by the program:

```
 1 +++Exposure of Window baseW occurred
 2 +++Exposure of Window editW occurred
 3 +++Exposure of Window fileW occurred
 4 +++Window baseW entered
 5 +++Window editW entered
 6 ---Leaving Window editW
 7 +++Window fileW entered
 8 ---Leaving Window fileW
 9 +++WindowbaseW entered
10 ---Leaving Window baseW
11 +++Window editW entered
```

When the mouse pointer entered the editW window, the editW window's foreground changes to grey and the background changes to white. When the mouse pointer moves to the fileW window, the editW window changes back to its original colouring, but the foreground of the fileW window changes to grey. When the mouse pointer enters the baseW window, the original colouring of the fileW window is restored, with no change in the colouring of the baseW window. When the mouse pointer finally enters the editW window, its foreground changes to grey and the background goes to white.

In the second run, the mouse followed the same circuit. In this case, the left-hand mouse button was pressed and then released in the editW window before the mouse pointer moves into the fileW window. The trace of events produced by the program is:

```
 1 +++Exposure of Window baseW occurred
 2 +++Exposure of Window editW occurred
 3 +++Exposure of Window fileW occurred
 4 +++Window baseW entered
 5 +++Window editW entered
 6 Button pressed in Window editW
 7 Button released in Window editW
 8 ---Leaving Window editW
 9 +++Window fileW entered
10 ---Leaving Window fileW
11 +++Window baseW entered
12 ---Leaving Window baseW
13 +++Window editW entered
```

When the mouse pointer entered the editW window, its foreground changed to grey and its background changed to white. Pressing and releasing the left-hand mouse button did not change any window colours. When the mouse pointer moved to the fileW window, its foreground changed to grey and its background remained white. Together with these changes, the foreground of the editW window reverted to the initial white and the background to black. Moving the mouse pointer to the baseW window did not change the colouring of the baseW window. However, the foreground of the fileW window changed back to black and the background to white. When the mouse pointer moved from the baseW window into the editW window, the colouring of the baseW window remained unchanged while the foreground of the editW window changed to grey while its background remained white.

In the third run, the left-hand mouse button is pressed while the mouse pointer is in the editW window, but is not released until the pointer had moved into the baseW window. The trace of events produced by the program is:

```
 1 +++Exposure of Window baseW occurred
 2 +++Exposure of Window editW occurred
 3 +++Exposure of Window fileW occurred
 4 +++Window baseW entered
```

```
 5 +++Window editW entered
 6 Button pressed in Window editW
 7 ---Leaving Window editW
 8 Button released in Window editW
 9 ---Leaving Window editW
10 +++Window baseW entered
11 ---Leaving Window baseW
12 +++Window editW entered
```

Upon the mouse pointer entering into the editW window, the foreground of that window changed to grey, and the background changes to white. Pressing of the left-hand mouse button did not change any window colouring. Moving the mouse pointer into the fileW window, and then the baseW window did not change the original colouring of those windows—all three windows (editW, fileW, and baseW) had their original colours. Releasing the button while over the baseW window produced no colour change. When the mouse pointer is moved into the editW window, the foreground of editW changed colour to grey, and the background changed to white.

In the fourth run, the left-hand mouse button is pressed while the mouse pointer was in the editW window, but was not released until its pointer returned to the editW window after completing the circuit. The trace of events produced by the program is:

```
1 +++Exposure of Window baseW occurred
2 +++Exposure of Window editW occurred
3 +++Exposure of Window fileW occurred
4 +++Window baseW entered
5 +++Window editW entered
6 Button pressed in Window editW
7 ---Leaving Window editW
8 +++Window editW entered
9 Button released in Window editW
```

Then, the mouse pointer entered the editW window, its foreground changed to grey. Upon moving to the fileW window, the fileW window did not change colour, but the editW window reverts to its initial colour. Movement of the mouse pointer into the baseW window resulted in no colour change to either the fileW or baseW windows. When the mouse pointer entered the editW window, its foreground changed to grey, but the colouring of the baseW window remained unchanged.

In the final trial, the left-hand mouse button was pressed in the editW window and released in the fileW window while the mouse pointer performed the circuit of movements. The trace of events produced by the program is:

```
1 +++Exposure of Window baseW occurred
2 +++Exposure of Window editW occurred
3 +++Exposure of Window fileW occurred
```

```
 4 +++Window baseW entered
 5 +++Window editW entered
 6 Button pressed in Window editW
 7 ---Leaving Window editW
 8 Button released in Window editW
 9 ---Leaving Window editW
10 +++Window fileW entered
11 ---Leaving Window fileW
12 +++Window baseW entered
13 ---Leaving Window baseW
14 +++Window editW entered
```

When the mouse pointer entered the editW window, its foreground changed to grey while its background remains white. Pressing the left-hand mouse button had no effect on the colouring of any window. As the mouse pointer moved into the fileW window, there was no change in colour of this window; however, the foreground and background colours of the editW window reverted to its initial colours. When the left-hand mouse button is released in the fileW window, the foreground of this window changed to grey (the background remained white). When the mouse button moved into the baseW window, the colours of the baseW window remained unchanged, while the foreground and background of the editW window reverted to its initial colours. Movement of the mouse pointer into the editW window changed its foreground colour to grey (background remained white).

The description above of running this program shows pressing the mouse button in a window makes the window the subject of all future events, until the button is released. When the mouse button is pressed in a window, only mouse pointer entry and leaving of this window generate events (and movement events—but this was not part of this program). The enter and leaving events of windows other than of the window in which the mouse button is pressed (and thus selected) are only restored upon release of the mouse button. This release itself also generates an event.

3.5.1   Exercises

1. Add pointer motion events to each window of the program in Fig. 3.8. When this program is run how does the trace produced differ from the above description of the behaviour of the original program?
2. Alter the program of Fig. 3.8 so it traces the mouse button behaviour but does not use bitmaps to decorate the windows involved. Do bitmap decorations of windows assist understanding the program's execution?

3.6   A Mouse Behaviour Application

A new mouse can present a problem in knowing what buttons are available. X Window can use 32 mouse buttons which are number 1–32. The correspondence between the mouse button number and the physical mouse button can be determined by the program in Fig. 3.10. This program uses mouse-generated events produced by the X Window System server in response to pressing buttons on the mouse, and moving the mouse while those buttons are depressed. The same program can be used to work through the mouse button assignments which have been made using such utilities as xmodmap in the current X11 session, or those stored in the $Home/.Xmodmap file which was possibly loaded when the current session begun.

The program draws a 200x200 pixel window having a white background on the screen. The mouse pointer is positioned over this window which acts as the target for the mouse-generated events. Three mouse events are recognised: a mouse button press, a mouse button release, and a movement of the mouse while the mouse button is repressed. The other available mouse event which occurs when the pointer is moved without a button depressed is not used. An event-relating message is printed on the terminal which launched the program. The button press and release events indicate the number of the button involved, together with the state of all the buttons and modifier keys immediately before the occurrence of the event. By contrast, motion events indicate the state of all the buttons and modifier keys before the occurrence of the motion reported. To assist in using the information produced in program using these mouse buttons and their states, the value printed is in octal notation.

An application of this program was to monitor the behaviour of a LogiTech Trackman Marble trackball being used as a mouse. This device had a left and right large button, and a smaller left and right button, with a trackball used to position the pointer. A sample of the output obtained is:

```
Button pressed:   button = 1   state = 0
Button released:  button = 1   state = 400
Button pressed:   button = 3   state = 0
Button released:  button = 3   state = 2000
Button pressed:   button = 8   state = 0
Button released:  button = 8   state = 0
Button pressed:   button = 9   state = 0
Button released:  button = 9   state = 0
Button pressed:   button = 1   state = 0
Motion event:     state = 400
Motion event:     state = 400
Motion event:     state = 400
Motion event:     state = 400
Button released:  button = 1   state = 400
Button pressed:   button = 3   state = 0
Motion event:     state = 2000
```

```
/*   This utility program responds to all mouse generated events
 *   under the X Window System.  A message indicating the nature
 *   of each mouse event received is sent to the console from
 *   where this * program was started.  However, the motion
 *   event without a button depressed is not used.  This can be
 *   used to determine the suitability and usefulness of the mouse
 *   under X which is plugged into the box running the X Window
 *   System.
 *
 *   Coded by:   Ross Maloney
 *   Date:       March 2009
 */

#include <X11/Xlib.h>
#include <X11/Xutil.h>
#include <stdio.h>

int main(int argc, char *argv)
{
    Display          *mydisplay;
    Window           baseW;
    XSetWindowAttributes  baseat;
    XSizeHints       wmsize;
    XWMHints         wmhints;
    XTextProperty    windowName, iconName;
    XEvent           myevents;
    char *window_name = "Xclick";
    char *icon_name   = "Xc";
    int              screen_num, done;
    unsigned long    valuemask;

                     /* 1.  open connection to the server */
    mydisplay = XOpenDisplay("");

                     /* 2.  create a top-level window */
    screen_num = DefaultScreen(mydisplay);
    baseat.background_pixel = WhitePixel(mydisplay, screen_num);
    baseat.border_pixel = BlackPixel(mydisplay, screen_num);
    baseat.event_mask = ExposureMask | ButtonPressMask
                        | ButtonReleaseMask | ButtonMotionMask;
    valuemask = CWBackPixel | CWBorderPixel | CWEventMask;
    baseW = XCreateWindow(mydisplay,
                          RootWindow(mydisplay, screen_num),
                          100, 100, 200, 200, 2,
                          DefaultDepth(mydisplay, screen_num),
                          InputOutput,
                          DefaultVisual(mydisplay, screen_num),
                          valuemask, &baseat);
```

Fig. 3.10 A program to print all mouse events

```
                    /* 3.   give the Window Manager hints */
wmsize.flags = USPosition | USSize;
XSetWMNormalHints(mydisplay, baseW, &wmsize);
wmhints.initial_state = NormalState;wmhints.flags = StateHint;
XSetWMHints(mydisplay, baseW, &wmhints);
XStringListToTextProperty(&window_name, 1, &windowName);
XSetWMName(mydisplay, baseW, &windowName);
XStringListToTextProperty(&icon_name, 1, &iconName);
XSetWMIconName(mydisplay, baseW, &iconName);
XMapWindow(mydisplay, baseW);


                    /* 4.   establish window resources */
                    /* 5.   create all the other windows needed */
                    /* 6.   select events for each window */
                    /* 7.   map the windows */


                    /* 8.   enter the event loop */
done = 0;
while ( done == 0 )  {
  XNextEvent(mydisplay, &myevents);
  switch (myevents.type)  {
  case  Expose:
    break;
  case  ButtonPress:
    printf("Button pressed: button = %d   state = %o\n",
           myevents.xbutton.button, myevents.xbutton.state);
    break;
  case  ButtonRelease:
    printf("Button released: button = %d   state = %o\n",
           myevents.xbutton.button, myevents.xbutton.state);
    break;
  case  MotionNotify:
    printf("Motion event:    state = %o\n",
           myevents.xmotion.state);
    break;
  default:
    printf("This should not happen\n");
  }
}


                    /* 9.   clean up before exiting */
XUnmapWindow(mydisplay, baseW);
XDestroyWindow(mydisplay, baseW);
XCloseDisplay(mydisplay);
}
```

Fig. 3.10 (continued)

```
Motion event:     state = 2000
Motion event:     state = 2000
Motion event:     state = 2000
Button released: button = 3   state = 2000
```

From this output together with observing the button used when the output was produced: the large left button was labelled 1, the large right button was 3, the small left
button was 8, and the small right button was 9. The bottom part of this output was
produced when button 1 and then button 2 was held down while the trackball was
moved. Notice how the state values during this motions are the same as reported when
the button was released. Additional output produced while holding down the small
left button and moving the trackball indicated this button implemented a scrolling
action.

3.6.1 Exercises

1. Each button and modifier key has a bit assigned to it in the value of the state
   variable which is printed by the program of Fig. 3.10. Experiment with the code
   of Fig. 3.10 so as to determine those bit assignments.
2. Use the program of Fig. 3.10 to *map* your particular mouse device. Is the behaviour
   of your mouse as you expect?

3.7 Implementing Hierarchical Menus

In Sect. 3.4 menus were shown to be combinations of windows which interact with
both the mouse pointer and its buttons. Also, one menu can be setup to lead into
another. The manner in which one menu leads into another and under what conditions
of the mouse which enables this to occur, together with which menus items remain
on the screen, gives rise to the *feel* of the graphics application. A graphics application
has both a look and a feel. But as stated on page xxii of Scheifler et al. (1988), one of
the principles of the X Window System is to *provide mechanism rather than policy*.
The *mechanism* provided by Xlib is shown in this section which enables variation of
policy in relation to behaviour of menus.

The *policy* adopted presents itself as the *look and feel* of the resulting application.
Toolkits for creating graphics applications impose their own look and feel in exchange
for simplification in the programming effort required in creating the application. The
look is the decoration associated with an item such as a menu button. The *feel* is
the manner in which, say, a menu item is selected, how one menu is positioned on
the screen relative to the button which led to its appearance, and how successive
menu entries remain on the screen once selected. Xlib allows, in fact requires, the
programmer to create all look and feel. This section demonstrates creating *look and*

feel of how one menu relates and appears in relation to the menu item which selected it, that is handling of menus hierarchies. Sections 4.3 and 7.1 deal with techniques which can further assist in generating the *look* of a menu.

Hierarchical menus impose relationships between individual menu items. A single menu consists of one or more menu items which can be selected. Each of those menu items can select a different menu which itself contains one or more selection items. This process can continue to any require level, but a practical limit is generally introduced due to human factor issues coming into play. The relationship of menu items in one menu to the next menu can be shown pictorially as a menu tree. How such relationships are managed is an important issue.

A menu tree is useful for both displaying and removing menus. Proceeding from the root of the menu tree to the leaves results in corresponding menus being displayed on the screen. Each menu is composed of selection items, and each of those menu items is implemented as a window in the context of Xlib. So, the displaying of a menu containing five menu items is achieved by displaying, or more correctly *mapping*, five windows to the screen. When the menu is no longer required, those five windows are removed from the screen, or *unmapped*. To assist this to occur, all the windows representing the menu items need to be created, and then mapped and unmapped to the screen according to menu activity. Not only those windows need to be created, but also their link into a menu and the windows (menu items) which follow on from it.

The program example in Fig. 3.12 shows implementing a simplified menu hierarchy. Each menu contains one or more items. Those menu items can be either connected, or not connected, to other menu items further in the menu tree. A simplification in this program is of not connecting many of those possible connections resulting in reduction in the size of the resulting code. The code following from this menu configuration is still a practical program. Here, its purpose is to show the management of displaying and removing menus on the screen.

The *feel* of the program of Fig. 3.12 results from the manner of handling the menu, which is the following. When the mouse pointer enters a menu item, it is highlighted and if a menu leads from it, the linked menu of items is displayed. When the mouse button leaves a menu item, the menu item is no longer highlighted. If there was a menu linked to this vacated menu item, then that collection of menu items is removed from the screen. A menu item is selected when the left mouse button is pressed while the mouse pointer is over the menu item (and thus highlighted).

The program of Fig. 3.12, which is shown operating in Fig. 3.13, consists of two buttons located on a 400x400 pixel base window which has a *navajo white* colour. These two buttons form a menu bar. They are not shown adjacent to one another on the screen to demonstrate it is not required in the programming perspective; having them adjacent is a visual convention. Figure 3.11 shows the menu tree of all the menu items and the connections between them. This shows only one, the left hand, menu bar button is connected to a menu, which in turn contains three menu items. In the menu tree of Fig. 3.11, each menu item is shown as a small circle, menus are shown as rectangles enclosing their contained menu items, and the link between a menu item and a menu is depicted by a solid line. All menus are shown rooted on the base window, with the dashed vertical lines indicating the depth of each menu.

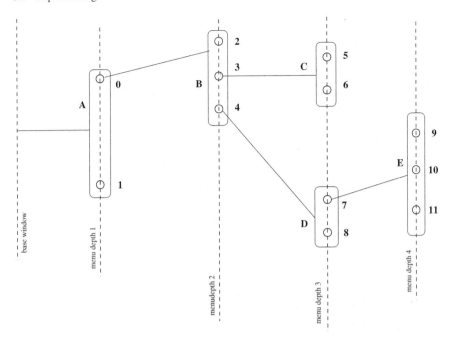

Fig. 3.11 Menu tree of the example program

In the program of Fig. 3.12, if a menu item is not connected to another menu, it is set to sound the keyboard bell if the item is clicked in an attempt to select it. No lettering, which is a form of decoration, is used on any menu items in the program in an attempt to shorten the program code. This was done to attempt to introduce *look* without affecting the *feel* of the program's operation. The resulting program is composed of 13 windows (12 menu items and the base window).

Each of the 13 windows are created individually. This allows adjusting the position parameters of each XCreateWindow() call to take into account the size of the other windows with which a window is linked. Correct positioning can be tested by mapping all the created windows to the display. The identification number of each window together with its relationship information is stored in the array W[] where each element, corresponding to one menu item, is of the data structure:

```
struct {
    Window   id;
    int      homemenu;
    int      menudepth
    int      shown;
    int      action;
}
```

```
/*  This program implements hierarchical menus.  The base 400x400
 *  pixel window contains two menu-bar buttons.  The button on
 *  the left hand side is connected to a menu of three menu items.
 *  The bottom item of that menu is connected to a menu of two
 *  items, and the top one of those menu items is connected to
 *  another three item menu.  Each menu item is a blank window
 *  which changes colour when the mouse pointer moves over it.
 *
 *  As the mouse pointer enters a menu item window, it is
 *  highlighted and if a menu leads from it, that is displayed.
 *  When the mouse pointer leaves a menu item, it ceases to be
 *  highlighted and any menu of menu items leading from it are
 *  removed from the display.  The left-hand mouse button is used
 *  to select a menu item.
 *
 *  Coded by:   Ross Maloney
 *  Date:       June 2009
 */

#include <X11/Xlib.h>
#include <X11/Xutil.h>

int main(int argc, char *argv)
{
  Display          *mydisplay;
  Window           baseW;
  struct {
    Window  id;
    int     homemenu;
    int     menudepth;
    int     shown;
    int     action;
  } W[13] = {
       {0,  1,  1,  0,  2},
       {1,  1,  1,  0,  1100},
       {2,  2,  2,  0,  1000},
       {3,  2,  2,  0,  3},
       {4,  2,  2,  0,  4},
       {5,  3,  3,  0,  1000},
       {6,  3,  3,  0,  1000},
       {7,  4,  3,  0,  5},
       {8,  4,  3,  0,  1100},
       {9,  5,  4,  0,  1000},
       {10, 5,  4,  0,  1000},
       {11, 5,  4,  0,  1000},
       {12, 0,  0,  0,  0}
  };
  XSetWindowAttributes  myat;
  XSizeHints        wmsize;
  XWMHints          wmhints;
  XTextProperty     windowName, iconName;
```

Fig. 3.12 A program demonstrating hierarchical menus

```
XEvent            baseEvent;
GC                mygc;
char *window_name = "Hierarchy";
char *icon_name   = "Hie";
int               screen_num, done, status, i, window;
unsigned long     mymask;

                  /* 1.  open  connection  to  the  server */
mydisplay = XOpenDisplay("");

                  /* 2.  create  a top−level  window */
screen_num = DefaultScreen(mydisplay);
myat.border_pixel = 0xFF0000;        /* red */
myat.background_pixel = 0xFFDEAD;  /* navajo white */
myat.event_mask = ExposureMask | EnterWindowMask;
mymask = CWBackPixel | CWBorderPixel | CWEventMask;
baseW = XCreateWindow(mydisplay,
                      RootWindow(mydisplay, screen_num),
                      350, 400, 400, 400, 2,
                      DefaultDepth(mydisplay, screen_num),
                      InputOutput,
                      DefaultVisual(mydisplay, screen_num),
                      mymask, &myat);

                  /* 3.  give the Window Manager hints */
wmsize.flags = USPosition | USSize;
XSetWMNormalHints(mydisplay, baseW, &wmsize);
wmhints.initial_state = NormalState;
wmhints.flags = StateHint;
XSetWMHints(mydisplay, baseW, &wmhints);
XStringListToTextProperty(&window_name, 1, &windowName);
XSetWMName(mydisplay, baseW, &windowName);
XStringListToTextProperty(&icon_name, 1, &iconName);
XSetWMIconName(mydisplay, baseW, &iconName);

                  /* 4.  establish window resources */
                  /* 5.  create all the other windows needed */
myat.background_pixel = 0xFFFFFF; /* white */
myat.event_mask = ButtonPressMask | ButtonReleaseMask
           | ExposureMask | EnterWindowMask | LeaveWindowMask;
mymask = CWBackPixel | CWBorderPixel | CWEventMask;
W[0].id = XCreateWindow(mydisplay, baseW,
                        50, 50, 90, 20, 2,
                        DefaultDepth(mydisplay, screen_num),
                        InputOutput,
                        DefaultVisual(mydisplay, screen_num),
                        mymask, &myat);
W[1].id = XCreateWindow(mydisplay, baseW, 250, 100, 70, 30, 2,
                        DefaultDepth(mydisplay, screen_num),
                        InputOutput,
                        DefaultVisual(mydisplay, screen_num),
                        mymask, &myat);
```

Fig. 3.12 (continued)

```
W[2].id = XCreateWindow(mydisplay, baseW, 70, 60, 90, 20, 2,
                        DefaultDepth(mydisplay, screen_num),
                        InputOutput,
                        DefaultVisual(mydisplay, screen_num),
                        mymask, &myat);
W[3].id = XCreateWindow(mydisplay, baseW, 70, 80, 90, 20, 2,
                        DefaultDepth(mydisplay, screen_num),
                        InputOutput,
                        DefaultVisual(mydisplay, screen_num),
                        mymask, &myat);
W[4].id = XCreateWindow(mydisplay, baseW, 70, 100, 90, 20, 2,
                        DefaultDepth(mydisplay, screen_num),
                        InputOutput,
                        DefaultVisual(mydisplay, screen_num),
                        mymask, &myat);
W[5].id = XCreateWindow(mydisplay, baseW, 140, 90, 60, 10, 2,
                        DefaultDepth(mydisplay, screen_num),
                        InputOutput,
                        DefaultVisual(mydisplay, screen_num),
                        mymask, &myat);
W[6].id = XCreateWindow(mydisplay, baseW, 140, 100, 60, 10, 2,
                        DefaultDepth(mydisplay, screen_num),
                        InputOutput,
                        DefaultVisual(mydisplay, screen_num),
                        mymask, &myat);
W[7].id = XCreateWindow(mydisplay, baseW, 140, 110, 60, 10, 2,
                        DefaultDepth(mydisplay, screen_num),
                        InputOutput,
                        DefaultVisual(mydisplay, screen_num),
                        mymask, &myat);
W[8].id = XCreateWindow(mydisplay, baseW, 140, 120, 60, 10, 2,
                        DefaultDepth(mydisplay, screen_num),
                        InputOutput,
                        DefaultVisual(mydisplay, screen_num),
                        mymask, &myat);
W[9].id = XCreateWindow(mydisplay, baseW, 200, 110, 100, 30, 2,
                        DefaultDepth(mydisplay, screen_num),
                        InputOutput,
                        DefaultVisual(mydisplay, screen_num),
                        mymask, &myat);
W[10].id = XCreateWindow(mydisplay, baseW, 200, 140, 100, 30, 2,
                        DefaultDepth(mydisplay, screen_num),
                        InputOutput,
                        DefaultVisual(mydisplay, screen_num),
                        mymask, &myat);
W[11].id = XCreateWindow(mydisplay, baseW, 200, 170, 100, 30, 2,
                        DefaultDepth(mydisplay, screen_num),
                        InputOutput,
                        DefaultVisual(mydisplay, screen_num),
                        mymask, &myat);
                        W[12].id = baseW;
```

Fig. 3.12 (continued)

```
                    /* 6.  select events for each window */
                    /* 7.  map the windows */
XMapWindow(mydisplay , baseW );
for ( i =0; i <2; i++)   {
  XMapWindow(mydisplay , W[ i ]. id );
  W[ i ]. shown = 1;
}


                    /* 8.  enter the event loop */
done = 0;
while ( done == 0 )   {
  XNextEvent(mydisplay , &baseEvent );
  window = -1;
  for ( i =0; i <13; i++)
    if ( W[ i ]. id == baseEvent . xany . window )   {
      window = i ;
      break;
    }
  switch (baseEvent . type)   {
  case   Expose :
    XMapWindow(mydisplay , baseW );
    for ( i =0; i <12; i++)
      if ( W[ i ]. shown == 1 )   XMapWindow(mydisplay , W[ i ]. id );
    break;
  case   ButtonPress :
    XUngrabPointer(mydisplay , CurrentTime );
    switch ( W[window ]. action )   {
    case  1000:
      XBell(mydisplay , 50);
      break ;
    case  1100:
      done = 1;
      break ;
    }
    break;
  case   ButtonRelease :
    break;
  case   EnterNotify :
    if ( i == 12 )
      for ( i =2; i <12; i++)  W[ i ]. shown = 0;
    else   {
      XSetWindowBackground(mydisplay , W[window ]. id , 0xFF0000);
      XClearWindow(mydisplay , W[window ]. id );
      for ( i =0; i <12; i++)   {
        if ( W[ i ]. menudepth > W[window ]. menudepth )
              W[ i ]. shown = 0;
        if ( W[ i ]. homemenu == W[window ]. action )
              W[ i ]. shown = 1;
      }
```

Fig. 3.12 (continued)

```
      }
      for  ( i =0;  i <12;  i++)
        if  ( W[ i ] . shown == 1  )   XMapWindow( mydisplay ,  W[ i ] . id );
        else   XUnmapWindow( mydisplay ,  W[ i ] . id );
      XFlush( mydisplay );
      break;
    case  LeaveNotify :
      XSetWindowBackground( mydisplay ,  W[ window ] . id ,  0xFFFFFF );
      XClearWindow( mydisplay ,  W[ window ] . id );
      break;
    }
  }

              /* 9.   clean up before exiting */
  XUnmapWindow( mydisplay ,  baseW );
  XDestroyWindow ( mydisplay ,  baseW );
  XCloseDisplay ( mydisplay );
}
```

Fig. 3.12 (continued)

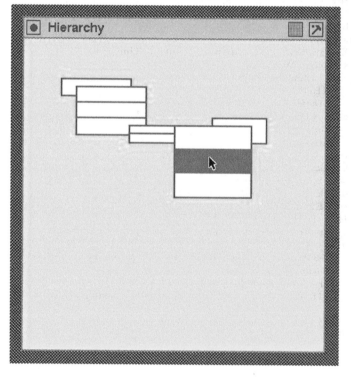

Fig. 3.13 Selection by using a hierarchy of menus

The identification number of each menu item window is computed during the program's execution. The other relationship information is constant. There are five menus which are number 1 through 5, rooted at the menu bar. These menus are assigned a depth, as shown in Fig. 3.11. The menu item is assigned membership of one of those menus together with the depth of the menu. The window identification number is inserted when the window representing the menu item is created by the corresponding XCreateWindow() call. Initially, each menu item is indicated as not being displayed by assigning a value of 0 to the shown member of the menu item structure. The action member is a label which shows what happens when the menu item is selected. In this program, there are three possible actions can be performed. If there is a following menu, then it can be displayed, in which case the action value is the number of the menu. Another action is to ring the bell, which is indicated by a 1000 value. The remaining action is to quit execution of the program which is indicated by a 1100 action value.

Displaying and removing menus are algorithmic in nature. This algorithm uses the pre-defined relationships between menu items, the menu in which each menu item exists, and the action to be performed when the menu item is selected, all of which is stored in the menu item relationship data structure. The number of both menu items and menus in this example was selected as a compromise between simplicity and being sufficient to show general functioning of the algorithm for handling menu display and removal. The algorithm has two parts: when the mouse pointer enters a menu item, and when the pointer leaves a menu item. The algorithm is:

```
pointer enters a menu item (window):
   colour the menu item as selected;
   find the menu in which this menu item resides;
   unmap all menu items in menus of higher depth;
   if a menu is linked to this menu item:
     display all menu items in that menu;

pointer leaves a menu item (window):
   colour the menu item as unselected;
```

The implementation of the menu display algorithm in the program of Fig. 3.12 proceeds as follows. The index in the W[] array corresponds to the window in which the mouse pointer enters or leaves as determined by matching the .xany.window member of the event received (in the baseEvent variable). The background colour of each button window is changed to red using a XSetWindowBackground() call when the pointer enters the window, and back to white when the pointer leaves the window. For the change to take effect immediately, a call to XClearWindow() is made followed by XFlush() which forces the server to send the window changes immediately to the client program.

The program operates by using events. Entering and leaving events together with the button press event. Only one button press event is generated by pressing any mouse button, but in the event message generated by X Window the actual button is identified. All three mouse events are enabled for each of the menu item windows. When the mouse pointer enters one of these windows, an entering window event is generated identifying the window. Similarly when the mouse pointer leaves one of these windows, a leaving window event is generated, also identifying the window.

A problem can arise due to positioning of menu item windows, giving rise a race condition. A race condition exists when one menu item window overlays a menu item window which has links to a menu item being displayed. If the mouse pointer entering the top menu item window is used to indicate the window should be unmapped, then the mouse pointer immediately falls on the menu item immediately below it. But the mouse pointer entering the menu item window is linked to the top menu item window being mapped to the display. The exposure/deletion cycle then occurs in rapid succession—a race condition.

This overlapping arrangement of menu item windows occurs in the code of Fig. 3.12. To void the occurrence of the race condition in the code of Fig. 3.12, use is made of EntryNotify events in collaboration with the known menu configuration on screen at any instance of time by use of the shown member of the W[] array which holds the menu item information. The generated LeaveNotify events are only used to change the menu item window's background colour indicating the item is no longer selected.

The program starts with two menu items shown. As the mouse pointer enters the left menu item, another menu appears. Moving the mouse pointer into each menu item colours the item red to indicate it to be selected. If another menu leads on from this menu item (as stored in the W[] array), then this menu of menu items is bought onto the screen. Moving the mouse pointer to menu items in a menu previously bought to screen removes the current lead-on menus from the screen.

Another positioning of the mouse pointer also must be considered. How should the chain of displayed menus behave if the pointer is moved out of the menu item windows currently being displayed? The easiest strategy to implement this is to leave the menu items unchanged. The mouse pointer can then be returned to the menu list where it was left.

An alternative strategy if the pointer moves out of the stack of menu items being displayed is to collapse the menu stack back to the situation where the menu bar buttons at the base (or root) of the menu structure alone appear. In that case, none of the menu bar buttons are selected by default. This is the strategy implemented in the code of Fig. 3.12.

As with most X Window programs, the operation of the code in Fig. 3.12 is centred upon the handling of events. To simplify such handling, the base window is first to generate events when the window is exposed, and when the mouse pointer enters this window. This window is then added to the menu item window list (W[]), and subsequently handled as a special case within this list. The moving in, or moving out from, a menu item by the mouse pointer results in changing the shown member of the array associated with menu window. The manner of changing is determined by the relationships between the homemenu, menudepth, and action of each menu item window and the window which raised the most recent entry or leaving event. Whether to display, or remove from the display, a menu item window is controlled by the value present in the `shown` member of each menu items structure in the menu item list. Entry and leaving a menu item window also change the background colour of that window using a `XSetWindowBackground()` and `XClearWindow()` pair of calls. It is necessary to ensure the base window is mapped to the display before any of the menu item windows so they are not obscured by this base window.

The handling of the `Expose` event in the code of Fig. 3.12 takes care of preserving the state of the operating program if it were to be obscured by another program on the screen.

One limitation of the code in Fig. 3.12 is the number of windows must be less than the action code which indicates a mouse button event, in this code 1000. This is easily changed but a 1000 menu windows is large.

As an aside, X Window handling of mouse events can impose a challenging problem if the mouse pointer is moved into or out of a window while any mouse button is held down. In this situation, entering and leaving events are only produced for the window in which the mouse pointer was located when the mouse button was pressed. This results from the default automatic *grab* of the pointer by the X Window server. This grabbed state is removed by releasing the mouse button, but between the pressing and releasing of the button, window entry and leaving events are not generated. One way to overcome this is by issuing a `XUngrapPointer()` call. Although releasing the button will remove the *grabbed state*, the client program will only receive a release button event if a `ButtonReleaseMask` is included in the event structure of the window involved. Notice, with the mouse movement specified for the program of Fig. 3.12, these conditions do not apply. However, this movement philosophy appears to have been used on the original Apple Macintosh.

3.7.1 Exercises

1. By using the technique of Sect. 7.1, create labels for the menu items used in the program of Fig. 3.12. Modify the program so the program can use those labels without diminishing the overall behaviour of the original program. Hint: A different Pixmap will be required to indicate when the mouse pointer is over, and not over, for each menu item window.
2. Modify the code in Fig. 3.12 so the original Macintosh manner of menu traversing is obtained. In this, menu traversing is performed with the mouse button pressed. As the mouse button enters a menu item, the item's colour changes and the menu leading from it is displayed. Moving to a different menu item deletes the visible menu chain linked to the previous highlighted menu item. Use the left-hand mouse button in this traversal process. Notice this produces a different *feel* than in the original program.
3. Write a program, using the code of Fig. 3.12 as a guide, which shows and identifies the menu item window in which the mouse button is depressed.

4. Modify the code of Fig. 3.12 so the mouse philosophy of the old Apple Macintosh is implemented, i.e. menus are only displayed when they are traversed while the mouse button is depressed, and the menu item is selected when the mouse button is released over the menu item. Use the left-hand mouse button as the subject mouse button.

5. A window which forms a menu item has a pattern in its foreground chich partially covers the entire window. What happens to that foreground pattern when the background colour of the window is changed? Prove your answer by appropriate modification to the code of Fig. 3.12. The answer to this question is linked to implementing labelled menu items.

6. Design, implement, and test a menu display algorithm which does not use the shown member of the menu item relationship structure of Fig. 3.12. Is this algorithm more efficient than that used in the code of Fig. 3.12?

7. Modify the code of Fig. 3.12 so it follows the *leave unchanged* menu selection strategy when the mouse pointer is moved outside of the menu items which are currently being displayed.

3.8 Which Window Gets the Event?

The members of the Xlib XSetWindowAttributes structure are used to define a number of the properties of a window. In previous example codes, members background_pixel, border_pixel, and event_mask of this structure have been used. Windows also have a hierarchical relationship which is also estab-lished in the XCreateWindow() library function used to create each window. Handling of events in a window follows the same hierarchical window relation-ship, i.e. an event occurring in a child window is passed to its parent window. This behaviour can be changed by using the do_not_propagate_mask in the XSetWindowAttribute structure when the window is created. A consequence of this propagation behaviour is the action which has been bound to a window for the occurrence an event may not occur when the event *appears* to occur in the window.

The members event_mask and do_not_propagate_mask together with the hierarchical relationship of the windows in which these members are defined come into play when an event occurs in a window involved in such a relationship. For demonstration purposes, consider the window relationship shown in Fig. 3.14. Window A is the parent of windows B and C. Window C is the parent of windows D and E. The focus here is on the behaviour of a mouse button pressing. Such a button press is designated as a ButtonPress event. A window links to such an event by including ButtonPressMask in the event_mask member of the variable of type XSetWindowAttributes which was used when creating the window.

Assume ButtonPressMask | ExposureMask | KeyPressMask is assigned as the value of the event_mask member of the XSetWindow Attributes variable used in creating windows A, B, C, D, and E of Fig. 3.14.

Fig. 3.14 Windows with
different relationships

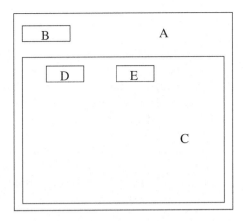

Then, when the mouse is over any of those windows and a mouse button is pressed,
this window is indicated as having received the event.

An event is only associated with a window when the mask associated with the
event is set in the `event_mask` member. So far, there are three event types for
each of the five windows will respond to. Remove the `ButtonPressMask` from
the `event_mask` of window D. Now when the user presses a mouse button over
window D, window C receives the event. Since window D is no longer associated
with a `ButtonPress` event, the event is passed to those window's parent, in this
case only window C. Now remove the `ButtonPressMask` from window C's
`event_mask`. When a mouse button is pressed above window D, window A receives
the event. As before, when the event occurs on window D, the X Window event system
passes the event down the chain until a window liked to it appears. But window C
is not associated with this type of event. So it is passed to its parent, window A. If
the mouse pointer is pressed above window E, B, or A, then those windows receive
the event. The rule here is if an event is received by a window, but if the window is
not linked to the event, the event will be passed to the parent of the window. This
passing is recursive.

Passing of events in a hierarchy of windows can have undesirable consequences.
The member `do_not_propagate_mask` in the `XSetWindowAttributes`
variables can be used to prevent propagation of specific events from a window. Say
all the windows in the arrangement of Fig. 3.14, except windows D and C, have the
`ButtonPushMask` set. A mouse button pressed while over windows C or D will
hand the event down to window A. However, if the `do_not_propagate_mask`
member of the `XSetWindowAttributes` variables used in creating those windows have the variable set to contain `ButtonPressMask`, then the event will not
propagate; it will just disappear. The contents of the `do_not_propagate_mask`
member for a window will only be noticed if the `CWDontPropagate` flag is
included in the `valuemask` parameter of the library call used to create the window.

3.8.1 Exercises

1. Describe a graphical programming situation where the window layout of Fig. 3.14 occurs. For this situation, what purpose would each of the five windows serve?
2. Using the coding model of the previous exercise, write an Xlib program which produces the window structure of Fig. 3.14. Use this program to establish the truth of the above discussion about event propagation.
3. Give a number of situations where passing of events in a hierarchy of windows is undesirable.
4. For the window arrangement of Fig. 3.14, what provisions need to be made so a mouse button press over window B does not propagate into window E or C? Explain your answer.

3.9 Summary

The prerequisites for this chapter were a window created using Xlib. This chapter grouped multiple windows to form menus. Events were then introduced in this chapter. This combinations enabled the construction of menus, together with studying of X11 events.

Menus are shown in this chapter to be formed from windows, and events which are linked to those windows. Each of the items in a menu, whether it be a button on the root window or a member of a menu list appear as a transients on the screen. Different menu behaviour and looks follow from modification of the properties of those windows. The selection of events, linking of them to a window, and processing their occurrence underlies most X11 programs. Each of these aspects of events is developed by example, using calls from Xlib to implement the required interface to services provided by the X Window System. All X11 programs contain an event processing loop with events either assigned explicitly or implicitly. Most stand-alone graphics programs contain buttons and menus. These observations make this chapter fundamental. As more familiarity with the services provided by X11 is obtained, these fundamentals can be built upon.

Events are central to creating dynamic behaviour in a graphics-based program. Buttons and menus implement some such behaviour. There are other techniques, also based on events, which will be covered in following chapters.

Chapter 4
Pattern Maps and Labels

Most, if not all, computer-based windowing systems have a means of displaying a fixed pattern on a window in such a way as to involve minimal processing. This is the generic pattern format of the windowing system. For the X Window System this format is a Pixmap. There are two sub-categories of Pixmap: the single bit (or black and white) bitmap and the more general PixMap which is capable of representing colour. A complication is X Window System refers to the analogue of a window as a Pixmap. But all what can be done on, or with, a window is not true for a map-type Pixmap.

A Pixmap is analogous to a window, but is not associated with a screen. As a consequence, it is off-line and invisible. What can be done in a window can also be done in such a Pixmap, but it is not visible with a Pixmap. Just as in the case of a window to which Xlib gives the storage type as Window, a Pixmap has the storage type Pixmap.

A further complication is the X Window System also has an image type which has the Xlib storage type XImage as discussed in Sect. 3.5. An image is similar to a Pixmap. It differs in how it is stored in the client program as opposed to being stored in the server as in the case of a Pixmap. As a consequence, an image does not take up server memory and their manipulation does not require the generation X Protocol requests to manipulate them as is the case with a Pixmap.

The pattern handling offered by a Pixmap can assist the production of buttons and menus, thus increasing their visual appeal. Two techniques for creating patterns for incorporating in a program for Pixmap use will be shown.

Electronic supplementary material The online version of this chapter (https://doi.org/10.1007/978-3-319-74250-2_4) contains supplementary material, which is available to authorized users.

4.1   The Pixmap Resource

Pixmaps are a significant resource of the X Window System. They are used as both as a cursor marker and as a tile pattern on a window. The tile pattern is repeated over the window. But if the tile is the same size as the as the window, then the tile is repeated once, increasing the scale of a Pixmap. Modern X Window distributions are more flexible in handling Pixmaps than earlier versions of X11. However, Pixmaps do have more limitations than do windows.

When a Pixmap is used as a tile on a window, then it takes on the following properties:

- A Pixmap has both a foreground and background colour;
- In reality, the Pixmap is a map of screen pixels;
- Once a Pixmap is created by a `XCreatePixmapFromBitmapData()`, the foreground and background colours cannot be changed;
- A Pixmap only becomes visible on the screen when it is linked to a window which is then displayed;
- A Pixmap can only be placed on the background of a window;
- A Pixmap is linked to a window by a `XSetWindowBackgroundPixmap()` Xlib call;
- Once linked to a window, any drawing operations performed on a Pixmap before or after the linking will be visible in the window;
- A Pixmap background does not have to be redrawn after a window is exposed;
- A Pixmap linked to a window is stored in the server, not the client;
- A `XSetWindowBackground()` call sets the background colour of a window, and if a Pixmap had been linked to the window, it is overwritten by this plane colour—the Pixmap link to the window is lost;
- `XCopyArea()` and `XFillRectangle()` calls can be used to draw into a Pixmap;
- A Pixmap can be drawn into at any time in contrast to a window which can only be drawn on when it is visible on the screen;
- If a Pixmap is created using a `XCreatePixmap()` call, then the initial contents of the Pixmap are undefined;
- A window can only have a single Pixmap linked to it at any one time;
- The one Pixmap can be linked to more than one window at any one time.

Some of these properties also apply when a Pixmap is used as cursor marker.

4.2   Pattern Patches

Patterns can be used for many things. One of those uses is as a decoration of a button, whether the button occurs on its own, or in combination with others in the form of menus. Section 3.4 considered creating such menus using buttons of a uniform colour and maybe including text. By using patterns, visually more complex buttons can be created. Another application is for display of a logo. A further use might be to indicate the position of the mouse pointer (or cursor) on a window. Patterns, whether they be small in on-screen appearance or large, warrant consideration.

Patterns in the X Window System are described as *Pixmaps*, and they come in two varieties. One variety is the *bitmap*, or XBM format, which is composed of two colours. The two colours are the foreground and background colours which are active in the graphics context (GC) at the moment the Pixmap is displayed. In the commonly use of Pixmaps as cursors, this is the manner of their colouring. The other variety is called a *PixMap*, or XPM format, which is composed of multiple colours which are encoded in the format of the Pixmap. These are explored in Sect. 4.7.

4.3   Bitmap Patterns

During the development of the X Window System, a need was seen for bitmaps. A result of this was library functions to handle such maps were included in the X Window System distribution. Such bitmaps labelled and decorated buttons, together with forming cursors to indicate the position of the pointer on a window.

Although a bitmap can be created by hand using an editor, the program bitmap which is part of the X Window System distribution is generally used. Running this program with the command line:

```
bitmap -size 50x25 shapes.bmp &
```

a grid of 50 pixel cells horizontally by 25 pixel cells vertically is presented for creating the drawing which is to be saved in a file called shapes.bmp upon exiting the bitmap program. A drawing consisting of one circle outline, three filled circles and a filled triangle was drawn, and the contents of the resulting shapes.bmp file was:

```
#define shapes_width 50
#define shapes_height 25
static unsigned char shapes_bits[] = {
    0x00, 0x00, 0x00, 0x00, 0x00, 0x00, 0x00, 0x00, 0x00, 0x00,
    0x00, 0x00, 0x00, 0x00, 0x00, 0x00, 0x00, 0x1f, 0x00, 0x00,
    0x00, 0x00, 0x00, 0xc0, 0x7f, 0x00, 0x00, 0x00, 0x00, 0x00,
    0xe0, 0xff, 0x00, 0x0e, 0x00, 0x00, 0x1f, 0xe0, 0xff, 0xc0,
    0x7f, 0x00, 0xc0, 0x60, 0xf0, 0xff, 0xe1, 0xff, 0x00, 0x30,
    0x80, 0xf1, 0xff, 0xf1, 0xff, 0x01, 0x08, 0x00, 0xf2, 0xff,
    0xf9, 0xff, 0x03, 0x08, 0x00, 0xf2, 0xff, 0xfd, 0xff, 0x03,
    0x04, 0x00, 0xf4, 0xff, 0xfd, 0xff, 0x03, 0x04, 0x00, 0xe4,
    0xff, 0xfc, 0xff, 0x03, 0xfa, 0x03, 0xe8, 0xff, 0xfe, 0xff,
    0x03, 0xfe, 0x07, 0xc8, 0x7f, 0xfe, 0xff, 0x03, 0xfe, 0x0f,
```

```
0x08, 0x1f, 0xfe, 0xff, 0x03, 0xfe, 0x0f, 0x08, 0x00, 0xfc,
0xff, 0x03, 0xfe, 0x0f, 0x08, 0x18, 0xfc, 0xff, 0x03, 0xfe,
0x0f, 0x04, 0x3c, 0xfc, 0xff, 0x03, 0xfe, 0x0f, 0x04, 0x3e,
0xf8, 0xff, 0x03, 0xfe, 0x0f, 0x02, 0x7f, 0xf0, 0xff, 0x01,
0xfe, 0x0f, 0x02, 0xff, 0xe0, 0xff, 0x00, 0xfc, 0x87, 0x81,
0xff, 0xc0, 0x7f, 0x00, 0xf8, 0x63, 0xc0, 0xff, 0x01, 0x0e,
0x00, 0x00, 0x1f, 0xe0, 0xff, 0x01, 0x00, 0x00, 0x00, 0x00,
0x00, 0xf0, 0x03, 0x00, 0x00};
```

This bitmap is the screen pattern used in the following program example. It is an array of 0 or 1 values which represent each pixel in the 50 by 25 block of cells (pixels) given as its limits.

This array of data is converted into the internal X Window System form of a Pixmap by the Xlib function `XCreatePixmapFromBitmapData()`. The internal *Pixmap* form is an analogue of a Window, with the same attributes as a Window, but having an invisible existence in the X Window server's memory. The Pixmap can be made visible by inserting it into a window by use of the Xlib function `XCopyPlane()`.

Important: The Pixmap created by the `XCreatePixmapFromData()` call is composed only of a foreground and a background. The distribution of 1 and 0 bits in the bit pattern gives the required appearance of the foreground and background over the extent of the bit pattern. Internally in the server, the foreground is interpreted as being black and the background as white. Whether black or white is specified as the `foreground` (argument 6) in the `XCreatePixmapFromData()` call defines whether the 1's in the Pixmap represents the foreground or background, respectively. The complement is then applied to the `background` (argument 7) of the `XCreatePixmapFromData()` call. The colours for the appearance of the foreground and the background of the pattern are set by the foreground and background colours assigned in the GC in use when the Pixmap is copied to a window. Specifying whether a 1 in a Pixmap represents the foreground or background is done once, when the Pixmap is created. So one set of Pixmap data could be used to create more than one Pixmaps with opposite foreground/background combinations. The visual colour of the foreground and background can be changed by the colours specified in the GC used to move the Pixmap to the screen.

The program in Fig. 4.1 shows application of the bitmap processing capacity of the X Window System. A window coloured red is first created. A previously prepared bitmap is stored in the program, and the graphics context is used to display it using the foreground of black and the background as white. This pattern is drawn on the red window when the left-hand button of the mouse is pressed, with the pattern positioned at the position of the mouse pointer when the button is pressed. The program execution must be terminated separate from the program.

In coding this example, default values of the GC `mygc` were set using the `XCreateGC()` call. White and black colours were then assigned to the foreground and background of the GC using the `XSetForeground()` and `XSetBackground()` calls, respectively. The function `XCopyPlane()` copies the Pixmap

```
/*   The program displays a window coloured red.  When the
 *   left-hand mouse button is pressed while the pointer is in
 *   that window, a pattern patch is displayed at the location
 *   of the pointer.  The  pattern is recorded as a bitmap in the
 *   program and is displayed with a black foreground and a white
 *   background.
 *
 *   Coded by:  Ross Maloney
 *   Date:      May 2008
 */

#include <X11/Xlib.h>
#include <X11/Xutil.h>

#define shapes_width 50
#define shapes_height 25
static unsigned char shapes_bits[] = {
   0x00, 0x00, 0x00, 0x00, 0x00, 0x00, 0x00, 0x00, 0x00, 0x00,
   0x00, 0x00, 0x00, 0x00, 0x00, 0x00, 0x00, 0x1f, 0x00, 0x00,
   0x00, 0x00, 0x00, 0xc0, 0x7f, 0x00, 0x00, 0x00, 0x00, 0x00,
   0xe0, 0xff, 0x00, 0x0e, 0x00, 0x00, 0x1f, 0xe0, 0xff, 0xc0,
   0x7f, 0x00, 0xc0, 0x60, 0xf0, 0xff, 0xe1, 0xff, 0x00, 0x30,
   0x80, 0xf1, 0xff, 0xf1, 0xff, 0x01, 0x08, 0x00, 0xf2, 0xff,
   0xf9, 0xff, 0x03, 0x08, 0x00, 0xf2, 0xff, 0xfd, 0xff, 0x03,
   0x04, 0x00, 0xf4, 0xff, 0xfd, 0xff, 0x03, 0x04, 0x00, 0xe4,
   0xff, 0xfc, 0xff, 0x03, 0xfa, 0x03, 0xe8, 0xff, 0xfe, 0xff,
   0x03, 0xfe, 0x07, 0xc8, 0x7f, 0xfe, 0xff, 0x03, 0xfe, 0x0f,
   0x08, 0x1f, 0xfe, 0xff, 0x03, 0xfe, 0x0f, 0x08, 0x00, 0xfc,
   0xff, 0x03, 0xfe, 0x0f, 0x08, 0x18, 0xfc, 0xff, 0x03, 0xfe,
   0x0f, 0x04, 0x3c, 0xfc, 0xff, 0x03, 0xfe, 0x0f, 0x04, 0x3e,
   0xf8, 0xff, 0x03, 0xfe, 0x0f, 0x02, 0x7f, 0xf0, 0xff, 0x01,
   0xfe, 0x0f, 0x02, 0xff, 0xe0, 0xff, 0x00, 0xfc, 0x87, 0x81,
   0xff, 0xc0, 0x7f, 0x00, 0xf8, 0x63, 0xc0, 0xff, 0x01, 0x0e,
   0x00, 0x00, 0x1f, 0xe0, 0xff, 0x01, 0x00, 0x00, 0x00, 0x00,
   0x00, 0xf0, 0x03, 0x00, 0x00};

int main(int argc, char *argv)
{
   Display           *mydisplay;
   Window            baseWindow;
   XSetWindowAttributes   myat;
   XSizeHints        wmsize;
   XWMHints          wmhints;
   XTextProperty     windowName, iconName;
   XEvent            baseEvent;
   Xcolor            exact,closest;
   GC                mygc;
   Pixmap            pattern;
   char *window_name = "BWclick";
   char *icon_name   = "BW";
   int               screen_num, done;
   unsigned long     mymask;
```

Fig. 4.1   A red-coloured window showing image pattern placements

```
int                   x, y;

                    /* 1.  open connection to the server */
mydisplay = XOpenDisplay("");


                    /* 2.  create a top-level window */
screen_num = DefaultScreen(mydisplay);
myat.border_pixel = BlackPixel(mydisplay, screen_num);
XAllocNamedColor(mydisplay,
                 XDefaultColormap(mydisplay, screen_num),
                 "red", &exact, &closest);
myat.background_pixel = closest.pixel;
myat.event_mask = ButtonPressMask | ExposureMask;
mymask = CWBackPixel | CWBorderPixel | CWEventMask;
baseWindow = XCreateWindow(mydisplay,
                 RootWindow(mydisplay, screen_num),
                 300, 300, 350, 400, 3,
                 DefaultDepth(mydisplay, screen_num),
                 InputOutput,
                 DefaultVisual(mydisplay, screen_num),
                 mymask, &myat);


                    /* 3.  give the Window Manager hints */
wmsize.flags = USPosition | USSize;
XSetWMNormalHints(mydisplay, baseWindow, &wmsize);
wmhints.initial_state = NormalState;
wmhints.flags = StateHint;
XSetWMHints(mydisplay, baseWindow, &wmhints);
XStringListToTextProperty(&window_name, 1, &windowName);
XSetWMName(mydisplay, baseWindow, &windowName);
XStringListToTextProperty(&icon_name, 1, &iconName);
XSetWMIconName(mydisplay, baseWindow, &iconName);


                    /* 4.  establish window resources */
pattern = XCreatePixmapFromBitmapData(mydisplay, baseWindow,
                    shapes_bits, shapes_width,
                    shapes_height,
                    BlackPixel(mydisplay, screen_num),
                    WhitePixel(mydisplay, screen_num),
                    DefaultDepth(mydisplay, screen_num));
mygc = XCreateGC(mydisplay, baseWindow, 0, NULL);
XSetForeground(mydisplay, mygc,
                    WhitePixel(mydisplay, screen_num));
XSetBackground(mydisplay, mygc,
                    BlackPixel(mydisplay, screen_num));


                    /* 5.  create all the other windows needed */
                    /* 6.  select events for each window */


                    /* 7.  map the windows */
XMapWindow(mydisplay, baseWindow);
```

Fig. 4.1 (continued)

```
                /* 8.   enter the event loop */
done = 0;

while ( done == 0 )  {
  XNextEvent(mydisplay, &baseEvent);
  switch( baseEvent.type )  {
  case Expose:
    break;
  case ButtonPress:
    if ( baseEvent.xbutton.button == Button1 )  {
      x = baseEvent.xbutton.x;
      y = baseEvent.xbutton.y;
      XCopyPlane(mydisplay, pattern, baseWindow, mygc, 0, 0,
                 shapes_width, shapes_height, x, y, 1);
    }
    break;
  }
}

                /* 9.   clean up before exiting */
XUnmapWindow(mydisplay, baseWindow);
XDestroyWindow(mydisplay, baseWindow);
XCloseDisplay(mydisplay);
}
```

Fig. 4.1 (continued)

Fig. 4.2 A distribution of black and white patches at mouse points

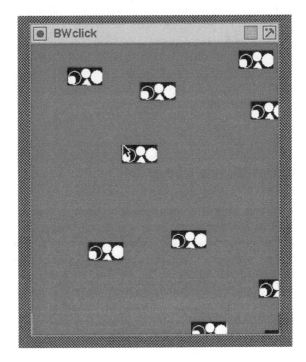

created by the XCreatePixmapFromBitmapData() call to the screen in the
window at the point required for as many times as required. In Sect. 7.1, this code is
used as the basis for producing multicolour patterns using the XPM library.

Figure 4.2 shows the screen display produced when executing the program of
Fig. 4.1. Notice:

1. The red background colour of the base window was applied when the window
   was first created as opposed to later through its graphics context (GC).
2. An event awareness (by setting the CWEventMask) is set into the top-level window when it was created.
3. The program is driven by such events, notably the ButtonPress event which occurs
   when a button on the mouse is pressed.
4. The colours set as the foreground and background in the graphics context (GC)
   of the top-level window when an image is put to the screen determine the colours
   in which the pattern is displayed.

4.3.1 Exercises

1. Modify the program so it uses the right-hand mouse button to perform the function
   originally performed by the left-hand mouse button.
2. Extend the program so the colours green, yellow, and black are used in the pattern
   produced replacing the black and white used originally. Group the colours in all
   possible combinations of two colours. At each click of the mouse button, rotate
   the group of colours used to display the pattern.
3. Modify the program of Fig. 4.1 so it uses a XCopyArea() function in place of
   the XCopyPlane() call. What advantages and disadvantages result from this
   modification?

4.4 A Bitmap Cursor

A Pixmap in general, or a bitmap to be more specific, can be used to indicate the
position of the mouse pointer. Unlike other bitmaps, cursor bixmaps are transient
as the pointer passes over a window; as the pointer moves, so does the associated
bitmap, with automatic reinstatement of what the cursor obscured. Such bitmaps are
generally 16x16 pixels in size. They are created using two bitmaps each containing
a similar pattern, but with one pattern slightly larger than the other. This is described
in Nye (1995) (p. 182). An additional attribute of these bitmaps is they contain a
hot point which is the single pixel which is to precisely represent the pointer on the
screen. This is nominated when the bitmap is created and its position within the map
is stored as part of the bitmap data structure.

```
/*   This program creates a window coloured red a then two other
 *   windows contained inside it.  One of those additional windows
 *   is coloured white and the other is coloured black.  A cursor
 *   shaped, defined by two bitmaps created externally to this
 *   program are then linked to the mouse pointer which it is over
 *   the white window.
 *
 *   Coded by:   Ross Maloney
 *   Date:       May 2008
 */

#include <X11/Xlib.h>
#include <X11/Xutil.h>

#define arrow_width 16
#define arrow_height 16
static unsigned char arrow_bits [] = {
    0x00, 0x00, 0x06, 0x00, 0x0e, 0x00, 0x3c, 0x00, 0xf8, 0x00,
    0xf8, 0x01, 0xf0, 0x07, 0xf0, 0x0f, 0xf0, 0x1f, 0xe0, 0x7f,
    0xe0, 0x7f, 0xc0, 0x7f, 0x80, 0x7f, 0x80, 0x7f, 0x00, 0x7f,
    0x00, 0x00 };

#define arrowmask_width 16
#define arrowmask_height 16
#define arrowmask_x_hot 0
#define arrowmask_y_hot 0
static unsigned char arrowmask_bits [] = {
    0x1f, 0x00, 0x3f, 0x00, 0xff, 0x00, 0xff, 0x03, 0xff, 0x07,
    0xfe, 0x0f, 0xfc, 0x1f, 0xfc, 0x3f, 0xf8, 0x7f, 0xf8, 0xff,
    0xf0, 0xff, 0xf0, 0xff, 0xe0, 0xff, 0xc0, 0xff, 0x80, 0xff,
    0x80, 0xff };

int main(int argc, char *argv)
{
    Display              *mydisplay;
    Window               baseWindow, wWindow, bWindow;
    XSetWindowAttributes myat, wat, bat;
    XSizeHints           wmsize;
    XWMHints             wmhints;
    XTextProperty        windowName, iconName;
    XEvent               baseEvent;
    XColor               exact, closest, front, backing;
    Pixmap               backArrow, foreArrow;
    Cursor               cursor;
    char *window_name = "CursorPlay";
    char *icon_name   = "Play";
    int                  screen_num, done;
    unsigned long        mymask;

                    /* 1.  open connection to the server */
    mydisplay = XOpenDisplay ("");
```

Fig. 4.3 Three windows demonstrating cursor visibility

```
                    /* 2.  create a top-level window */
screen_num = DefaultScreen(mydisplay);
myat.border_pixel = BlackPixel(mydisplay, screen_num);
XAllocNamedColor(mydisplay,
                    XDefaultColormap(mydisplay, screen_num),
                    "red", &exact, &closest);
myat.background_pixel = closest.pixel;
myat.event_mask = ButtonPressMask | ExposureMask;
mymask = CWBackPixel | CWBorderPixel | CWEventMask;
baseWindow = XCreateWindow(mydisplay,
                    RootWindow(mydisplay, screen_num),
                    400, 500, 600, 340, 3,
                    DefaultDepth(mydisplay, screen_num),
                    InputOutput,
                    DefaultVisual(mydisplay, screen_num),
                    mymask, &myat);


                    /* 3.  give the Window Manager hints */
wmsize.flags = USPosition | USSize;
XSetWMNormalHints(mydisplay, baseWindow, &wmsize);
wmhints.initial_state = NormalState;
wmhints.flags = StateHint;
XSetWMHints(mydisplay, baseWindow, &wmhints);
XStringListToTextProperty(&window_name, 1, &windowName);
XSetWMName(mydisplay, baseWindow, &windowName);
XStringListToTextProperty(&icon_name, 1, &iconName);
XSetWMIconName(mydisplay, baseWindow, &iconName);


                    /* 4.  establish window resources */
backArrow = XCreatePixmapFromBitmapData(mydisplay, baseWindow,
                    arrowmask_bits, arrowmask_width,
                    arrowmask_height, 1, 0, 1);
foreArrow = XCreatePixmapFromBitmapData(mydisplay, baseWindow,
                    arrow_bits, arrow_width, arrow_height,
                    1, 0, 1);
XAllocNamedColor(mydisplay,
                    XDefaultColormap(mydisplay, screen_num),
                    "black", &exact, &front);
XAllocNamedColor(mydisplay,
                    XDefaultColormap(mydisplay, screen_num),
                    "white", &exact, &backing);
cursor = XCreatePixmapCursor(mydisplay, foreArrow, backArrow,
                    &front, &backing,
                    arrowmask_x_hot, arrowmask_y_hot);
XDefineCursor(mydisplay, baseWindow, cursor);


                    /* 5.  create all the other windows needed */
wat.event_mask = ButtonPressMask | ExposureMask;
wat.background_pixel = WhitePixel(mydisplay, screen_num);
bat.event_mask = ButtonPressMask | ExposureMask;
bat.background_pixel = BlackPixel(mydisplay, screen_num);
```

Fig. 4.3 (continued)

```
wWindow = XCreateWindow(mydisplay, baseWindow,
                        100, 50, 200, 200, 1,
                        DefaultDepth(mydisplay, screen_num),
                        InputOutput,
                        DefaultVisual(mydisplay, screen_num),
                        mymask, &wat);
bWindow = XCreateWindow(mydisplay, baseWindow,
                        400, 50, 100, 100, 1,
                        DefaultDepth(mydisplay, screen_num),
                        InputOutput,
                        DefaultVisual(mydisplay, screen_num),
                        mymask, &bat);

                /* 6.  select events for each window */

                /* 7.  map the windows */
XMapWindow(mydisplay, baseWindow);
XMapWindow(mydisplay, wWindow);
XMapWindow(mydisplay, bWindow);

                /* 8.  enter the event loop */
done = 0;
while ( done == 0 )  {
   XNextEvent(mydisplay, &baseEvent);
   switch( baseEvent.type)  {
   case Expose:
     break;
   case ButtonPress:
     break;
   }
}
                /* 9.  clean up before exiting */
XUnmapWindow(mydisplay, baseWindow);
XDestroyWindow(mydisplay, baseWindow);
XCloseDisplay(mydisplay);
}
```

Fig. 4.3 (continued)

The code in Fig. 4.3 shows this process. First, the bitmaps were created using the `bitmap` program and the resulting bitmap data structures loaded into the file which contained the rest of the program's code. A window coloured red is used to contain a black window and a white window. A cursor, in the form of a double-arrowhead, is created externally to the program and inserted in this code. The data associated with this arrowhead were stored in the `arrow_bits` array, with the associated outline bitmap with a foreground arrowhead shape slightly larger than shape contained in the `arrow_bits` array, stored in the `arrowmask_bits` array. The default foreground colour of the arrowhead is set to black and its outline set to white, when these Pixmaps are created by the `XCreatePixmapFromBitmapData()` calls.

The program in Fig. 4.3 shows why a cursor is created with a shape and with an outline of that shape. The black and white colours used in creating the cursor correspond to the background colours of two of the windows. Without the outline, the cursor would *be lost* when the mouse pointer enters the black window. Moving the cursor over each of the three windows in this example demonstrates the visibility of the cursor being used. This particular design of a cursor is not good: Can you think of reasons for this observation? The program is terminated externally to this program.

Notice:

1. The size of the border pixels for the black and white windows has been decreased to 1 pixel as opposed to the 3 pixel size for the containing red window. This is only for aesthetics.
2. The actual colour of the cursor is assigned when the cursor is made using the XCreatePixmapCursor() function, not when the associated bitmaps are created. As a result, dummy values can be used when such bitmaps are created using the XCreatePixmapFromData() function.
3. The depth of the cursor bitmaps (Pixmaps) is unity (1).

Figure 4.4 shows the displayed output of the program of Fig. 4.3 at an instant of time. As the mouse pointer is moved over the red, white, and black windows, the pointer indicator (which looks like two arrowheads facing in diagonal opposite directions) shows its position. A closer look at the cursor indicates a white border around the black centre. The border is created by the appropriate colouring and sizing of the two bitmaps which make up the cursor's shape. Without the white border, the black cursor would disappear when over a black window.

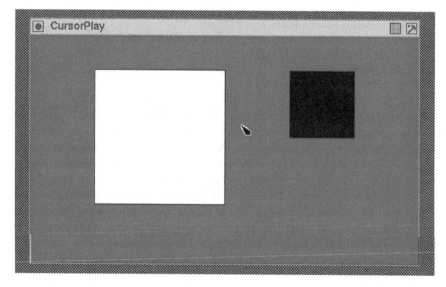

Fig. 4.4 A user designed cursor pointer on a window

4.4.1 Exercises

1. Modify the background and foreground colours so they are different from red, black, or white.
2. Extend the program of Fig. 4.3 so there is a second cursor which is associated only with the black-coloured window.
3. Modify the shape of the cursor so it is significantly different from that shown in the program of Fig. 4.3.

4.5   A Partially Transparent Pixmap

The Pixmaps previously considered when displayed on the screen had a rectangular footprint. There are situations where such a footprint is not desirable. A cursor is such a situation. The cursor pattern is a Pixmap, but the footprint on the screen is not rectangular. This is achieved by having transparent parts in the rectangular Pixmap pattern which allows the portion of the screen they cover to remain visible. Cursors are considered a particular situation in X and are handled in a unique manner. But the idea of transparency in a portion of a Pixmap has application beyond cursors. One example of this is drawing the arrow of a cursor on a window as an indicator of a previous pointer position for taking a screenshot. For example, a partially transparent window in the shape of a magnifying glass might be moved across the window to locate a portion of the screen to be magnified. Having such a magnifier obscuring the magnification target would not be reasonable but also the pattern of the magnified is required to be larger than a cursor.

Figure 4.6 is an example screen output of a program which places a partially transparent Pixmap on the screen where the pointer is positioned when the right-handle mouse button is pressed. The Pixmap is of a black arrow with a narrow white boarder around it. A hole is located in the centre of the arrow. The red colour of the screen is seen to surround the outer white border of the arrow and fill the hole inside the arrow centre. Figure 4.5 contains the code used to produce this result.

With respect to the code of Fig. 4.5, note the following. The arrow is drawn from a Pixmap with a black foreground and a white background. If this Pixmap was displayed on the screen, the black figure of the arrow would appear in a white square. A mask is loaded into the GC used for drawing this Pixmap. This mask is a Pixmap with 1's positioned above pixels of the arrow Pixmap which are to be shown on the screen. This means the shape contained in the mask Pixmap is slightly larger than the arrow so some of the arrow Pixmap's background is covered by the mask bits. The hole appears in the arrow on the screen is also set in this Pixmap and not in the Pixmap of the original arrow. The mask is positioned relative to the destination drawable, not with respect to the bitmap which is to be filtered. This requires the use of the XSetClipOrigin() call in the event loop to adjust the position of the mask

```
/*   This program displays a window coloured red.  When the
 *   right-hand mouse button is pressed while the pointer is
 *   in that window, a pattern patch is displayed at the
 *   location of the pointer.  The pattern is of an arrow
 *   pointing to the top-left which is coloured black,
 *   surrounded by a thin white border.  This pattern is
 *   recorded as a bitmap in the program and is displayed
 *   using a clipping mask which also is stored as a Pixmap.
 *   A transparent Pixmap pattern results.
 *
 *   Coded by:   Ross Maloney
 *   Date:       March 2009
 */

#include <X11/Xlib.h>
#include <X11/Xutil.h>

#define arrow_width 16
#define arrow_height 16
static unsigned char arrow_bits[] = {
    0x00, 0x00, 0x06, 0x00, 0x1e, 0x00, 0x7c, 0x00, 0xfc, 0x01,
    0xf8, 0x07, 0xf8, 0x1f, 0xf8, 0x7f, 0xf0, 0x7f, 0xf0, 0x03,
    0xe0, 0x07, 0xe0, 0x06, 0xc0, 0x0c, 0xc0, 0x18, 0x80, 0x30,
    0x00, 0x00};

#define mask_width 16
#define mask_height 16
static unsigned char mask_bits[] = {
    0x07, 0x00, 0x1f, 0x00, 0x7f, 0x00, 0xf6, 0x01, 0xc6, 0x07,
    0x8e, 0x1f, 0x0c, 0x3e, 0x1c, 0xfc, 0x38, 0xfc, 0x38, 0xfc,
    0x78, 0x0f, 0xf0, 0x1f, 0xf0, 0x3f, 0xe0, 0x7d, 0xe0, 0x79,
    0xc0, 0x71};

int main(int argc, char *argv)
{
    Display             *mydisplay;
    Window              baseWindow;
    XSetWindowAttributes  myat;
    XSizeHints          wmsize;
    XWMHints            wmhints;
    XTextProperty       windowName, iconName;
    XEvent              baseEvent;
    XColor              exact, closest;
    GC                  mygc;
    XGCValues           myGCValues;
    Pixmap              pattern, mask;
    char *window_name = "Transparent";
    char *icon_name   = "Tr";
    int                 screen_num, done;
    unsigned long       mymask;
```

Fig. 4.5 A program while draws transparent arrow at each pointer click

```
int                x, y;

                   /* 1.   open connection to the server */
mydisplay = XOpenDisplay("");

                   /* 2.   create a top-level window */
screen_num = DefaultScreen(mydisplay);
myat.border_pixel = BlackPixel(mydisplay, screen_num);
XAllocNamedColor(mydisplay,
                 XDefaultColormap(mydisplay, screen_num),
                 "red", &exact, &closest);
myat.background_pixel = closest.pixel;
myat.event_mask = ButtonPressMask | ExposureMask;
mymask = CWBackPixel | CWBorderPixel | CWEventMask;
baseWindow = XCreateWindow(mydisplay,
                           RootWindow(mydisplay, screen_num),
                           300, 300, 350, 400, 3,
                           DefaultDepth(mydisplay, screen_num),
                           InputOutput,
                           DefaultVisual(mydisplay, screen_num),
                           mymask, &myat);

                   /* 3.   give the Window Manager hints */
wmsize.flags = USPosition | USSize;
XSetWMNormalHints(mydisplay, baseWindow, &wmsize);
wmhints.initial_state = NormalState;
wmhints.flags = StateHint;
XSetWMHints(mydisplay, baseWindow, &wmhints);
XStringListToTextProperty(&window_name, 1, &windowName);
XSetWMName(mydisplay, baseWindow, &windowName);
XStringListToTextProperty(&icon_name, 1, &iconName);
XSetWMIconName(mydisplay, baseWindow, &iconName);

                   /* 4.   establish window reqources */
pattern = XCreatePixmapFromBitmapData(mydisplay, baseWindow,
                   arrow_bits, arrow_width, arrow_height,
                   WhitePixel(mydisplay, screen_num),
                   BlackPixel(mydisplay, screen_num),
                   DefaultDepth(mydisplay, screen_num));
mask = XCreatePixmapFromBitmapData(mydisplay, baseWindow,
                   mask_bits, mask_width, mask_height,
                   1, 0, 1);
mymask = GCForeground | GCBackground | GCClipMask;
myGCValues.background = WhitePixel(mydisplay, screen_num);
myGCValues.foreground = BlackPixel(mydisplay, screen_num);
myGCValues.clip_mask = mask;
mygc = XCreateGC(mydisplay, baseWindow, mymask, &myGCValues);

                   /* 5.   create all the other windows needed */
```

Fig. 4.5 (continued)

```
                /* 6.   select events for each window */

                /* 7.   map the windows */
XMapWindow( mydisplay ,  baseWindow );

                /* 8.   enter the event loop */
done = 0;
while ( done == 0 )  {
  XNextEvent( mydisplay ,  &baseEvent );
  switch( baseEvent.type )  {
  case Expose :
    break;
  case ButtonPress :
    if ( baseEvent.xbutton.button == Button3 )  {
      x = baseEvent.xbutton.x;
      y = baseEvent.xbutton.y;
      XSetClipOrigin( mydisplay ,  x,  y );
      XCopyPlane( mydisplay ,  pattern ,  baseWindow ,  mygc ,  0,  0,
                  arrow_width ,  arrow_height ,  x,  y,  1);
    }
    break;
  }
}

                /* 9.   clean up before exiting */
XUnmapWindow( mydisplay ,  baseWindow );
XDestroyWindow( mydisplay ,  baseWindow );
XCloseDisplay( mydisplay );
}
```

Fig. 4.5 (continued)

to align to where the arrow Pixmap is copied to the screen. For this, the coordinates of the pointer are used with both the XSetClipOrigin() and XCopyPlane() calls to correctly position the arrow shape.

This code indicates when the GC is created, the value mask does not have to indicate the clipping mask is going to change. However, if it is included by adding GCClipMask to the bit mask used when creating the GC (where the mask contains as a minimum GCForeground | GCBackground), then a mask must be assigned to the clip_mask member of the XGCValues passed to the XCreateGC() call.

Fig. 4.6 A red screen covered by transparent arrows

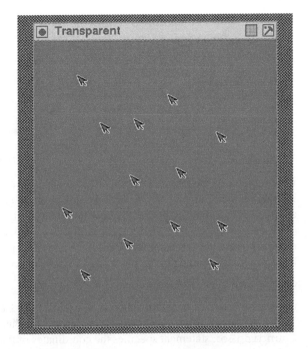

4.6 Using Postscript to Create Labels

The example in Fig. 3.6 is one way of creating a menu of labelled entries. This was done by creating a menu item as a window and then drawing a string into the window using the `XDrawImageString()` call. An alternate approach is considered here in which Pixmaps which were considered in Fig. 4.1 are used. This approach has the advantages over the string drawing of the:

- transmission cost for displaying the label letters is reduced and
- characters available to form the label is increased.

Forming labels with this technique enables a combination of letters with symbols. The problem is obtaining the letter and symbol combination which looks correct when the label appears on the display. Such combinations could be created by hand by using an editor. That technique is reasonably time-consuming, and the results can be uncertain. An alternative is the use the `bitmap` program as was done in Sect. 4.3. However, the program `bitmap` provides no assistance in creating characters. The technique used here is to create the label using a small Encapsulated Postscript (EPS) program. Then, this program is transformed into a bitmap using the `convert` program, which is part of the `ImageMagick` open software package.

As an example of this label generation progress, the EPS program:

```
%!PS-Adobe-2.0 EPSF-1.2
%%BoundingBox: 0 5 50 25

/Times-Bold findfont
18 scalefont
setfont
10 10 moveto
(View) show

showpage
```

which produced the label View was created using an editor. Assume this program is stored in the file string.eps. Since this program is an EPS program, it can be executed on a Postscript printer or programs such as ghostscript or display (which is part of the open source ImageMagick package). They provide a means of inspecting what the label will look like. Then, the required bitmap form of the label would be obtained in the file view.xbm by the command:

```
convert string.eps view.xbm
```

using the convert program which is also part of the ImageMagick package.

An advantage of this technique comes from the flexibility of Postscript. The BoundingBox statement specifies the coordinates of the lower left-hand corner (x and y values, respectively) and the upper right-hand coordinates in which the label is to be drawn; anything outside of this box will disappear. The /Times-Bold statement selects the font in which the label is to be drawn, while the 18 scalefont statement indicates the font is to be 18 points in height. The characters in the required label are specified in the (View) show statement, which produce View as output. By changing these four statements, different labels, composed from different sized fonts, can be generated.

Postscript is designed to use fine divisions in coordinates. This results in smooth representation of geometric shapes, in particular curves. Postscript generates all character shapes by drawing them as a series of (Bézier) curves. Such curves are designed to perform well on the printed page. By contrast, X uses a bitmap display in which the coordinates are fixed by the screen hardware's pixel density and are today generally packed in a higher density than *Printer's points* on which Postscript is designed. Despite this density difference, a graphic or string of characters which Postscript generates on a printed page will be viable on a screen. This is particularly the case if Postscript is converted to a bitmap representation as proposed in the above procedure. From the bitmap (in the form of Pixmaps), X produces menu labels.

Postscript is supplied with 35 standard fonts. Two of those fonts are of symbols and standard small patterns, leaving 33 for creating text. Those standard fonts, or *typefaces*, for creating text are listed in Table 4.1. The name of the font is used with the findfont Postscript language construct, as in the example EPS program above.

A bitmap is transformed into a Pixmap, and it is the Pixmap which X uses. There is no loss in precision or accuracy in going from a bitmap to a Pixmap. A Pixmap is a generalized version of a bitmap (from version 11 of X, bitmaps are

Table 4.1 Names of the 33 standard postscript text fonts

No.	Font name	No.	Font name
1	AvantGrade-Book	2	AvantGrade-BookOblique
3	AvantGrade-Demi	4	AvantGrade-DemiOblique
5	Bookman-Demi	6	Bookman-DemiItalic
7	Bookman-Light	8	Bookman-LightItalic
9	Courier	10	Courier-Bold
11	Courier-BoldOblique	12	Courier-Oblique
13	Helvetica	14	Helvetica-Bold
15	Helvetica-BoldOblique	16	Helvetica-Narrow
17	Helvetica-Narrow-Bold	18	Helvetica-Narrow-BoldOblique
19	Helvetica-Narrow-Oblique	20	Helvetica-Oblique
21	NewCenturySchlbk-Bold	22	NewCenturySchlbk-BoldItalic
23	NewCenturySchlbk-Italic	24	NewCenturySchlbk-Roman
25	Palatino-Bold	26	Palatino-BoldItalic
27	Palatino-Italic	28	Palatino-Roman
29	Times-Bold	30	Times-BoldItalic
31	Times-Italic	32	Times-Roman
33	ZapfChancery-MediumItalic		

no longer directly handled by X but are considered as Pixmaps). Once a Pixmap is created, it is a one-to-one mapping between a bit of the Pixmap and a pixel on the screen. This is the reason for their use as menu labels. Xlib provides the `XCreatePixmapFromBitmapData()` function to convert a bitmap created externally into a Pixmap for use by X. However, the conversion of Postscript output to a bitmap can result in precision loss; what appears clear and precise from Postscript be less so in the corresponding bitmap representation. But Postscript provides a easier creation approach.

To assist selection of Postscript fonts for use in creating bitmap labels, a program was written to display all 33 standard Postscript text fonts. The output of this program is in Fig. 4.7. Each of the 33 fonts is shown displaying the same sentence at 12, 14, and 18 point sizes in consecutive columns of Fig. 4.7. The numbers in the left column of Fig. 4.7 correspond to the number against each of the fonts shown in Table 4.1. The most common font size for menu labels is 12 point.

Postscript programs each similar to the above, were written for each of the 33 fonts, and their 3 font sizes separately. A bitmap equivalent was obtained by applying the `convert` program to each Postscript program. The resulting bitmap wasbrought into the X window program using a `#include` for each bitmap. The Xlib function used to create a Pixmap from the bitmap was `XCreatePixmapFromBitmapData()`. A `XCopyArea()` Xlib call was used to place the Pixmap on the display.

1	The quick brown fox jumped.	The quick brown fox jumped.	The quick brown fox jumped.
2	The quick brown fox jumped.	The quick brown fox jumped.	The quick brown fox jumped.
3	The quick brown fox jumped.	The quick brown fox jumped.	The quick brown fox jumped.
4	The quick brown fox jumped.	The quick brown fox jumped.	The quick brown fox jumped.
5	The quick brown fox jumped.	The quick brown fox jumped.	The quick brown fox jumped.
6	The quick brown fox jumped.	The quick brown fox jumped.	The quick brown fox jumped.
7	The quick brown fox jumped.	The quick brown fox jumped.	The quick brown fox jumped.
8	The quick brown fox jumped.	The quick brown fox jumped.	The quick brown fox jumped.
9	The quick brown fox jumped.	The quick brown fox jumped.	The quick brown fox jumped.
10	The quick brown fox jumped.	The quick brown fox jumped.	The quick brown fox jumped.
11	The quick brown fox jumped.	The quick brown fox jumped.	The quick brown fox jumped.
12	The quick brown fox jumped.	The quick brown fox jumped.	The quick brown fox jumped.
13	The quick brown fox jumped.	The quick brown fox jumped.	The quick brown fox jumped.
14	The quick brown fox jumped.	The quick brown fox jumped.	The quick brown fox jumped.
15	The quick brown fox jumped.	The quick brown fox jumped.	The quick brown fox jumped.
16	The quick brown fox jumped.	The quick brown fox jumped.	The quick brown fox jumped.
17	The quick brown fox jumped.	The quick brown fox jumped.	The quick brown fox jumped.
18	The quick brown fox jumped.	The quick brown fox jumped.	The quick brown fox jumped.
19	The quick brown fox jumped.	The quick brown fox jumped.	The quick brown fox jumped.
20	The quick brown fox jumped.	The quick brown fox jumped.	The quick brown fox jumped.
21	The quick brown fox jumped.	The quick brown fox jumped.	The quick brown fox jumped.
22	The quick brown fox jumped.	The quick brown fox jumped.	The quick brown fox jumped.
23	The quick brown fox jumped.	The quick brown fox jumped.	The quick brown fox jumped.
24	The quick brown fox jumped.	The quick brown fox jumped.	The quick brown fox jumped.
25	The quick brown fox jumped.	The quick brown fox jumped.	The quick brown fox jumped.
26	The quick brown fox jumped.	The quick brown fox jumped.	The quick brown fox jumped.
27	The quick brown fox jumped.	The quick brown fox jumped.	The quick brown fox jumped.
28	The quick brown fox jumped.	The quick brown fox jumped.	The quick brown fox jumped.
29	The quick brown fox jumped.	The quick brown fox jumped.	The quick brown fox jumped.
30	The quick brown fox jumped.	The quick brown fox jumped.	The quick brown fox jumped.
31	The quick brown fox jumped.	The quick brown fox jumped.	The quick brown fox jumped.
32	The quick brown fox jumped.	The quick brown fox jumped.	The quick brown fox jumped.
33	The quick brown fox jumped.	The quick brown fox jumped.	The quick brown fox jumped.

Fig. 4.7 Bitmap rendering in 12, 14, and 18 point of 33 standard Postscript text fonts

Inspection of Fig. 4.7 indicates properties of the standard Postscript text fonts relevant to their selection for use in creating menu labels. Font 33 (ZapfChancery-MediumItalic) appears the most inappropriate due to its compactness. The Courier fonts (number 9–12) are too spaced out. Fonts 1 (AvantGrade-Book), 16 (Helvetica-Narrow), 28 (Palatino-Roman), and 32 (Times-Roman) appear to retain their clarity across the three point sizes of the tabulation, particularly at 12 point. These fonts might be used as first choices in obtaining the font thought most appropriate for menu items. Such selection is inexact and is subject to the opinion of whom is making the selection. For example, should bold or normal weight fonts be used?

4.7 Changing the Colour of a Pixmap

One means of indicating to the program user what selection is about to be made is to change the colour of a button on which the mouse button currently rests. This gives a more positive indication of the mouse pointer's position than finding the mouse cursor. This can be implemented using the Pixmap handling idea contained in the example of Fig. 4.1. The Pixmap used for the label is created by the Postscript conversion technique given in Sect. 4.6.

Fig. 4.8 Inverted Pixmaps
on a window

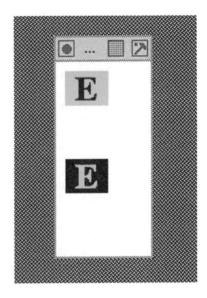

The program in Fig. 4.9 shows the basis of this process. It uses bitmap data of a 36-point E character. This is converted to a Pixmap in the program and then placed in two fixed positions on a window coloured white. The black and green colours of the respective foreground and background are swapped over between the two positions. As with all X11 programs, it is event driven, and in this case, the exposure event is used. Notice in Fig. 4.9 this exposure event is linked to the base window when it is created.

Figure 4.8 shows the screen display produced when executing the program of Fig. 4.9.

Notice in the program of Fig. 4.9 the XCopyPlane() function call is used to move the Pixmap to the window so as to make it visible. The function XCopyArea() cannot be used for this purpose as it does not make reference to the foreground and background members of the GC included in the call. The XCopyArea() uses the GC, but not its foreground and background members. It is those members which are used to colour the Pixmap on the window.

```
/*   This program draws a 100 by 200 pixel base window.  An image
 *   is created from a bitmap pattern of the character E that had
 *   been created externally to this program.  That bitmap
 *   pattern is stored in this program.  The program converts that
 *   pattern to the X Window System Pixmap format and that Pixmap
 *   format is written onto the base window using two different
 *   sets of foreground and background colours.
 *
 *   Coded by:   Ross Maloney
 *   Date:       July 2008
 */

#include <X11/Xlib.h>
#include <X11/Xutil.h>


#define e_width 45
#define e_height 35
static char e_bits [] = {
   0x00,  0x00,  0x00,  0x00,  0x00,  0x00,  0x00,  0x00,  0x00,  0x00,
   0x00,  0x00,  0x00,  0x00,  0x00,  0x00,  0x00,  0x00,  0x00,  0x00,
   0x00,  0x00,  0x00,  0x00,  0x00,  0x00,  0x00,  0x00,  0x00,  0x00,
   0x00,  0x00,  0x00,  0x00,  0x00,  0x00,  0x00,  0xfc,  0xff,  0xff,
   0x00,  0x00,  0x00,  0xf8,  0xff,  0xff,  0x00,  0x00,  0x00,  0xe0,
   0x0f,  0xf8,  0x00,  0x00,  0x00,  0xc0,  0x0f,  0xe0,  0x00,  0x00,
   0x00,  0xc0,  0x0f,  0xe0,  0x00,  0x00,  0x00,  0xc0,  0x0f,  0xc6,
   0x00,  0x00,  0x00,  0xc0,  0x0f,  0xc6,  0x00,  0x00,  0x00,  0xc0,
   0x0f,  0x06,  0x00,  0x00,  0x00,  0xc0,  0x0f,  0x07,  0x00,  0x00,
   0x00,  0xc0,  0x0f,  0x07,  0x00,  0x00,  0x00,  0xc0,  0xcf,  0x07,
   0x00,  0x00,  0x00,  0xc0,  0xff,  0x07,  0x00,  0x00,  0x00,  0xc0,
   0xff,  0x07,  0x00,  0x00,  0x00,  0xc0,  0x8f,  0x07,  0x00,  0x00,
   0x00,  0xc0,  0x0f,  0x07,  0x00,  0x00,  0x00,  0xc0,  0x0f,  0x06,
   0x00,  0x00,  0x00,  0xc0,  0x0f,  0x06,  0x01,  0x00,  0x00,  0xc0,
   0x0f,  0x86,  0x01,  0x00,  0x00,  0xc0,  0x0f,  0xc0,  0x01,  0x00,
   0x00,  0xc0,  0x0f,  0xc0,  0x01,  0x00,  0x00,  0xc0,  0x0f,  0xe0,
   0x01,  0x00,  0x00,  0xe0,  0x0f,  0xf8,  0x01,  0x00,  0x00,  0xf8,
   0xff,  0xff,  0x00,  0x00,  0x00,  0xfc,  0xff,  0xff,  0x00,  0x00,
   0x00,  0x00,  0x00,  0x00,  0x00,  0x00,  0x00,  0x00,  0x00,  0x00,
   0x00,  0x00,  0x00,  0x00,  0x00,  0x00,  0x00,  0x00,  0x00,  0x00,
   0x00,  0x00,  0x00,  0x00,  0x00,  0x00,  0x00,  0x00,  0x00,  0x00 };

int main(int argc, char *argv)
{
   Display            *mydisplay;
   XSetWindowAttributes  myat;
   Window             mywindow;
   XSizeHints         wmsize;
   XWMHints           wmhints;
   XTextProperty      windowName, iconName;
   char *window_name = "Image";
```

Fig. 4.9 Inverting the foreground and background of a Pixmap

```
char  *icon_name = "Im";
XEvent         myevent;
XGCValues      myGCvalues;
GC             imageGC;
Pixmap         pattern;
XImage         *local;
int            screen_num, done, x, y;
unsigned long  valuemask;

               /* 1.   open connection to the server */
mydisplay = XOpenDisplay("");

               /* 2.   create a top-level window */
screen_num = DefaultScreen(mydisplay);
myat.background_pixel = WhitePixel(mydisplay, screen_num);
myat.border_pixel = BlackPixel(mydisplay, screen_num);
myat.event_mask = ButtonPressMask | ExposureMask;
valuemask = CWBackPixel | CWBorderPixel | CWEventMask;
mywindow = XCreateWindow(mydisplay,
                    RootWindow(mydisplay, screen_num),
                    300, 50, 100, 200, 3,
                    DefaultDepth(mydisplay, screen_num),
                    InputOutput,
                    DefaultVisual(mydisplay, screen_num),
                    valuemask, &myat);

               /* 3.   give the Window Manager hints */
wmsize.flags = USPosition | USSize;
XSetWMNormalHints(mydisplay, mywindow, &wmsize);
wmhints.initial_state = NormalState;
wmhints.flags = StateHint;
XSetWMHints(mydisplay, mywindow, &wmhints);
XStringListToTextProperty(&window_name, 1, &windowName);
XSetWMName(mydisplay, mywindow, &windowName);
XStringListToTextProperty(&icon_name, 1, &iconName);
XSetWMIconName(mydisplay, mywindow, &iconName);

               /* 4.   establish window reqources */
pattern = XCreatePixmapFromBitmapData(mydisplay, mywindow,
                    e_bits, e_width, e_height,
                    WhitePixel(mydisplay, screen_num),
                    BlackPixel(mydisplay, screen_num),
                    DefaultDepth(mydisplay, screen_num));
imageGC = XCreateGC(mydisplay, mywindow, 0, NULL);

               /* 5.   create all the other windows needed */

               /* 6.   select events for each window */

               /* 7.   map the windows */
```

Fig. 4.9 (continued)

```
XMapWindow( mydisplay ,  mywindow );

              /* 8.  enter the event loop */
done = 0;
while ( done == 0 )  {
  XNextEvent( mydisplay ,  &myevent );
  switch ( myevent . type )  {
  case Expose :
    XSetBackground( mydisplay ,  imageGC,  0xff00 );
    XSetForeground( mydisplay ,  imageGC,
                    BlackPixel( mydisplay ,  screen_num ));
    XCopyPlane( mydisplay ,  pattern ,  mywindow,  imageGC,  0,  0,
                e_width ,  e_height ,  10,  10,  1);
    XSetForeground( mydisplay ,  imageGC,  0xff00 );
    XSetBackground( mydisplay ,  imageGC,
                    BlackPixel( mydisplay ,  screen_num ));
    XCopyPlane( mydisplay ,  pattern ,  mywindow,  imageGC,  0,  0,
                e_width ,  e_height ,  10,  100,  1);
    break;
  case ButtonPress :
    break;
  }
}

              /* 9.  clean up before exiting */
XUnmapWindow( mydisplay ,  mywindow );
XDestroyWindow( mydisplay ,  mywindow );
XCloseDisplay ( mydisplay );
}
```

Fig. 4.9 (continued)

4.8 Reducing Server–Client Interaction by Images

An image is a modification of the Pixmap provided by the X Window System. Whereas a Pixmap is stored on the server, an image is stored in the client program. This (at least) reduces the possibility of resource limitations on a X program due to the server. Another consequence of this is any manipulation of an image by a program does not require the exchange of protocol messages between the client and the server to access the image, and as a result, the program should run faster. Interaction by the program user with menus formed from Pixmaps is an example of such a manipulation. Advantage can be gained by using image format for formulating menus.

To indicate the basic technique, the example of Fig. 4.9 for screen displaying two versions of the one Pixmap is redone in Fig. 4.11. In this instance, the Pixmap is changed to image format which is then sent to the screen. The use of red (0xff0000) and yellow (0xffff00) in the foreground and background of those image dumps to screen is applicable to both the Pixmap and image format techniques.

Fig. 4.10 Two Pixmaps handled in image format dumped on a window

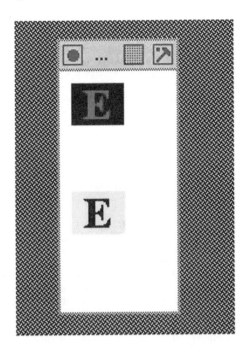

There are some important differences in how a Pixmap is used directly, as in the program of Fig. 4.9, and indirectly using the image format. The starting point in both cases is the pattern of bits indicating the foreground and background which is then converted to a `Pixmap` structure by the `XCreatePixmapFromBitmapData()` call. The Pixmap can then be made visible on a window using a `XCopyPlane()` call. For the image approach, an image in the form of a `XImage` structure is created from a Pixmap using the `XGetImage()` call. This image is made visible on a window by using the `XPutImage()` function. The `XPutImage()` function will only use the colours in the GC which are included in the call, if the image is of `XYBitmap` format. But the `XYBitmap` format is not one of the two formats the `XGetImage()` function recognizes. This is overcome by explicitly setting the `format` member of the image created by the `XGetImage()` to be `XYBitmap` after setting the depth parameter of the `XCreatePixmapFromBitmapData()` to unity (1) to indicate the Pixmap is in fact to be a bitmap. Alternately, the call `XCreatePixmapFromBitmapData()` could be used as a replacement for the `XCreateBitmapFromData()` call. That approach would require fewer parameters in the call, but the call could not be used if the direct use of the Pixmap was being used.

The screen output of the program in Fig. 4.11 is shown in Fig. 4.10. This output is very similar to that in Fig. 4.8 (aside from colour differences) which was produced by the program in Fig. 4.1.

```
/*    This program draws a 100 by 200 pixel base window.  An image
 *    is created from a bitmap pattern of the character E that had
 *    been created externally to this program.  That bitmap pattern
 *    is stored in this program.  The program converts that pattern
 *    to the X Window System image format and that image format is
 *    written onto the base window using two different sets of
 *    foreground and background colours.
 *
 *    Coded by:    Ross Maloney
 *    Date:        July 2008
 */

#include <X11/Xlib.h>
#include <X11/Xutil.h>
#include <stdio.h>

#define e_width 45
#define e_height 35
static char e_bits [] = {
   0x00, 0x00, 0x00, 0x00, 0x00, 0x00, 0x00, 0x00, 0x00, 0x00,
   0x00, 0x00, 0x00, 0x00, 0x00, 0x00, 0x00, 0x00, 0x00, 0x00,
   0x00, 0x00, 0x00, 0x00, 0x00, 0x00, 0x00, 0x00, 0x00, 0x00,
   0x00, 0x00, 0x00, 0x00, 0x00, 0x00, 0x00, 0xfc, 0xff, 0xff,
   0x00, 0x00, 0x00, 0xf8, 0xff, 0xff, 0x00, 0x00, 0x00, 0xe0,
   0x0f, 0xf8, 0x00, 0x00, 0x00, 0xc0, 0x0f, 0xe0, 0x00, 0x00,
   0x00, 0xc0, 0x0f, 0xe0, 0x00, 0x00, 0x00, 0xc0, 0x0f, 0xc6,
   0x00, 0x00, 0x00, 0xc0, 0x0f, 0xc6, 0x00, 0x00, 0x00, 0xc0,
   0x0f, 0x06, 0x00, 0x00, 0x00, 0xc0, 0x0f, 0x07, 0x00, 0x00,
   0x00, 0xc0, 0x0f, 0x07, 0x00, 0x00, 0x00, 0xc0, 0xcf, 0x07,
   0x00, 0x00, 0x00, 0xc0, 0x0ff, 0x07, 0x00, 0x00, 0x00, 0xc0,
   0xff, 0x07, 0x00, 0x00, 0x00, 0xc0, 0x8f, 0x07, 0x00, 0x00,
   0x00, 0xc0, 0x0f, 0x07, 0x00, 0x00, 0x00, 0xc0, 0x0f, 0x06,
   0x00, 0x00, 0x00, 0xc0, 0x0f, 0x06, 0x01, 0x00, 0x00, 0xc0,
   0x0f, 0x86, 0x01, 0x00, 0x00, 0xc0, 0x0f, 0xc0, 0x01, 0x00,
   0x00, 0xc0, 0x0f, 0xc0, 0x01, 0x00, 0x00, 0xc0, 0x0f, 0xe0,
   0x01, 0x00, 0x00, 0xe0, 0x0f, 0xf8, 0x01, 0x00, 0x00, 0xf8,
   0xff, 0xff, 0x00, 0x00, 0x00, 0xfc, 0xff, 0xff, 0x00, 0x00,
   0x00, 0x00, 0x00, 0x00, 0x00, 0x00, 0x00, 0x00, 0x00, 0x00,
   0x00, 0x00, 0x00, 0x00, 0x00, 0x00, 0x00, 0x00, 0x00, 0x00,
   0x00, 0x00, 0x00, 0x00, 0x00, 0x00, 0x00, 0x00, 0x00, 0x00 };


int main(int argc, char *argv)
{
   Display           *mydisplay;
   XSetWindowAttributes   myat;
   Window            mywindow;
   XSizeHints        wmsize;
   XWMHints          wmhints;
   XTextProperty     windowName, iconName;
   char *window_name = "Image";
```

Fig. 4.11 Two versions of a Pixmap handled in image format

```
char        *icon_name = "Im";
XEvent      myevent;
XGCValues   myGCvalues;
GC          imageGC;
Pixmap      pattern;

XImage      *local;
int         screen_num, done;
unsigned long valuemask;

                /* 1.  open connection to the server */
mydisplay = XOpenDisplay("");

                /* 2.  create a top-level window */
screen_num = DefaultScreen(mydisplay);
myat.background_pixel = WhitePixel(mydisplay, screen_num);
myat.border_pixel = BlackPixel(mydisplay, screen_num);
myat.event_mask = ExposureMask;
valuemask = CWBackPixel | CWBorderPixel | CWEventMask;
mywindow = XCreateWindow(mydisplay,
                         RootWindow(mydisplay, screen_num),
                         300, 50, 100, 200, 3,
                         DefaultDepth(mydisplay, screen_num),
                         InputOutput,
                         DefaultVisual(mydisplay, screen_num),
                         valuemask, &myat);

                /* 3.  give the Window Manager hints */
wmsize.flags = USPosition | USSize;
XSetWMNormalHints(mydisplay, mywindow, &wmsize);
wmhints.initial_state = NormalState;
wmhints.flags = StateHint;
XSetWMHints(mydisplay, mywindow, &wmhints);
XStringListToTextProperty(&window_name, 1, &windowName);
XSetWMName(mydisplay, mywindow, &windowName);
XStringListToTextProperty(&icon_name, 1, &iconName);
XSetWMIconName(mydisplay, mywindow, &iconName);

                /* 4.  establish window reqources */
pattern = XCreatePixmapFromBitmapData(mydisplay, mywindow,
                         e_bits, e_width, e_height,
                         WhitePixel(mydisplay, screen_num),
                         BlackPixel(mydisplay, screen_num), 1);
local = XGetImage(mydisplay, pattern, 0, 0, e_width, e_height,
                  1, XYPixmap);
local->format = XYBitmap;
imageGC = XCreateGC(mydisplay, mywindow, 0, NULL);

                /* 5.  create all the other windows needed */
                /* 6.  select events for each window */
                /* 7.  map the windows */
XMapWindow(mydisplay, mywindow);
```

Fig. 4.11 (continued)

```
                    /* 8.  enter the event loop */
  done = 0;
  while ( done == 0 ) {
    XNextEvent(mydisplay , &myevent);
    switch (myevent.type)  {
    case Expose:
      XSetBackground(mydisplay , imageGC,
                     BlackPixel(mydisplay , screen_num));
      XSetForeground(mydisplay , imageGC, 0xff0000);
      XPutImage(mydisplay , mywindow, imageGC, local , 0, 0, 10, 10,
                e_width , e_height);
      XSetBackground(mydisplay , imageGC, 0xffff00);
      XSetForeground(mydisplay , imageGC,
                     BlackPixel(mydisplay , screen_num));
      XPutImage(mydisplay , mywindow, imageGC, local , 0, 0, 10, 100,
                e_width , e_height);
      break;
    }
  }

                    /* 9.  clean up before exiting */
  XUnmapWindow(mydisplay , mywindow);
  XDestroyWindow(mydisplay , mywindow);
  XCloseDisplay(mydisplay);
}
```

Fig. 4.11 (continued)

4.8.1 Exercises

1. Why would the use of the XCreateBitmapFromData() call be inappropriate for the direct use of the bitmap data as in the program of Fig. 4.9?
2. Design and perform an experiment to determine whether using Pixmap format or image format as the implementation media for labels leads to a performance advantage. Such performance measurement should include both execution/response time and memory usage.

4.9 Creating Menus by Using the Image Format

Menu bars, pull-down menus, and pop-up menu are collections of labels. In most instances, actions are associated with selections from those labels, and this selection process is dynamic. This rapid appearance and disappearance, and providing visual indication of an individual label, is of interest here. A blend of group and individual behaviours is required from the labels to form such menus. Labels formed from Pixmaps are ideal for this application. This is particularly the case if the image format is used. It adds potential performance advantages over Pixmaps following on

Fig. 4.12 Menus
implemented by labels in
image format in use

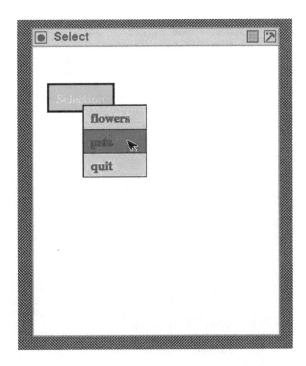

from the labels being stored complete within the client program. How this can be
done is the purpose of this section.

The program in Fig. 4.13 uses menus formed from labels which are built in the
X11 image format. Figure 4.12 shows the resulting screen output. This menu has the
same operation as the program of Fig. 3.6. A single selection button coloured green is
located on a background window. On the selection button is the word Selection
in pink characters. By clicking the left-hand mouse button on this selection button, an
option menu appears containing the options flowers, pets, and quit. Each
option is labelled in blue with a pink background. On moving the mouse pointer
to each option, the pick background of the options changes to red. Clicking the
right-hand mouse button above, the quit option terminates the program. All menu
labels in this program were implemented using image format created from Pixmaps
which were created externally to this program by the Encapsulated Postscript process
outlined in previous sections. All labels were made up of 18 point characters of the
Times Roman bold font type. So in their creation, only the BoundingBox and show
statements in the previous Encapsulated Postscript program needed to be changed
between each run to generated the required labels. The colours are applied through
the graphics context (GC) used to map the labels to the screen.

Since the XCreateSimpleWindow() call is used to create the menu window,
the events this window is to be sensitive to are established via the XChangeWindow
Attributes() call. With the XCreateSimpleWindow() call, the attributes

```
/*   This  program  creates  a  main  window  on  which  is  a  selection
 *   button.    That  button  is  green  in  colour  with  the  label
 *   'Selection'  in  pink  characters.   By  clicking  the  left  mouse
 *   button  on  this  button  an  option  menu  of  'flowers',  'pets',
 *   and  'quit'  appears.   Each  option  is  labelled  in  blue  with  a
 *   pink  background.   On  moving  the  mouse  pointer  over  each
 *   option,  the  pink  background  changes  to  red.   Clicking  the
 *   right-hand  mouse  button  over  the  'quit'  option  terminates
 *   the  program.
 *
 *   Coded  by:   Ross  Maloney
 *   Date:        July  2008
 */

#include <X11/Xlib.h>
#include <X11/Xutil.h>
#include <stdio.h>
#include "labels.h"        /* bitmap representing all labels */

int main(int argc, char *arcv)
{
    Display            *mydisplay;
    XSetWindowAttributes   myat, buttonat, popat;
    Window             baseW, buttonW, optionW, panelsW[3];
    XSizeHints         wmsize;
    XWMHints           wmhints;
    XTextProperty      windowName, iconName;
    XEvent             myevent;
    XColor             exact, closest;
    GC                 myGC1, myGC2, myGC3;
    Pixmap             pattern;
    XImage             *buttonL, *image2panels[3];
    unsigned long      valuemask;
    char *window_name  = "Select";
    char *icon_name    = "Sel";
    int                screen_num, done, i;
    char *colours[]    = {"white", "black", "green", "pink",
                          "blue", "red"};
    unsigned long      colourBits[6];

                    /* 1.  open connection to the server */
    mydisplay = XOpenDisplay("");

                    /* 2.  create a top-level window */
    screen_num = DefaultScreen(mydisplay);
    for (i=0; i<6; i++) {
        XAllocNamedColor(mydisplay,
                         XDefaultColormap(mydisplay, screen_num),
                         colours[i], &exact, &closest);
        colourBits[i] = exact.pixel;
    }
```

Fig. 4.13 Menu selection implemented using image format

```
myat.background_pixel = colourBits[0];
myat.border_pixel = colourBits[1];
valuemask = CWBackPixel | CWBorderPixel;
baseW = XCreateWindow(mydisplay,
                      RootWindow(mydisplay, screen_num),
                      300, 300, 350, 400, 3,
                      DefaultDepth(mydisplay, screen_num),
                      InputOutput,
                      DefaultVisual(mydisplay, screen_num),
                      valuemask, &myat);

                /* 3.  give the Window Manager hints */
wmsize.flags = USPosition | USSize;
XSetWMNormalHints(mydisplay, baseW, &wmsize);
wmhints.initial_state = NormalState;
wmhints.flags = StateHint;
XSetWMHints(mydisplay, baseW, &wmhints);
XStringListToTextProperty(&window_name, 1, &windowName);
XSetWMName(mydisplay, baseW, &windowName);
XStringListToTextProperty(&icon_name, 1, &iconName);
XSetWMIconName(mydisplay, baseW, &iconName);

                /* 4.  establish window resources */
myGC1 = XCreateGC(mydisplay, baseW, 0, NULL);
XSetBackground(mydisplay, myGC1, colourBits[2]);
XSetForeground(mydisplay, myGC1, colourBits[3]);
myGC2 = XCreateGC(mydisplay, baseW, 0, NULL);
XSetBackground(mydisplay, myGC2, colourBits[3]);
XSetForeground(mydisplay, myGC2, colourBits[4]);
myGC3 = XCreateGC(mydisplay, baseW, 0, NULL);
XSetBackground(mydisplay, myGC3, colourBits[5]);
XSetForeground(mydisplay, myGC3, colourBits[4]);

                /* 5.  create all the other windows needed */
buttonW = XCreateSimpleWindow(mydisplay, baseW, 20, 50,
                      selection_width, selection_height, 3,
                      colourBits[1], colourBits[0]);
pattern = XCreateBitmapFromData(mydisplay, buttonW,
                      selection_bits, selection_width,
                      selection_height);
buttonL = XGetImage(mydisplay, pattern, 0, 0,
                      selection_width, selection_height,
                      1, XYPixmap);
buttonL->format = XYBitmap;
optionW = XCreateSimpleWindow(mydisplay, baseW, 70, 80,
                      quit_width, 3*quit_height, 1,
                      colourBits[1], colourBits[1]);
for (i=0; i<3; i++)
  panelsW[i] = XCreateSimpleWindow(mydisplay, optionW, 0,
                      i*quit_height, quit_width, quit_height,
                      1, colourBits[1], colourBits[0]);
```

Fig. 4.13 (continued)

```
pattern = XCreateBitmapFromData(mydisplay, buttonW, flowers_bits,
                                flowers_width, flowers_height);
image2panels[0] = XGetImage(mydisplay, pattern, 0, 0,
                            flowers_width, flowers_height,
                            1, XYPixmap);
image2panels[0]->format = XYBitmap;
pattern = XCreateBitmapFromData(mydisplay, buttonW, pets_bits,
                                pets_width, pets_height);
image2panels[1] = XGetImage(mydisplay, pattern, 0, 0,
                            pets_width, pets_height, 1,
                            XYPixmap);
image2panels[1]->format = XYBitmap;
pattern = XCreateBitmapFromData(mydisplay, buttonW, quit_bits,
                                quit_width, quit_height);
image2panels[2] = XGetImage(mydisplay, pattern, 0, 0,
                            quit_width, quit_height, 1,
                            XYPixmap);
image2panels[2]->format = XYBitmap;

               /* 6.  select events for each window */
myat.event_mask = ButtonPressMask | ExposureMask;
valuemask = CWEventMask;
XChangeWindowAttributes(mydisplay, buttonW, valuemask, &myat);
myat.event_mask = ButtonPressMask | EnterWindowMask
                  | LeaveWindowMask;
for ( i=0; i<3; i++)
  XChangeWindowAttributes(mydisplay, panelsW[i],
                          valuemask, &myat);

               /* 7.  map the windows */
XMapWindow(mydisplay, baseW);
XMapWindow(mydisplay, buttonW);

               /* 8.  enter the event loop */
done = 0;
while ( done == 0 ) {
  XNextEvent(mydisplay, &myevent);
  switch (myevent.type) {
  case Expose:
    XPutImage(mydisplay, buttonW, myGC1, buttonL, 0, 0, 0, 0,
              selection_width, selection_height);
    break;
  case ButtonPress:
    if ( myevent.xbutton.button == Button1
         && myevent.xbutton.window == buttonW ) {
      printf("that_is_the_button\n");
      XMapWindow(mydisplay, optionW);
      for (i=0; i<3; i++) {
        XMapWindow(mydisplay, panelsW[i]);
        XPutImage(mydisplay, panelsW[i], myGC2, image2panels[i],
                  0, 0, 0, 0, quit_width, quit_height);
```

Fig. 4.13 (continued)

```
                }
        }
        if  (myevent.xbutton.button  ==  Button3
                && myevent.xbutton.window  ==  panelsW[2]  )
                done = 1;     /* exit */
        break;
    case    EnterNotify:
        printf("window_entered\n");
        for  (i=0; i<3; i++)  {
          if  ( myevent.xcrossing.window  ==  panelsW[i] )  {
            XPutImage(mydisplay,  panelsW[i],  myGC3,  image2panels[i],
                        0, 0, 0, 0, quit_width,  quit_height);
          break;
          }
        }
        break;
    case    LeaveNotify:
        printf("window_just_left\n");
        for  (i=0; i<3; i++)  {
          if  ( myevent.xcrossing.window  ==  panelsW[i] )  {
            XPutImage(mydisplay,  panelsW[i],  myGC2,  image2panels[i],
                        0, 0, 0, 0, quit_width,  quit_height);
          break;
          }
        }
        break;
      }
    }

                /* 9.   clean up before exiting */
    XUnmapWindow(mydisplay,  baseW);
    XDestroyWindow(mydisplay,  baseW);
    XCloseDisplay(mydisplay);
}
```

Fig. 4.13 (continued)

of the parent window are inherited by the window being created. In this program, the parent is the base window which does not have any event sensitivity set. But the menu window needs such sensitivity. In the case of the option window which has the menu window as a parent, a change in attributes is not necessary as the option window needs the same attributes.

Other points worthy of note in the code of Fig. 4.13 are:

1. The three labels (flowers, pets, quit) are put into their own window so the mouse pointer entering and leaving them can be detected and the colouring of the label can be changed.
2. Each of the three labels in the menu is assembled into a container window (optionsW) so they can all be removed together by unmapping this parent window.

3. Each of the three labels has the same width and height; therefore, the container window is three times the height of each label and the same width as each label since together the labels are to cover the container window completely on the screen.

4. Both the identifiers of the label containing windows and the identifiers of the images formed from those labels are stored in an array so there is a one-to-one correspondence across the array indices.

5. As much of the set-up associated with the production of the different windows is done before the event loop is entered so as to maximize the response time to the program user's actions.

6. The background colour specified for a window in its attribute structure overrides that given in the `XCreateSimpleWindow()` call.

7. The Pixmap patterns from which the four labels used in the program are not reproduced here as they take the same form as used in Figs. 4.8 and 4.10.

8. Although the Pixmap is created for a particular window, it, and the image derived from it, can be applied to other windows as well.

4.9.1 Exercises

1. Modify the program of Fig. 4.13 so it uses the Pixmap format only in place of the image format.

2. Compare and contrast the programs in Figs. 4.13 and 3.6 which essentially do the same thing. Provide experimental evidence to support the points you use.

4.10 Forming Text Messages from Bitmap Glyphs

Bitmaps are considered in Sect. 4.2 as specific examples of Pixmap patterns. In such patterns, each pixel on the screen is either *coloured* or left blank. In the case of a default bitmap foreground colouring is black with a white background. Standard bitmap editors such as `bitmap`, which is contained in a standard X Window distribution, are available for manually creating such patterns. However, using a bitmap editor to combine characters for creating text messages is difficult warranting a different approach. This difficulty is magnified by the variations which occur across the *fonts* available today. Each font is built up from *glyphs*, and there is one glyph for each character in a font. A glyph is a graphical representation of a character in a font. To assemble a combination of characters which look pictorially correct requires knowing the properties of glyphs and how those properties determine how one glyph can be packed adjacent to another.

In Sect. 4.6, creating of bitmap representation of text for use in labels was approached using Postscript. This has the advantage of simplicity. It uses *Type 1* fonts initially created by Adobe Systems. A larger variety of font styles are now available as *TrueType Fonts*, a font specification initially created by Apple Inc. True-Type Fonts are widely used, with http://www.dafont.com being one of many Web-sites containing freely downloadable archives of such fonts. Such TrueType Fonts can be converted to Type 1 fonts by programs such as `ttf2pt1` which is available as open source from the `http://ttf2pt1.sourceforge.net` Website. By downloading TrueType fonts and then converting them to Type 1 fonts, the range of fonts which can be used with the approach of Sect. 4.6 increases significantly above using the *standard* Type 1 fonts.

There is a problem with both Type 1 and TrueType fonts. Each is a mathematical font defined with points and connecting mathematical equations. The pattern which represents an individual character in a font is called its *glyph*. The shape of each glyph in each of these fonts is defined by Bézier (cubic) and B-spline (quadratic) equations, respectively. These curves have to be rendered into pixels on the screen. Algorithmic mapping of a continuous curve onto a fixed, discrete grid can led to complications resulting in an unattractive or indistinct character. To overcome this problem, fonts which are created/defined only on such a fixed grid are also available. Because of this grid definition, these fonts are size specific. In most cases, the sizes are multiples of 8pt (8, 16, 24, etc.), other sizes being less common. Such fonts are know as *pixel* or *bitmap* fonts. They are also available from such archive sites as http://www.dafont.com.

X Window comes with a large set of bitmap fonts. Each glyph of these bitmap fonts in the point sizes available can be viewed using the `xfontsel` program which is also a standard part of the X distribution. It is logical to use such available fonts directly. To do this, glyphs are selected from such a font and arrange adjacent to one another to form words. This is known as *glyph packing*. The assembled glyphs are then formed into a bitmap which can then be used for such things as menu items or labelling of items such as a text entry window.

4.10.1 Accessing X11 Standard Bitmap Fonts

The font files of X Window are stored in sub-directories `100dpi`, `75dpi`, `misc`, `encoding` and `Type1` of the /usr/share/fonts/X11 directory. Sub-directories `100dpi`, `75dpi` and `misc` contain bitmap font files in Portable Compiled Format (PCF) which is then compressed using `gzip`. Each sub-directory contains a file `fonts.dir` which tabulates the correspondence between the name of the file and the name of the font as specified using the X Logical Font Description (XLFD). Sub-directories `100dpi` and `75dpi` contain the same number and font types, but at different pixel densities. A summary of the types of fonts contained in those two sub-directories is contained in Table 4.2.

Each file in sub-directories `100dpi` and `75dpi` contains a single size font. Font compliance with International Standards ISO8859-1 and ISO10646-1 is varied (the -1 part of each standard font name denotes the part associated with the Latin 1 character set). If a file contains a font complying to ISO10646-1, the file is larger

Table 4.2 Styles of selected bitmap font files in X11 dpi sub-directories

Name	08	10	12	14	18	19	24	iso8859-1	iso10646-1	Extra
charB	*	*	*	*	*		*	*		
charBI	*	*	*	*	*		*	*		
charI	*	*	*	*	*		*	*		
charR	*	*	*	*	*		*	*		
courB	*	*	*	*	*		*	*	*	
courBO	*	*	*	*	*		*	*	*	
courO	*	*	*	*	*		*	*	*	
helvB	*	*	*	*	*		*	*	*	
helvBO	*	*	*	*	*		*	*	*	
helvO	*	*	*	*	*		*	*	*	
helvR	*	*	*	*	*		*	*	*	
luBIS	*	*	*	*	*	*	*	*	*	
luBS	*	*	*	*	*	*	*	*	*	
luIS	*	*	*	*	*	*	*	*	*	
luRS	*	*	*	*	*	*	*	*	*	
lubB	*	*	*	*	*	*	*	*	*	
lubBI	*	*	*	*	*	*	*	*	*	
lubI	*	*	*	*	*	*	*	*	*	
lubR	*	*	*	*	*	*	*	*	*	
lutBS	*	*	*	*	*	*	*	*	*	
lutRS	*	*	*	*	*	*	*	*	*	
ncenB	*	*	*	*	*		*	*	*	
ncenBI	*	*	*	*	*		*	*	*	
ncenI	*	*	*	*	*		*	*	*	
ncenR	*	*	*	*	*		*	*	*	
symb	*	*	*	*	*		*	*		fontspecific
tech			*							dectech
techB			*							dectech
term			*					*		
termB			*					*		
timB	*	*	*	*	*		*	*	*	
timBI	*	*	*	*	*		*	*	*	
timR	*	*	*	*	*		*	*	*	

than the corresponding ISO8859-1 compliant font file due to containing approximately 4 times as many glyphs/characters. This means all the glyphs/characters in the ISO8859-1 file are contained in the ISO10646-1 file, plus more. ISO10644-1, or the Universal Character Set, is a later standard than ISO8859-1. When a font is present

Table 4.3 Styles of selected bitmap font files in X11 misc sub-directories

Name	1	2	3	4	5	7	8	9	10	11	13	14	15	16	KOI8	iso10646-1	iso646
10x20	*	*	*	*	*	*	*	*	*	*	*	*	*	*	*	*	
12x13ja																*	
12x24																*	
12x24rk																*	
18x18ja																*	
18x18ko																*	
4x6	*	*	*	*	*	*	*	*	*		*	*	*	*	*	*	
5x7	*	*	*	*	*	*	*	*	*		*	*	*	*	*	*	
5x8	*	*	*	*	*	*	*	*	*		*	*	*	*	*	*	
6x10	*	*	*	*	*	*	*	*	*		*	*	*	*	*	*	
6x12	*	*	*	*	*	*	*	*	*		*	*	*	*	*	*	
6x13	*	*	*	*	*	*	*	*	*		*	*	*	*	*	*	
6x13B	*	*	*	*	*	*	*	*	*		*	*	*	*		*	
6x13O	*	*	*	*	*	*		*	*		*	*	*	*		*	
6x9	*	*	*	*	*	*	*	*	*		*	*	*	*	*	*	
7x13	*	*	*	*	*	*	*	*	*	*	*	*	*	*	*	*	
7x13B	*	*	*	*	*	*	*	*	*	*	*	*	*	*		*	
7x13O	*	*	*	*	*	*	*	*	*	*	*	*	*	*		*	
7x14	*	*	*	*	*	*	*	*	*		*	*	*	*	*	*	
7x14B	*	*	*	*	*	*	*	*	*		*	*	*	*		*	
8x13	*	*	*	*	*	*	*	*	*		*	*	*	*	*	*	
8x13B	*	*	*	*	*	*		*	*		*	*	*	*		*	
8x13O	*	*	*	*	*	*	*	*	*		*	*	*	*		*	
8x16																*	
8x16rk																*	
9x15	*	*	*	*	*	*	*	*	*	*	*	*	*	*	*	*	
9x15B	*	*	*	*	*	*	*	*	*	*	*	*	*	*		*	
9x18	*	*	*	*	*	*	*	*	*	*	*	*	*	*	*	*	
9x18B	*	*	*	*	*	*	*	*	*		*	*	*	*		*	
arabic24																*	
clB6x10																	*
clB8x12																	*
clB8x10																	*
clB8x12																	*
clB8x13																	*
clB8x14																	*

(continued)

Table 4.3 (continued)

Name	1	2	3	4	5	7	8	9	10	11	13	14	15	16	KOI8	iso10646-1	iso646
clB8x16																	*
clB8x8																	*
clB9x15																	*
clI6x12																	*
clB8x8																	*
clR4x6																	*
clR5x10																	*
clR5x6																	*
clR5x8																	*
clR6x10																	*
clR6x12																	*
clR6x10																	*
clR6x10																	*
clR6x12	*	*	*	*	*	*	*	*	*	*	*	*	*	*	*		
cu-pau12															*		

in files complying to both ISO standard, then ISO8859-1 is appended to the name of the file complying to ISO8859-1. As an example of this, the file containing font courB (courier bold) at 14 point size is called `courB14-ISO8859-1.pcf.gz`, while the ISO10646-1 compliant font is stored in file `courB14.pcf.gz`. Providing ISO8859-1 compliant version of a font when ISO10646-1 is also provided is for backward compatibility of the X11 distributions.

As indicated in Table 4.2, most fonts available from sub-directories `100dpi` and `75dpi` are in sizes from 8 to 24 point. With the exception of the courier and some of the lucidatypewriter fonts (respectively indicated as cour and lut in Table 4.2) which are mono-spaced fonts, all others are proportionally spaced fonts.

Sub-directory `misc` contains fonts designed specifically for use on computer displays. Several of these fonts are proportional spaced fonts, but most are character cell fonts, which is a form of mono-spacing. The numbers heading the columns of Table 4.3 indicate a font complying to different parts of ISO8859, with those parts pertaining to character of the different print languages of the world. Part 1 of ISO8859 relates to characters of Western European languages. Some fonts are provided to comply with the later ISO10646-1 standard, while others to the earlier ISO646 standard.

In each of these fonts, each glyph is contained within a cell size which is generally contained within its name; for example, the glyphs of a 10x20 font are contained within a 10x20 pixel cell. These fonts tend to be smaller when displayed on the screen than those in sub-directories `100dpi` and `75dpi`.

4.10.2 How to Use the Bitmap Fonts

To use an X11 bitmap font, it first needs to be decompressed, the resulting binary bitmap file is converted into another format, and then, the glyphys contained in the resulting file need to be composed into the required label using a program such as that in Fig. 4.14. Decompressing the font file is done using the $gzip$ program.

The file resulting is a binary file in Portable Compiled Format (PCF) which represents a font's glyphs in a manner efficiently handled by the X Window server together with needing less disc storage than the Bitmap Distribution Format (BDF) file from which it was generated. Such BDF files are defined in the specification available from http://partners.adobe.com/public/developer/en/font/5005.BDF_Spec.pdf and are themselves text files. The program $pcf2bdf$, available from http://www.tsg.ne. jp/GANA/S/pcf2bdf, is a decompiler for PCF files, producing BDF files. Conversely, the program $bdftopcf$ is the corresponding compiler, available from http://xorg. freedesktop.org/releases/individual/app.

The BDF file contains not only the detail of each defined glyph in the font, but also how those glyphs can be put together to construct a composition. Keywords are contained in the file to identify, or tag, such information. The BDF specification defines the keywords shown in Table 4.4. In Table 4.4, a *Level* is assigned to each of those keywords. A Level 1 indicates the data associated with each keyword go directly into forming the glyph. A Level 2 indicates a delimiting keyword which introduces some structure into the resulting file enabling checking for completeness. A Level 3 indicates an information additives, while a Level of $*$ indicates keywords associated with glyph assembly in other than left-to-right ordering on a page (which are not considered here). The $pcf2bdf$ program when acting on a bitmap file in a standard X Window distribution/server produces a BDF containing keywords of levels 1, 2, and 3. Additional non-standard keywords are also generated between STARTPROPERTIES and ENDPROPERTIES keywords. These are surplus to the need for generating the glyphs. Each BDF file defines a font, and each STARTCHAR keyword in the file specifies a character in that font. Consecutive lines in the file following that STARTCHAR keyword, up to the closing ENDCHAR keyword, define all the details of the glyph representing the character.

Joining glyphs into a composition is done via *attachment points*. Each glyph has a *left attachment point* defined on its left side where its pattern is to be connected to the glyph on its left (i.e. the glyph it follows). The position of this point is defined by the parameters on the BBX keyword. Defined in the parameters of a DWIDTH keyword is a *right attachment point* where the next glyph is to be attached to it (on the right). This is specified relative to the left-hand attachment point of the glyph. Each of these two points is specified relative to the individual glyph.

Within each Bitmap Distribution Format font file, a bounding box is defined for all the glyphs there contained. This is the FONTBOOUNDINGBOX keyword. The FBBy parameter gives the total height in pixels needed to contain all glyphs of the font individually. The *starting point* in bounding box where the first glyph is to be

```
/*   This program composes a message given on the command line
 *   using a font described in a Bitmap Distribution Format
 *   (BDF) and outputs the resultant bitmap.
 *
 *   Coded by:         Ross Msloney
 *   Initial code:     August 2011
 */

#include  <stdio.h>
#include  <stdlib.h>      /* for exit() */
#include  <string.h>      /* for strcat() */

FILE    *fileIn, *fileOut, *fopen();
int     count, checkChars, ready, ii, k, attachx, attachy;
int     number, value;
int     FBBx, FBBy, Xoff, Yoff;   /* glyphs Boundingbox info. */
struct  glyph {
   int    BBx, BBy, BBxoff, BByoff, dwx, dwy, number, lines;
   char   name[40], encoding[10], pattern[40][6];
}   pallet[200];     /* Information storage for glyph in font */

char    lineoftype[40][400];      /* Storage for composed message */

int main(int argc, char *argv[])
{
   char   c, line[300], filename[30];
   int    i;
   void   extract(char *);
   void   compose(char *);
   void   xbmout(char *, int, int);

                    /* check the command line, then setup processing */
   if ( ( fileIn = fopen(argv[argc-1], "r") ) == NULL )  {
      printf("Name_of_BDF_file_needs_to_be_supplied\n");
      exit(1);
   }
   count = 0;
   while ( fscanf(fileIn, "%[^\n]", line) != EOF )
      fscanf(fileIn, "%c", &c);  { /* Store glyphs */
      if ( line[0] != '\0' )  extract(line);  /* 0 length skip */
      line[0] = '\0';
   }
   compose(argv[1]);    /* compose the command line message */
   strcat(filename, argv[2]);
   strcat(filename, ".xbm");
   if ( ( fileOut = fopen(filename, "w") ) == NULL )   {
      printf("Could_not_open_file_for_output\n");
      exit(1);
   }
   xbmout(argv[2], FBBy, attachx);     /* file composed message */
}
```

Fig. 4.14 Creating bitmap messages by packing glyphs

```
/*   Function to examine a BDF file and recovers required
 *   information associated with it's keywords.
 */

void extract(char *fileLine)
{
  char    command[40];
  int     i, j;
  void    printglyph(char);

  sscanf(fileLine, "%s", command);
  if ( !strcmp(command, "FONTBOUNDINGBOX") )   {
    sscanf(fileLine, "%s %d %d %d %d",
           command, &FBBx, &FBBy, &Xoff, &Yoff);
    return;
  }
  if ( !strcmp(command, "CHARS") )   {
    sscanf(fileLine, "%s %d", command, &checkChars);
    ii = 0;
    return;
  }
  if ( !strcmp(command, "STARTCHAR") )   {
    sscanf(fileLine, "%s %s", command, &pallet[ii].name);
    count++;
    return;
  }
  if ( !strcmp(command, "ENDCHAR") )   {
    pallet[ii].lines = k;
    ii++;
    ready = 0;
    return;
  }
  if ( !strcmp(command, "ENCODING") )   {
    sscanf(fileLine, "%s %s", command, &pallet[ii].encoding);
    ready = 1;
    checkChars--;
    return;
  }
  if ( !strcmp(command, "DWIDTH") )   {
    sscanf(fileLine, "%s %d %d",
           command, &pallet[ii].dwx, &pallet[ii].dwy);
    if ( ready != 1 )   {
      printf("ENCODING statement required before");
      printf("DWIDTH statement: %s\n", fileLine);
      exit(1);
    }
    ready = 2;
    return;
  }
  if ( !strcmp(command, "BBX") )   {
    sscanf(fileLine, "%s %d %d %d %d", command,
           &pallet[ii].BBx, &pallet[ii].BBy, &pallet[ii].BBxoff,
```

Fig. 4.14 (continued)

```
                 &pallet [ ii ]. BByoff );
          if ( ready != 2 ) {
            printf ("DWIDTH statement required before");
            printf ("BBX statement: %s\n", fileLine );
            exit (1);
          }
          ready = 3;
                    /* Calculates number of data hex per line */
          pallet [ ii ]. number = pallet [ ii ]. BBx/4;
          if (pallet [ ii ]. number*4 != pallet [ ii ]. BBx)
            pallet [ ii ]. number++;
          return;
        }
        if ( !strcmp (command, "BITMAP") ) {
          if ( ready != 3 ) {
            printf ("No BBX statement for encoding %d\n",
                     pallet [ ii ]. encoding );
            exit (1);
          }
          ready = 4;
          k =0;
          return;
        }
        if ( ready == 4 ) {
          sscanf (fileLine , "%s", command );
          for (j=0; j<pallet [ ii ]. number; j++)
            pallet [ ii ]. pattern [k][ j ] = command[ j ];
          k++;
        }
        return;
}

/* Function to typeset the glyph pattern.
 */

void   compose (char *message)
{
  int    i , j , k , n, topx, topy, currentx, currenty;
  void putglyph (char, int, int );

  for (i=0; i<FBBy; i++)
    for (j=0; j<400; j++)  lineoftype [i][ j ] = '.';
  attachx = −Xoff;       /* Calculate location of initial point */
  attachy = FBBy + Yoff;
  k = 0;
  lineoftype [attachy ][ attachx ] = 'M'; /* Show attachment point */
  while ( message [k] != '\0' ) {        /* Get each character */
    for (j=0; j<ii ; j++)
      if ( pallet [ j ]. name [0] == message [k] )  break;
    topy = attachy − (pallet [ j ]. BBy + pallet [ j ]. BByoff);
    topx = attachx − pallet [ j ]. BBxoff;
    currentx = topx;
```

Fig. 4.14 (continued)

```
    currenty = topy;
    if ( topx < 0 )  currentx = 0;
            /* Show top-left glyph pattern position */
    lineoftype[topy][topx] = 'T';
    for (n=0; n<pallet[j].lines; n++)  {
      currentx = topx;
      for (i=0; i<pallet[j].number; i++)  {
        putglyph(pallet[j].pattern[n][i], currenty, currentx);
        currentx = currentx + 4;
      }
      currenty++;
    }
    k++;
    attachx = attachx + pallet[j].dwx;
    attachy = attachy + pallet[j].dwy;
    lineoftype[attachy][attachx] = 'M';
/* Show next attachment */
  }
}


/*  Function to insert the black/white bits contained in single
 *  glyph into the bitmap of the overall composition */

void  putglyph(char hex, int y, int x)
{
  int   value;

  switch ( hex )  {
  case '0':   lineoftype[y][x] = '+';      lineoftype[y][x+1] = '+';
              lineoftype[y][x+2] = '+';    lineoftype[y][x+3] = '+';
              break;
  case '1':   lineoftype[y][x] = '+';      lineoftype[y][x+1] = '+';
              lineoftype[y][x+2] = '+';    lineoftype[y][x+3] = 'm';
              break;
  case '2':   lineoftype[y][x] = '+';      lineoftype[y][x+1] = '+';
              lineoftype[y][x+2] = 'm';    lineoftype[y][x+3] = '+';
              break;
  case '3':   lineoftype[y][x] = '+';      lineoftype[y][x+1] = '+';
              lineoftype[y][x+2] = 'm';    lineoftype[y][x+3] = 'm';
              break;
  case '4':   lineoftype[y][x] = '+';      lineoftype[y][x+1] = 'm';
              lineoftype[y][x+2] = '+';    lineoftype[y][x+3] = '+';
              break;
  case '5':   lineoftype[y][x] = '+';      lineoftype[y][x+1] = 'm';
              lineoftype[y][x+2] = '+';    lineoftype[y][x+3] = 'm';
              break;
  case '6':   lineoftype[y][x] = '+';      lineoftype[y][x+1] = 'm';
              lineoftype[y][x+2] = 'm';    lineoftype[y][x+3] = '+';
              break;
  case '7':   lineoftype[y][x] = '+';      lineoftype[y][x+1] = 'm';
              lineoftype[y][x+2] = 'm';    lineoftype[y][x+3] = 'm';
              break;
```

Fig. 4.14 (continued)

```
case '8':   lineoftype[y][x] = 'm';       lineoftype[y][x+1] = '+';
            lineoftype[y][x+2] = '+';     lineoftype[y][x+3] = '+';
            break;
case '9':   lineoftype[y][x] = 'm';       lineoftype[y][x+1] = '+';
            lineoftype[y][x+2] = '+';     lineoftype[y][x+3] = 'm';
            break;
case 'A':   lineoftype[y][x] = 'm';       lineoftype[y][x+1] = '+';
            lineoftype[y][x+2] = 'm';     lineoftype[y][x+3] = '+';
            break;
case 'B':   lineoftype[y][x] = 'm';       lineoftype[y][x+1] = '+';
            lineoftype[y][x+2] = 'm';     lineoftype[y][x+3] = 'm';
            break;
case 'C':   lineoftype[y][x] = 'm';       lineoftype[y][x+1] = 'm';
            lineoftype[y][x+2] = '+';     lineoftype[y][x+3] = '+';
            break;
case 'D':   lineoftype[y][x] = 'm';       lineoftype[y][x+1] = 'm';
            lineoftype[y][x+2] = '+';     lineoftype[y][x+3] = 'm';
            break;
case 'E':   lineoftype[y][x] = 'm';       lineoftype[y][x+1] = 'm';
            lineoftype[y][x+2] = 'm';     lineoftype[y][x+3] = '+';
            break;
case 'F':   lineoftype[y][x] = 'm';       lineoftype[y][x+1] = 'm';
            lineoftype[y][x+2] = 'm';     lineoftype[y][x+3] = 'm';
            break;
default:    printf("Error in printing a hex value\n");
  }
}


/*  Function to write the glyph composition as an X Window bitmap
 *  (XBM) file using the naming information supplied on the
 *  command line which invoked this program.
 *
 *  Note with respect to xbm files:
 *  .  the least significant bit is on the left
 *  .  the most significant hex digit is on the right of a hex-pair
 *  .  each row of bits are completely contained in bytes
 *          representing that row
 */

void  xbmout(char *message, int height, int width)
{
  int  i, j, result, value, k, bit;
  int  copy, swing;

  fprintf(fileOut, "#define %s_width %d\n", message, width);
  fprintf(fileOut, "#define %s_height %d\n", message, height);
  fprintf(fileOut, "static char %s_bits[] = {\n", message);
      /* main test part */
  for (i=0; i<height; i++)  {
    k = 0;
    bit = 1;
    value = 0;
```

Fig. 4.14 (continued)

```
        copy  =  0;
        swing  =  1;
        for  (j=0;  j<width;  j++)  {
          if  (  lineoftype[i][j]  ==  'm'  )   value  =  value  |  bit;
          bit  =  bit*2;
          k++;
          if  (  k  ==  4  )  {
            if  (  swing  >  0  )   copy  =  value;
            else   fprintf(fileOut ,  "  0x%x%x,",  value ,  copy);
            swing  =  −swing;
            value  =  0;
            bit  =  1;
            k  =  0;
          }
        }
        if  (  k  ==  0  )      /* selecting  end  of  row  output */
          if  (  swing  >  0  )   fprintf(fileOut ,  "\n");
          else   fprintf(fileOut ,  " 0x0%x,\n",  copy);
        else
          if  (  swing  >  0  )   fprintf(fileOut ,  " 0x0%x,\n",  value);
          else   fprintf(fileOut ,  " 0x%x%x,\n",  value ,  copy);
      }
      fprintf(fileOut ,  "};\n");
    }
```

Fig. 4.14 (continued)

Table 4.4 Keywords defined in the BDF specification

Level	Keyword	Level	Keyword
1	STARTFONT	*	VVECTOR
3	COMMENT	3	METRICSSET
3	CONTENTVERSION	2	STARTCHAR
3	FONT	1	ENCODING
3	SIZE	2	SWIDTH
1	FONTBOUNDINGBOX	1	DWIDTH
2	STARTPROPERTIES	1	BBX
2	ENDPROPERTIES	1	BITMAP
2	CHARS	2	ENDCHAR
*	SWIDTH1	2	ENDFONT
*	DWIDTH1		

located is also specified, relative to the bottom left-hand pixel of the bounding box. This is the first attachment point.

The composing algorithm for representing a given sequence of characters using a specified BDF font file is:

zeroarray to contain composition
select start position of glyph attachment point in composition array
for each character to be composed
      calculate location of left attachment point in this glyph's pattern
      calculate of location of top-left glyph pattern in composition array
      map glyph onto composition array
      recalculate glyph attachment point in composition array

The program of Fig. 4.14 implements this algorithm.

The program of Fig. 4.14 needs a little assistance. First, BDF file with which it is used is edited. The program matches a character in the string being composed with a character in the BDF file. But in a lot of instances, the STARTCHAR keyword has a word, containing multiple characters, following it, for example STARTCHAR one. Those multiple words need to be replaced with their single character equivalent, in the example, one by 1. Most BDF files also contain more characters that are going to be used in composing, and typically, these contain multiple character words in their corresponding STARTCHAR keyword. These surpluses should also be eliminated. Of special interest is the STARTCHAR space keyword. Replacing the space word with a space keyboard entry would result in the STARTCHAR keyword not denoting any character. Another keyboard character, which is not going to be used in any composing in this BDF file, is needed. One possible replacement is to use the \ character. If this is done, then a space character in a string presented to the program of Fig. 4.14 to be composed would have the \ replacement used in a string.

The procedure for processing a X11 bitmap font is as follows. A PCF file is selected from either the 100dpi, 75dpi or misc sub-directories of the directory /usr/share/fonts/X11/75dpi for use in creating a label. This file is copied into the directory where the work is to be done. The file is then processed by the following steps:

- decompress using gzip
- convert the pcf file to a bdf file by using the pcf2bdf program
- replace the single parameter, a string which names the character, on each STARTCHAR line by the keyboard character it represents, e.g. parentleft is replace by) .
- the character/glyph name space is replaced with a *non-white* character such as \ for messages containing space characters but where replacement character is not present in the composition.
- characters/glyphs whose names cannot be replaced by a single keyboard character are deleted from the file since all messages are assumed to be composed from collections of single characters.

As an example, consider the BDF font file resulting from applying `pcf2bdf` to the font file `selection.bdf`. This BDF file is edited in that the `STARTCHAR` `space` keyword is replaced by `STARTCHAR\`. The label to be composed is `Mary` `had a little lamb`, and the resulting bitmap is to be named `example`. If the program of Fig. 4.14 has been compiled under the name `pack`, then it is run as:

```
pack "Mary\ had\ a\ little\ lamb" example selection.bdf
```

The bitmap representation of the message then appears as the file `example.xbm`. This file can be viewed using any graphics viewing program, for example xv. The three variables defined in the file are `example_width`, `example_height`, and `example_bits`.

4.10.3 Exercises

1. Modify the program of Fig. 4.14 so to remove two pixels from the top of the composed glyphs so to make the text more central to the overall height of the block of text.
2. Write a program which displays a single 200x200 window containing a 50x50 button which has the label OK centred in it. When the mouse pointer is over this button and the left button is pressed down, the program terminates. Construct the label for this button using the program of Fig. 4.14.

4.11 Using Pixmaps to Colour a Window's Background

One of the powerful properties of the X Window System is attributes which can be associated with individual windows. A window can be linked to the occurrence of particular events and set to ignore others. When an event occurs, the colour of a window could be changed in response to the event alerting the user of the program to a particular situation. Pixmaps are another window attribute which can be applied if needed. A Pixmap might be used to label a window. A Pixmap has a foreground and a background, each of which can have a colour associated with it. There is also a special form of Pixmap called a *bitmap*. The advantage of bitmaps over Pixmaps is that the former takes up less storage due to its set colouring.

Window labelling and linking to events are considered in Sect. 3.5 where bitmaps are converted to images. Images are held on the client machine, processed there, and displayed after the whole image is retransmitted to the server. So using images introduces less network traffic. By contrast, bitmap and Pixmaps are held on the server. They are transferred from the client machine to the server once. However, each bitmap and Pixmap consumes memory and other resources on the server and thus should be used sparingly. So reuse of any Pixmap should be considered where possible. Also the server can change the colour of the background of a Pixmap upon receiving only an instruction from the client program. Another instruction can place such recoloured Pixmap onto a window without retransmitting the window nor the bitmap. This can reduce client/server communications.

The program of Fig. 4.15 uses colour change in response to the mouse pointer entering and leaving two windows. A base window with an initial background colour of red contains a second window. This second window has a background covered by a checkerboard Pixmap. Initially, the checkerboard is coloured with a blue background and a black foreground. When the mouse pointer enters the first window, its background changes to a yellow colour. When the pointer enters the second window, the background colour of the second window changes to green and the foreground changes to blue. When the pointer leaves the second window, the checkerboard background changes back to its original blue–black colouring. This mouse movement also means the mouse pointer has entered the surrounding base window. This results in the background of the base window changing back to yellow. Figure 4.16 gives two screenshots of the windows produced by the program with different mouse positions.

This example demonstrates important properties of windows and Pixmaps under the X Window System.

A window and a Pixmap are a related pair. A window has a foreground and a background. Drawing is done on the foreground of a window or onto a Pixmap. A window foreground and a Pixmap are collectively called *drawables*. All Xlib graphics calls require a drawable to be specified, and these can be either a window foreground or a Pixmap. However, a drawing can only be done onto the foreground of a window when the window is exposed to view on a screen; i.e. it is unobscured. By contrast, a Pixmap can always be drawn. But a Pixmap can only be seen on the screen when it is mapped onto the foreground or the background of a window. If a Pixmap is mapped onto the foreground of a window and that window becomes obscured and then unobscured, it is necessary to move the Pixmap to the window again. By contrast, if the Pixmap is mapped to the background of the window, this renewal is not required (the server takes care of it).

A Pixmap also has a foreground and a background (ignoring multicoloured Pixmaps considered in Sect. 7.1 for the moment). A Pixmap is a pattern which is held in the server's memory for rapidly mapping onto a window. A common way of introducing the Pixmap pattern is to include it in the source code as a static array, for example `b_bits[]`. It is made up from hexadecimal digits. In the binary representation of each hexadecimal value, each bit indicates the corresponding pixel in the Pixmap's foreground, while a zero indicates the corresponding Pixmap background. Each value in the array (e.g. `0xf2`) represents 8 pixels in the bitmap. The pixels are laid out on the screen with width indicated by the value assigned to `b_width` measured in pixels and of height indicated by the corresponding `b_height`, again measured in pixels. These width and height values are applied to the given hexadecimal values to produce the bitmap. If there are more hexadecimal values given than the number of pixels contained in the array formed from the width and height given, then they are discarded.

A `bitmap` is a particular type of Pixmap. It has a predefined (default) foreground colour of black and a background colour of white. The Xlib function calls

```
/*   This program consists of a main window on which is placed a
 *   second window.  Initially the main window is coloured red.
 *   When the mouse pointer enters this window, that background
 *   changes to yellow and then back to red when the mouse
 *   pointer exits this window.  Onto this first window a second
 *   window is placed.  This second window carries a
 *   checker-board bitmap which only covers the background of the
 *   whole window.  When the mouse pointer is inside this window
 *   the background of that checker-board is coloured green and
 *   blue, and when outside it is coloured black and blue.
 *
 *   Coded by:   Ross Maloney
 *   Date:       March 2012
 */

#include <X11/Xlib.h>
#include <X11/Xutil.h>

#define b_width 32
#define b_height 32
static char b_bits[] = {
0xff, 0xff, 0x00, 0x00,
0xff, 0xff, 0x00, 0x00,
0xff, 0xff, 0x00, 0x00,
0xff, 0xff, 0x00, 0x00,
0xff, 0xff, 0x00, 0x00,
0xff, 0xff, 0x00, 0x00,
0xff, 0xff, 0x00, 0x00,
0xff, 0xff, 0x00, 0x00,
0xff, 0xff, 0x00, 0x00,
0xff, 0xff, 0x00, 0x00,
0xff, 0xff, 0x00, 0x00,
0xff, 0xff, 0x00, 0x00,
0xff, 0xff, 0x00, 0x00,
0xff, 0xff, 0x00, 0x00,
0xff, 0xff, 0x00, 0x00,
0xff, 0xff, 0x00, 0x00,
0x00, 0x00, 0xff, 0xff,
0x00, 0x00, 0xff, 0xff,
0x00, 0x00, 0xff, 0xff,
0x00, 0x00, 0xff, 0xff,
0x00, 0x00, 0xff, 0xff,
0x00, 0x00, 0xff, 0xff,
0x00, 0x00, 0xff, 0xff,
0x00, 0x00, 0xff, 0xff,
0x00, 0x00, 0xff, 0xff,
0x00, 0x00, 0xff, 0xff,
0x00, 0x00, 0xff, 0xff,
0x00, 0x00, 0xff, 0xff,
0x00, 0x00, 0xff, 0xff,
0x00, 0x00, 0xff, 0xff,
```

Fig. 4.15 Changing window colour as mouse enters and leaves

```
   0x00,  0x00,  0xff,  0xff,
   0x00,  0x00,  0xff,  0xff
};

int main(int argc,  char *argv)
{
   Display         *mydisplay;
   XSetWindowAttributes  baseat,  secondat;
   Window          baseW,  secondW;
   XSizeHints      wmsize;
   XWMHints        wmhints;
   XTextProperty   windowName,  iconName;
   XEvent          myevent;
   XColor          exact,  closest;
   GC              baseGC;
   XGCValues       myGCValues;
   Pixmap          ck_board1,  ck_board2;
   char *window_name = "Background";
   char *icon_name   = "Bk";
   int             screen_num,  done;
   unsigned long valuemask,  red,  green,  yellow,  blue;

                   /* 1.  open connection to the server */
   mydisplay = XOpenDisplay("");

                   /* 2.  create a top-level window */
   screen_num = DefaultScreen(mydisplay);
   baseat.background_pixel = WhitePixel(mydisplay,  screen_num);
   baseat.border_pixel = BlackPixel(mydisplay,  screen_num);
   baseat.event_mask = EnterWindowMask | LeaveWindowMask
                     | ExposureMask;
   valuemask = CWBackPixel | CWBorderPixel | CWEventMask;
   baseW = XCreateWindow(mydisplay,
                   RootWindow(mydisplay,  screen_num),
                   300,  300,  350,  200,  3,
                   DefaultDepth(mydisplay,  screen_num),
                   InputOutput,
                   DefaultVisual(mydisplay,  screen_num),
                   valuemask,  &baseat);

                   /* 3.  give the Window Manager hints */
   wmsize.flags = USPosition | USSize;
   XSetWMNormalHints(mydisplay,  baseW,  &wmsize);
   wmhints.initial_state = NormalState;
   wmhints.flags = StateHint;
   XSetWMHints(mydisplay,  baseW,  &wmhints);
   XStringListToTextProperty(&window_name,  1,  &windowName);
   XSetWMName(mydisplay,  baseW,  &windowName);
   XStringListToTextProperty(&icon_name,  1,  &iconName);
   XSetWMIconName(mydisplay,  baseW,  &iconName);
```

Fig. 4.15 (continued)

```
                    /* 4.  establish window resources */
XAllocNamedColor(mydisplay,
                 XDefaultColormap(mydisplay, screen_num),
                 "red", &exact, &closest);
red = closest.pixel;
XAllocNamedColor(mydisplay,
                 XDefaultColormap(mydisplay, screen_num),
                 "green", &exact, &closest);
green = closest.pixel;
XAllocNamedColor(mydisplay,
                 XDefaultColormap(mydisplay, screen_num),
                 "yellow", &exact, &closest);
yellow = closest.pixel;
XAllocNamedColor(mydisplay,
                 XDefaultColormap(mydisplay, screen_num),
                 "blue", &exact, &closest);
blue = closest.pixel;


                    /* 5.  create all the other windows needed */
XSetWindowBackground(mydisplay, baseW, red);
secondat.background_pixel = green;
secondat.border_pixel = BlackPixel(mydisplay, screen_num);
secondat.event_mask = EnterWindowMask | LeaveWindowMask
                      | ExposureMask;
valuemask = CWBackPixel | CWBorderPixel | CWEventMask;
secondW = XCreateWindow(mydisplay, baseW,
                 100, 50, 96, 80, 1,
                 DefaultDepth(mydisplay, screen_num),
                 InputOutput,
                 DefaultVisual(mydisplay, screen_num),
                 valuemask, &secondat);
ck_board1 = XCreatePixmapFromBitmapData(mydisplay, secondW,
                 b_bits, b_width, b_height,
                 BlackPixel(mydisplay, screen_num),
                 blue, DefaultDepth(mydisplay, screen_num));
XSetWindowBackgroundPixmap(mydisplay, secondW, ck_board1);
ck_board2 = XCreatePixmapFromBitmapData(mydisplay, secondW,
                 b_bits, b_width, b_height, blue,
                 green, DefaultDepth(mydisplay, screen_num));

                    /* 6.  select events for each window */

                    /* 7.  map the windows */
XMapWindow(mydisplay, baseW);
XMapWindow(mydisplay, secondW);

                    /* 8.  enter the event loop */
done = 0;
while ( done == 0 )  {
  XNextEvent(mydisplay, &myevent);
  switch (myevent.type)  {
```

Fig. 4.15 (continued)

```
    case    EnterNotify :
      if  (  myevent . xcrossing . window  ==  baseW  )  {
         XSetWindowBackground ( mydisplay ,  baseW ,  yellow );
         XClearWindow ( mydisplay ,  baseW );
      }
      if  (  myevent . xcrossing . window  ==  secondW  )  {
         XSetWindowBackgroundPixmap ( mydisplay ,  secondW ,  ck_board2 );
         XClearWindow ( mydisplay ,  secondW );
      }
      break ;
    case    LeaveNotify :
      if  (  myevent . xcrossing . window  ==  baseW  )  {
         XSetWindowBackground ( mydisplay ,  baseW ,  red );
         XClearWindow ( mydisplay ,  baseW );
      }
      if  (  myevent . xcrossing . window  ==  secondW  )  {
         XSetWindowBackgroundPixmap ( mydisplay ,  secondW ,  ck_board1 );
         XClearWindow ( mydisplay ,  secondW );
      }
      break ;
    }
  }

                /* 9.    clean  up  before  exiting */
  XUnmapWindow ( mydisplay ,  baseW );
  XDestroyWindow ( mydisplay ,  baseW );
  XCloseDisplay ( mydisplay );
}
```

Fig. 4.15 (continued)

XCreatePixmapFromBitmapData() and XCreateBitmapFromData() are used to generate a general Pixmap and a bitmap, respectively, which show this difference; foreground and background colours are required to be specified in the former call. The data included in both calls are the same and represent the required pattern. A bitmap is also limited to a depth of 2.

The foreground and background colours of a Pixmap are set when the Pixmap is created. In the particular case of a bitmap, they are set to black and white, respectively, by default. They cannot be changed. So, if a pattern which is appropriately displayed on a window as a Pixmap is required in more than one colour combination, then a Pixmap for each colour combination is required. Each of these Pixmaps can be created from the same data, but using different foreground and background colour assignments. The program of Fig. 4.15 is an example of the contrast in behaviour of Pixmaps and window colouring.

A window cannot be created with the background_Pixmap attribute set defining a background Pixmap. If this is done, a BadPixmap error is produced when the window creation executes. The reason for this is the attribute requires the Pixmap to exist, but creation of the Pixmap needs the window on which it is to be mapped to exist; i.e. it has already been created. Instead, the process used should:

Fig. 4.16 Simple and
bitmap window colouring
following mouse events

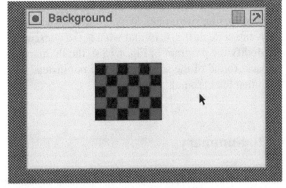

(g) Initially

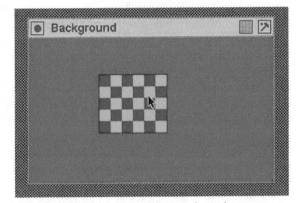

(h) Mouse entered second window

- create the window
- create the Pixmap which references this window and then
- use Xlib function `XSetWindowBackgroundPixmap()` to place the Pixmap
  on the window's background.

4.11.1 Exercises

1. Verify that covering the second window of the program in Fig. 4.15 with another,
   and then removing the overlayed window does not destroy the background pattern
   on the second window even if the X Window server does not have *backing store*
   activated.
2. Modify the code of Fig. 4.15 to demonstrate a window cannot be created with a
   Pixmap in its background (Hint: it is simple).

3. The mouse pointer can be inside or outside of a window. So for two windows, there are four such states. Why is one of those states missing in the visual produced by the code of Fig. 4.15 and what is the consequence?

4. Modify the program of Fig. 4.15 so the Pixmap pattern is not repeated across the background of the second window but instead occupies the top left-hand corner of that background.

4.12   Summary

Given the window creation process, this chapter showed decorating the body of such a window. Such a pattern could be a (generally simple) picture or a text label prepared outside of the X11 program and then linked to a window. One application of these techniques is when a window is used as a button or menu item.

A bitmap is a special case of a Pixmap. Both have their pattern content defined by a distribution of binary numbers, each number giving whether the foreground or background colour is to show at the pixel's location. In the case of a bitmap, the foreground colour is always black, while the background is always white. In the case of a Pixmap, the foreground and background colours can be specified in a program, either when the Pixmap is created or during its use. A Pixmap and a bitmap have only two colours. This binary colouring is analogous to the colouring of a window.

The bitmap approach for creating and using such patterns was used here. This approach has been standard in X11 since its release. An alternate, and added later, is the Pixmap technique which builds upon bitmaps. These will be used in later chapters. Generally, bitmaps are black and white patches which are applied to a window. However, as shown by example in this chapter, a transparency can be achieved by using a mask to enable the underlying window to show through the patch, producing a transparency. Creating of such bitmaps and masks for a simple diagram-type picture is relatively easy compared with a lettered label. In particular, correctly forming letters at the pixel level is difficult. The use of Postscript programs to generate a pattern, and then converting the program's output into appropriate maps, is demonstrated.

Chapter 5
Keyboard Entry and Displaying Text

Entering information to a program from a keyboard is a common task. The data entered is one form of text. In X Window, each key on a keyboard is considered to be like a mouse button in that they raise events. Like a mouse button each keyboard key can raise two different types of events; a key press event, and a key release event (although on some PC keyboards, the key release event may not be implemented). Since each key is identified uniquely, different patterns for presentation of the meaning of a key and displayed on a screen can be changed by selection of a mapping between the key identifier and a pattern. Because a keyboard is a *complex mouse* consisting of many buttons, it justifies a chapter of its own. Like a mouse, keyboards are serviced by the events they generate. Such events can be linked to achieve a variety of effects.

Each keystroke event is stored in a Xlib `XKeyEvent` structure on the server. This structure contains a `keycode` member which is a number in the range 8 to 255. This number is the representation of the key pressed (or released—they use the same keycode). Although the engravings on keys from different keyboard manufacturers may be similar, they can result in different keycodes being produced, for there is no fixed standard. Each keycode is given a symbolic name in the header file `keysym.h`. The function `XLookupSstring()` provides the mapping between the keycode and the character it maps to via the mapping table contained in the `keysym.h` header file. The corresponding character can then be displayed using the function `XDrawText()` if the character is one byte long. If the character is two bytes in length, as when using an international character set, then the function `XDrawText16()` is used. Notice characters are being received from the keyboard, not strings. So a line of text involves a keycode transmission, translation, and printing for each character in the text.

Electronic supplementary material The online version of this chapter (https://doi.org/10.1007/978-3-319-74250-2_5) contains supplementary material, which is available to authorized users.

All keys on the keyboard have a keycode. Keyboard keys considered as modifier keys, such as the shift key, the Alt key, Ctrl key, also generate a keycode when each is pressed. If after the shift key is depressed and held while an alphabetic character key is pressed, the keycode produced is different to the alphabetic key pressed without the shift key being depressed. This is as expected for a different keycode to be generated for lower-case and upper-case versions of a alphabetic key.

The technique commonly used to determine which keyboard key has been pressed is by using the XLookupString() function. An alternative is to use the XKeycodeToKeysym() function followed by the XKeysymToString() function. Only the first techniques will receive further consideration here.

Another form of text is where it is already stored in the computer and it is to be displayed in a window on the screen. This is similar to the keyboard entry situation, which is the reason it is presented here together with the keyboard entry situation. This output presents additional problems, such as only showing a portion of the text and enabling the program user to *scroll* through the text.

5.1   Elementary Keyboard Text X Entry

This example demonstrates the basic use of the X Window System keyboard model. In particular, it shows keyboard entry is not automatically echoed, that a sequence of characters can be assigned in a program to a keyboard key, and the process of recognising which key has been pressed and a means of associating meaning to it.

The program displays a plain white 300×300 window which contains two sub-windows each of the same height and width, one below the other. Each of the three windows is activated to receive an event produced by a button press from a mouse and a keyboard key press. Each of those events leads to text being printed on the console terminal (which is not part of this program, but from which the program is assumed to have been run). No matter in which of the three windows the mouse pointer is positioned, a mouse button click gives rise to the text I got a button press. If the mouse is positioned in the larger (background) window when a keyboard key is pressed, the text I got a key press is printed. If the mouse pointer is located in the top window, a keyboard key press results in the text In top window being printed. However, if the mouse is inside the bottom window when the keyboard key is pressed, then the text In bottom window is printed, followed by the value of the keycode, keysym, and character associated with the key pressed.

The program is written to print the keysym value as a hexadecimal number. This value can be searched for in the keysymdef.h header file which is usually stored in the /usr/include/X11 directory on Unix/Linux systems. This file is called into source code when the keysym.h header file is used, but in the example for Fig. 5.1 they are not needed. From either of these two header files, the keysym *XK_* corresponding to the keysym value can be found. It is this keysym which is used with the XRebindKeysym() function to link a program defined string to a keyboard key. In the program of Fig. 5.1, the Windows key, which has the Keysym value of

```
/*   This program consists of a main window on which is placed two
 *   text input windows. All three windows have white backgrounds
 *   with the boundary of each text window shown by its border.
 *   Each window responses to keyboard key presses and mouse.
 *   button presses. The nature of each press is printed on the
 *   console * screen.
 *
 *   Coded by:   Ross Maloney
 *   Date:       October 2008
 */

#include <X11/Xlib.h>
#include <X11/Xutil.h>
#include <stdio.h>

#define  BUFFER_LENGTH    10

int main(int argc, char *argv)
{
   Display            *mydisplay;
   Window             baseWindow, textWindow1, textWindow2;
   XSetWindowAttributes   myat;
   XSizeHints         wmsize;
   XWMHints           wmhints;
   XTextProperty      windowName, iconName;
   XEvent             baseEvent;
   GC                 mygc;
   KeySym             sym;
   char   *window_name = "Inout";
   char   *icon_name   = "IO";
   int                screen_num, done;
   unsigned long      mymask;
   int                x, i;
   char               buffer[BUFFER_LENGTH];

                   /* 1.  open connection to the server */
   mydisplay = XOpenDisplay("");

                   /* 2.  create a top-level window */
   screen_num = DefaultScreen(mydisplay);
   myat.border_pixel = BlackPixel(mydisplay, screen_num);
   myat.background_pixel = WhitePixel(mydisplay, screen_num);
   myat.event_mask = KeyPressMask | ButtonPressMask | ExposureMask;
   mymask = CWBackPixel | CWBorderPixel | CWEventMask;
   baseWindow = XCreateWindow(mydisplay,
                       RootWindow(mydisplay, screen_num),
                       300, 300, 350, 400, 2,
                       DefaultDepth(mydisplay, screen_num),
                       InputOutput,
                       DefaultVisual(mydisplay, screen_num),
                       mymask, &myat);
```

Fig. 5.1 A simple program to explore the keyboard

```
                    /* 3.  give the Window Manager hints */
wmsize.flags = USPosition | USSize;
XSetWMNormalHints(mydisplay, baseWindow, &wmsize);
wmhints.initial_state = NormalState;
wmhints.flags = StateHint;
XSetWMHints(mydisplay, baseWindow, &wmhints);
XStringListToTextProperty(&window_name, 1, &windowName);
XSetWMName(mydisplay, baseWindow, &windowName);
XStringListToTextProperty(&icon_name, 1, &iconName);
XSetWMIconName(mydisplay, baseWindow, &iconName);


                  /* 4.  establish window resources */
XRebindKeysym(mydisplay, XK_Meta_L, NULL, 0, "MetaL", 5);
                  /* 5.  create all the other windows needed */
textWindow1 = XCreateWindow(mydisplay, baseWindow,
                    30, 80, 200, 20, 2,
                    DefaultDepth(mydisplay, screen_num),
                    InputOutput,
                    DefaultVisual(mydisplay, screen_num),
                    mymask, &myat);
textWindow2 = XCreateWindow(mydisplay, baseWindow,
                    30, 200, 200, 20, 2,
                    DefaultDepth(mydisplay, screen_num),
                    InputOutput,
                    DefaultVisual(mydisplay, screen_num),
                    mymask, &myat);


                  /* 6.  select events for each window */
                  /* 7.  map the windows */
XMapWindow(mydisplay, baseWindow);
XMapWindow(mydisplay, textWindow1);
XMapWindow(mydisplay, textWindow2);


                  /* 8.  enter the event loop */
done = 0;
while ( done == 0 ) {
  XNextEvent(mydisplay, &baseEvent);
  switch( baseEvent.type ) {
  case Expose:
    break;
  case ButtonPress:
    printf("I got a button press\n");
    break;
  case KeyPress:
    printf("I got a key press\n");
    if ( baseEvent.xkey.window == textWindow1 )
      printf("In top window\n");
    if ( baseEvent.xkey.window == textWindow2 )  {
      printf("In bottom window\n");
      x = XLookupString(&baseEvent.xkey, buffer, BUFFER_LENGTH,
                        &sym, NULL);
```

Fig. 5.1 (continued)

```
                    printf (" Keycode  =  %d\n" ,  baseEvent . xkey . keycode );
                    sym  =  XKeycodeToKeysym ( mydisplay ,
                                          baseEvent . xkey . keycode ,  1 );
                    printf (" x  =  %d\n" ,  x );
                    printf (" Keysym  =  %x     character  =  %c " ,  sym,  buffer [0]);
                    for  ( i =1;  i<x;  i++)   printf("%c" ,  buffer [ i ]);
                    printf (" \n" );
                }
              break ;
          }
      }

                      /*  9.   clean  up  before  exiting  */
      XUnmapWindow ( mydisplay ,  baseWindow );
      XUnmapWindow ( mydisplay ,  textWindow1 );
      XUnmapWindow ( mydisplay ,  textWindow2 );
  }
```

Fig. 5.1 (continued)

Fig. 5.2 The windows of the
keyboard explorer

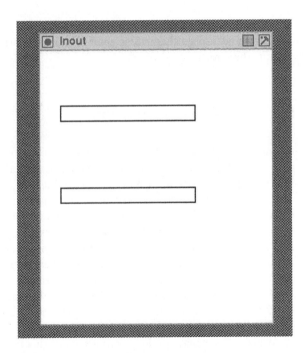

ffe7 corresponding to Keysym *XK_Meta_L* (Left meta), was assigned the character
sequence MetaL. The fundamental purpose of this program is to print on the terminal
the result of the keyboard entry directed through the simple window combination
shown in Fig. 5.2.

Notice each of the three windows in this example uses the same event structure,
for each is to receive the same inputs. The window which is to receive a keyboard
entry or a mouse button click is the one on which the mouse pointer is positioned.

But the window is only able to receive such events if it is encoded into the *event structure* active for the window. This is usually established (as in this example) when the window is created. However it can be changed after the window is created by using the XChangeWindowAttributes() Xlib call using parameters similar to the valuemask and attributes variables used with a XCreateWindow() call. Alternately, a XSelectInput() Xlib call could be used.

This program offers a means for exploring the codes generated by each of the keys on a keyboard connected to X. For example, by using this program the keycode generated by the *Enter* keyboard key was found to be the value 36 on a Linux system running on Intel x686 hardware.

5.1.1 Exercises

Modify the program so that:

1. The text entered in each window is displayed yellow in colour.
2. When a backspace character is entered, the last character on the line is removed from the screen.

5.2 What Fonts Are Available

A font is the pattern placed on the screen to represent a character. Thus to display a character (which is stored in the computer as a particular number) a font needs to be selected. In the case of the X Window System this pattern is a bitmap and a *font* is a collection of such patterns which share a common *style* across all members contained in that font. The alphabet of the font is the individual patterns which can be accessed from this collection. When a font is defined it sets up a correspondence between the members of its alphabet and a pattern for each member. Thus a character from an alphabet of a font defines a pattern which will appear on the screen. A graphics context (GC) is then used in association with this pattern to represent the character on the screen. Whereas the font contributes the pattern, the graphics context contributes (in relation to drawing of characters) such things as colour, clipping, and how overlaying is to appear on screen.

Available fonts may reside on a *font server*. This is a separate server to the X11 server which interacts with the X Window System screen. The font server xfs is included with the X Window System distribution and is often used in this serving roll, but not always. When xfs is used, the fonts appear to be contained in directories within the unpacked files of the X distribution and directly accessed from there. This is not the case. It is xfs that is accessing those file and making them available using a protocol. A defined protocol, separate to that for interacting with the X11 server, is used for interacting with any font server, including xfs. Functions in Xlib which are responsible for interacting with the font server use this protocol as their mechanism.

A font must be loaded, from the font server if it is used, onto the X11 server of the client/server pair executing a program before the font can be used. A font to be used in a program is then linked to the GC by setting the appropriate member in the XGCValues structure. If the font has not been loaded, an attempt to use the GC to draw text will occur without an error return, but nothing will appear on the screen. It is important all fonts to be used by a client program be available. If a font server is used, or in the server itself, only one copy of a font is kept on the server, that font being shared by many client programs. A font is only unloaded from the font server once all client programs using the font no longer need it. There is at least one font loaded on any server, and this is the *default font*. If a font is not specified when a GC is created, the default font is used. The default font is implementation dependent.

Generally, the XLoadQueryFont() function is used to load a font for Xlib into the server and establish links between this font and the client program. This function is composed of a XQueryFont() and a XLoadFont() function call with XLoadQueryFont() having the combined effect of both component calls.

Each font is identified by a name. It is this name which is used to load the font onto the X11 server and, through it, to connect it to the client program. The program of Fig. 5.3 lists the name of each font available on a font server, which is different from those which have been loaded onto an X11 server. Note the difference and similarities of this program with the other X Window programs included in this book. To assist this comparison, the template structure used in writing those X Window programs has also been used in Fig. 5.3. Notice that only the display needs to be opened by the program since fonts are related to the display, not to windows on the display. When this program was run, 2900 fonts were listed by name since those names matched the general wildcard search string "*" used in the XlistFonts() function. A similar list is produced using the xlsfonts command which is provided as a standard part of the X Window System distribution.

Full font names are composed of 12 fields separated by a hyphen (-). Those fields are:

- foundry [misc, mutt, schumacher, sony, adobe, b&h, bitstream];
- font family [palatino, courier, helvetica, avantgrade, times, symbol];
- font weight [medium, bold, book, demi, light];
- slant [roman, italic, oblique];
- set width [normal];
- size in pixels [8, 10, 12, 14, 18, 24];
- point size (in tenths of a point) [80, 100, 120, 140, 120, 150, 170, 230];
- horizontal resolution in dots per inch (dpi [75, 100]);
- vertical resolution in dots per inch (dpi) [75, 100];
- spacing [p, c];
- average width (in tenths of a pixel);
- character set name [iso8859-1];

with examples of each field given in [square brackets]. If the search field in the program of Fig. 4.14 is changed to "*-palatino-*iso8859-1", then 4 font names are listed.

```
/*   This program prints the name of all fonts available on the
 *   current X server.
 *
 *   Coded by:    Ross Maloney
 *   Date:        December 2008
 */

#include <X11/Xlib.h>
#include <X11/Xutil.h>
#include <stdio.h>

int main(int argc, char *carv)
{
  Display          *mydisplay;
  char             **fontNames;
  int              i, present;

                    /* 1.  open connection to the server */
  mydisplay = XOpenDisplay("");
  fontNames = XListFonts(mydisplay, "*", 4000, &present);
  for (i=0; i<present; i++)  printf("%s\n", fontNames[i]);
  printf("Number_of_those_fonts_present_=_%d\n", present);

                    /* 2.  create a top-level window */
                    /* 3.  give the Window Manager hints */
                    /* 4.  establish window resources */
                    /* 5.  create all the other windows needed */
                    /* 6.  select events for each window */
                    /* 7.  map the windows */
                    /* 8.  enter the event loop */
                    /* 9.  clean up before exiting */
}
```

Fig. 5.3 A program to print the names of all available fonts

The list created by a program such as in Fig. 4.14 provides a first step in using a font by identifying the fonts available. A program such as xfontsel available in the standard X Window System distribution can be used to view the appearance of a font corresponding to a name. This name can be used as a parameter in a XLoadFont() or XLoadQueryFont() function.

5.3 Keyboard Echoing on Windows

Generally, visual feedback of keyboard entry is required as it is entered. There are occasions when this is not the case, for example when a password is requested for entry. The separation by Xlib of keyboard entry from showing what has just been entered caters for both these situations. The technique used in the program of Fig. 5.1

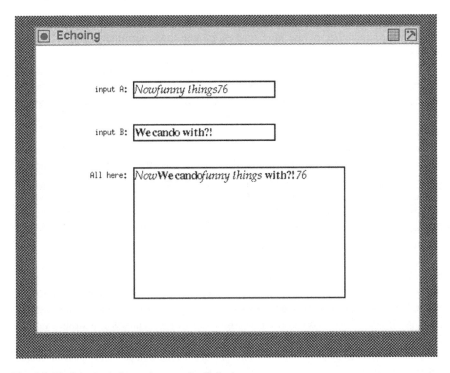

Fig. 5.4   Keyboard echoing and accumulated display

of printing the keyboard entry on the console assumes the console is available. If the window is not available, an alternate window could be used, or something completely different could be used to provide the keystroke feedback. In the case of the program in Fig. 5.1 a character font is used to show a representation of the character produced by each keystroke.

Both static processing and dynamic processing of text are used in the program of Fig. 5.5. The program starts with three text sub-windows arranged on a plain white window 300 × 400 pixels in size. These three sub-windows are used for displaying text. Figure 5.4 shows this window combination. The two top windows receive a sequence of characters from the keyboard, the user selecting which window is to be used via the mouse. As the characters are typed, they are displayed both in the selected window and in the third window. Different character fonts are defined in the program for each of the three of those character streams. Each of the three windows is labelled with a text string with these strings presented in a fourth font. The display of the text strings entered through the keyboard is dynamic, while static text is used to display the label of each window. Both the containing (background) window and the windows which show the accumulated entered text are insensitive to keyboard entry.

To implement control of this program, receiving of a *down arrow* key entry from the keyboard in either of the keyboard entry windows, terminates the program's execution.

The four windows used in this program fall into two classes; those which accept the mouse pointer click and keyboard entry, and those which will receive neither. A result of this is a different event mask that is required for each of these two classes: the first with keyboard, mouse button, and exposure events enabled, while the other has only the exposure event enabled.

Both the Xlib function XDrawText() and XDrawImageString() are used here to put text on the windows. For the labelling of the windows, the function XDrawImageString() is more appropriate since the X11 server only uses a limited part of the graphics context (GC) specified for drawing the text to achieve the required result. By contrast, the XDrawText() function allows more flexibility by the program (client) in the way the text is drawn, but at the cost of greater activity by the server.

Prior to the XDrawImageString() calls in the program of Fig. 5.5, no font had been referenced. When these calls make reference to the mygc graphics context (GC), the font used is the default. This default will vary with implementation of the X Window System being used in running the program, for the default used is assigned by the X11 server used. The alignment of those labels was done by trial-and-error to get the labels to be right-justified one under the other. But the length of each label text display is font dependent and so this alignment will be incomplete if a different default font was used.

All other text is written using fonts which are explicitly loaded. This is better means of drawing text. The steps involved are:

1. create a GC;
2. load the font;
3. link the loaded font to the GC;
4. draw the text referencing the GC.

The font is loaded from the font server of whatever form it takes into the X11 server of the client program. In the client program, a pointer is returned to the block of memory in the X11 server where the details of the loaded font are stored. The fid member of this block of information contains the identifier of the font, and it is the value of this member which is set as the font member in the GC structure.

Two graphics contexts (mygc and myGC1) are used, but it is myGC1 which is used for handling the text. Two fonts are loaded with their pointers stored as font1 and font2. Both fonts are proportional fonts which means each character in the font can take a different character width. The font identification member (fid) of the font structure is set as the default font in the myGC1 structure before it is used in the XDrawText() function call which echos the character received from the keyboard.

Characters are entered one after the other using the keyboard. Each character entered needs to be displayed immediately. So the call to XDrawText() is made using a string of one character in length. All characters are displayed in the position

```
/*   This program consists of a main window on which is placed
 *   three text windows: two windows for text input and the
 *   other for display of all the text entered through the other
 *   two windows.  The text entered is also echoed in that
 *   window.  All four text streams have a different font.  All
 *   four windows have white backgrounds with the boundary of
 *   each text window shown by its border.  A text label is
 *   displayed against each text window.  The program is
 *   terminated by typing the 'down arrow' key.
 *
 *   Coded by:   Ross Maloney
 *   Date:       November 2008
 */

#include <X11/Xlib.h>
#include <X11/Xutil.h>
#include <string.h>

#define   BUFFER_LENGTH    10

int main(int argc, char *argv)
{
   Display            *mydisplay;
   Window             baseWindow, textWindow1, textWindow2,
                         textWindow3;
   XSetWindowAttributes   myat;
   XSizeHints         wmsize;
   XWMHints           wmhints;
   XTextProperty      windowName, iconName;
   XEvent             baseEvent;
   GC                 mygc, myGC1, myGC2, myGC3;
   XGCValues          myGCvalues;
   KeySym             sym;
   XFontStruct        *font1, *font2;
   XTextItem          myText;
   char *window_name = "Echoing";
   char *icon_name    = "Ec";
   char *label1       = "input_A:";
   char *label2       = "input_B:";
   char *label3       = "All_here:";
   int                screen_num, done;
   unsigned long      mymask;
   int                x, i;
   int                yWindow1, yWindow2, yWindow3, width;
   char               buffer[BUFFER_LENGTH];

                /* 1.  open connection to the server */
   mydisplay = XOpenDisplay("");

                /* 2.  create a top-level window */
   screen_num = DefaultScreen(mydisplay);
   myat.border_pixel = BlackPixel(mydisplay, screen_num);
```

Fig. 5.5 Creating two text entry and a accumulate windows

```
myat.background_pixel = WhitePixel(mydisplay, screen_num);
myat.event_mask = ExposureMask;
mymask = CWBackPixel | CWBorderPixel | CWEventMask;
baseWindow = XCreateWindow(mydisplay,
                    RootWindow(mydisplay, screen_num),
                    300, 400, 550, 400, 2,
                    DefaultDepth(mydisplay, screen_num),
                    InputOutput,
                    DefaultVisual(mydisplay, screen_num),
                    mymask, &myat);
```

```
                    /* 3.  give the Window Manager hints */
wmsize.flags = USPosition | USSize;
XSetWMNormalHints(mydisplay, baseWindow, &wmsize);
wmhints.initial_state = NormalState;
wmhints.flags = StateHint;
XSetWMHints(mydisplay, baseWindow, &wmhints);
XStringListToTextProperty(&window_name, 1, &windowName);
XSetWMName(mydisplay, baseWindow, &windowName);
XStringListToTextProperty(&icon_name, 1, &iconName);
XSetWMIconName(mydisplay, baseWindow, &iconName);
```

```
                    /* 4.  establish window resources */
XRebindKeysym(mydisplay, XK_Meta_L, NULL, 0, "MetaL", 5);
myGCvalues.background = WhitePixel(mydisplay, screen_num);
myGCvalues.foreground = BlackPixel(mydisplay, screen_num);
mymask = GCForeground | GCBackground;
mygc = XCreateGC(mydisplay, baseWindow, mymask, &myGCvalues);
font1 = XLoadQueryFont(mydisplay,
    "-adobe-palatino-medium-i-normal--0-0-0-0-p-0-iso8859-1");
font2 = XLoadQueryFont(mydisplay,
    "-adobe-times-bold-r-normal--0-0-0-0-p-0-iso8859-1");
myGC1 = XCreateGC(mydisplay, baseWindow, mymask, &myGCvalues);
```

```
                    /* 5.  create all the other windows needed */
mymask = CWBackPixel | CWBorderPixel | CWEventMask;
textWindow3 = XCreateWindow(mydisplay, baseWindow,
                    140, 170, 300, 180, 2,
                    DefaultDepth(mydisplay, screen_num),
                    InputOutput,
                    DefaultVisual(mydisplay, screen_num),
                    mymask, &myat);
myat.event_mask = KeyPressMask | ButtonPressMask | ExposureMask;
textWindow1 = XCreateWindow(mydisplay, baseWindow,
                    140, 50, 200, 20, 2,
                    DefaultDepth(mydisplay, screen_num),
                    InputOutput,
                    DefaultVisual(mydisplay, screen_num),
                    mymask, &myat);

                    140, 110, 200, 20, 2,
                    DefaultDepth(mydisplay, screen_num),
```

Fig. 5.5 (continued)

```
                                       InputOutput,
                                       DefaultVisual(mydisplay, screen_num),
                                       mymask, &myat);


          /* 6.  select events for each window */
          /* 7.  map the windows */
XMapWindow(mydisplay, baseWindow);
XMapWindow(mydisplay, textWindow1);
XMapWindow(mydisplay, textWindow2);
XMapWindow(mydisplay, textWindow3);


          /* 8.  enter the event loop */
done = 0;
yWindow1 = yWindow2 = yWindow3 = 0;
myText.chars = buffer;
myText.nchars = 1;
while ( done == 0 )  {
  XNextEvent(mydisplay, &baseEvent);
  switch( baseEvent.type )  {
  case Expose:
    XDrawImageString(mydisplay, baseWindow, mygc,
                     85, 65, label1, strlen(label1));
    XDrawImageString(mydisplay, baseWindow, mygc,
                     85, 125, label2, strlen(label2));
    XDrawImageString(mydisplay, baseWindow, mygc,
                     78, 185, label3, strlen(label3));
    break;
  case ButtonPress:
    break;
  case KeyPress:
    if ( baseEvent.xkey.keycode == 88 )  {
      done = 1;
      break;
    }
    x = XLookupString(&baseEvent.xkey, buffer, BUFFER_LENGTH,
                      &sym, NULL);
    sym = XKeycodeToKeysym(mydisplay, baseEvent.xkey.keycode,
                           1);
    if ( baseEvent.xkey.window == textWindow1 )  {
      myText.font = font1 -> fid;
      XDrawText(mydisplay, textWindow1, myGC1, yWindow1, 15,
                &myText, 1);
      width = XTextWidth(font1, buffer, 1);
      yWindow1 += width;
    }
    if ( baseEvent.xkey.window == textWindow2 )  {
      myText.font = font2 -> fid;
      XDrawText(mydisplay, textWindow2, myGC1, yWindow2, 15,
                &myText, 1);
      width = XTextWidth(font1, buffer, 1);
        yWindow2 += width;
```

Fig. 5.5 (continued)

```
        }
        XDrawText(mydisplay, textWindow3, myGC1, yWindow3, 15,
                  &myText, 1);
        yWindow3 += width;
        break;
      }
   }
 }


                /* 9.  clean up before exiting */
    XUnmapWindow(mydisplay, baseWindow);
    XUnmapWindow(mydisplay, textWindow1);
    XUnmapWindow(mydisplay, textWindow2);
  }
```

Fig. 5.5 (continued)

passed as parameters to the XDrawText() function. To do this correctly a counter of the position in the window where the next character is to be shown is kept and is incremented by the width of that character after each character is shown. This width is determined by the function XTextWidth() based on the character and the font used to show that character on the screen.

5.3.1 Exercises

Modify the program of Fig. 5.5 so that:

1. The characters are echoed in the top window and inserted in the bottom window both of which are coloured red.
2. The bottom window holds the accumulated line of text so all characters remain visible when long character sequences are typed in the top two windows.

5.4 Putting Lines of Text in a Window

Displaying text comprising collections of characters available entirely before starting the display process is considered here. The process is similar to, but also enables refinements to be made to the techniques used in Sect. 5.3 for printing characters entered from a keyboard. Having all the text available presents different challenges to be resolved about the appearance of this text on a window.

There is a fundamental process which underlies placing of all text in a window. It consists of a number of steps. The characters, or collection of characters, which are to be displayed are assumed to be available. The window to be used is created or identified for use. Then the font to be used is selected and loaded into the server.

Fig. 5.6 Text being
displayed in a text window

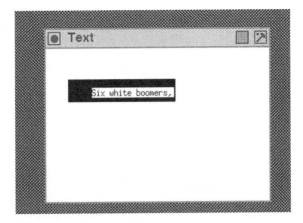

Finally the characters are drawn on the window using the selected font. The code
which performs this process is shown in Fig. 5.7. It prints the terminal output:

```
ascent = 16
decent = 4
```

which are characteristics of the font used. These two values contain all the glyphs
in the font; i.e., any character drawn with this font will be contained in a 20 pixel
height. Figure 5.6 shows the resulting text on the window of the program.

   The displayed text has a foreground colour which appears as the characters of the
text are drawn while the background colour underlies the box which contains, and
thus encloses, each glyph it can display in representing characters, i.e. the glyph of
each character. If text does not fill the window, then the colour of the window will
fill areas of the window not covered by the text. Text that falls beyond the window
in which it is drawn is cut (or *clipped*) off. So positioning of text in window can be
significant.

   The horizontal position of the text in the textWindow window is set by a
parameter passed in the XDrawImageString() call. If this parameter is greater
than zero, the start point where the first character of the string is displayed in the
window is shifted in the window. Vacant space appears in the window. Also, if
the length of the assembled glyphs representing the characters is shorter than the
horizontal dimension of the window, vacant space appears on the right of the window.
Such vacant space is filled by the window's background colour. This positioning is
of the text string inside the text window is different from having the text window
passing over the text and clipping text characters which is beyond the extent of the
window. Thus, the technique used here for displaying text differs from that shown
in Sect. 5.8 for scrolling text.

   The code in Fig. 5.7 also positions the glyphs of the text vertically. The height
of the text window (textWindow) is created as being 26 pixels high. The base-
line of the assembled glyphs characters of the string (textline) is positioned

```
/*   This program demonstrates placement of a single line of text
 *   in a window which is setup for that purpose.  The line of
 *   text is too long to be displayed in the window.
 *
 *   Coded by:   Ross Maloney
 *   Date:       February 2009
 */

#include <X11/Xlib.h>
#include <X11/Xutil.h>
#include <string.h>
#include <stdio.h>

int main(int argc, char *argv)
{
    Display              *mydisplay;
    Window               baseWindow, textWindow;
    XSetWindowAttributes myat;
    XSizeHints           wmsize;
    XWMHints             wmhints;
    XTextProperty        windowName, iconName;
    XEvent               baseEvent;
    GC                   mygc;
    XGCValues            myGCvalues;
    XFontStruct          *font1;
    char *window_name = "Text";
    char *icon_name   = "Te";
    char *textline = "Six_white_boomers,_Snow_white_boomers,_Racing";
    int                  screen_num, done;
    unsigned long        mymask;

                      /* 1.  open connection to the server */
    mydisplay = XOpenDisplay("");

                      /* 2.  create a top-level window */
    screen_num = DefaultScreen(mydisplay);
    myat.border_pixel = BlackPixel(mydisplay, screen_num);
    myat.background_pixel = WhitePixel(mydisplay, screen_num);
    myat.event_mask = ExposureMask;
    mymask = CWBackPixel | CWBorderPixel | CWEventMask;
    baseWindow = XCreateWindow(mydisplay,
                               RootWindow(mydisplay, screen_num),
                               100, 100, 300, 200, 2,
                               DefaultDepth(mydisplay, screen_num),
                               InputOutput,
                               DefaultVisual(mydisplay, screen_num),
                               mymask, &myat);

                      /* 3.  give the Window Manager hints */
    wmsize.flags = USPosition | USSize;
    XSetWMNormalHints(mydisplay, baseWindow, &wmsize);
    wmhints.initial_state = NormalState;
```

Fig. 5.7 A program to draw a string of text

```
wmhints.flags = StateHint;
XSetWMHints(mydisplay, baseWindow, &wmhints);
XStringListToTextProperty(&window_name, 1, &windowName);
XSetWMName(mydisplay, baseWindow, &windowName);
XStringListToTextProperty(&icon_name, 1, &iconName);
XSetWMIconName(mydisplay, baseWindow, &iconName);
wmsize.flags = USPosition | USSize;
XSetWMNormalHints(mydisplay, baseWindow, &wmsize);
wmhints.initial_state = NormalState;
wmhints.flags = StateHint;
XSetWMHints(mydisplay, baseWindow, &wmhints);
XStringListToTextProperty(&window_name, 1, &windowName);
XSetWMName(mydisplay, baseWindow, &windowName);
XStringListToTextProperty(&icon_name, 1, &iconName);

            /* 4.  establish window resources */
myGCvalues.background = WhitePixel(mydisplay, screen_num);
myGCvalues.foreground = BlackPixel(mydisplay, screen_num);
mymask = GCForeground | GCBackground;
mygc = XCreateGC(mydisplay, baseWindow, mymask, &myGCvalues);
font1 = XLoadQueryFont(mydisplay,
        "-adobe-times-bold-r-normal--0-0-0-0-p-0-iso8859-1");
printf("ascent_=_%d\ndescent_=_%d\n",
        font1->ascent, font1->descent);
XSetFont(mydisplay, mygc, font1->fid);

            /* 5.  create all the other windows needed */
myat.background_pixel = BlackPixel(mydisplay, screen_num);
mymask = CWBackPixel | CWBorderPixel | CWEventMask;
textWindow = XCreateWindow(mydisplay, baseWindow,
                    30, 40, 140, 26, 2,
                    DefaultDepth(mydisplay, screen_num),
                    InputOutput,
                    DefaultVisual(mydisplay, screen_num),
                    mymask, &myat);

            /* 6.  select events for each window */
            /* 7.  map the windows */
XMapWindow(mydisplay, baseWindow);
XMapWindow(mydisplay, textWindow);

            /* 8.  enter the event loop */
done = 0;
while ( done == 0 ) {
  XNextEvent(mydisplay, &baseEvent);
  switch ( baseEvent.type ) {
  case Expose:
    XDrawImageString(mydisplay, textWindow, mygc,
                30, 20, textline, strlen(textline));
    break;
```

Fig. 5.7 (continued)

```
        }
      }

                    /* 9.   clean up before exiting */
          XUnmapWindow(mydisplay, baseWindow);
      }
```

Fig. 5.7 (continued)

using the `XDrawImageString()` call to be 20 pixels down from the top of the
`textWindow`. The height of the font used (`font1`) is the sum of the
`font1->ascent` and `font1->descent`, which in this example are 16 and 4,
respectively. The result of these measures and settings is the text is not centred vertically in the text window, for there is uneven amounts of the window's background
above and below the line of text.

Note the `mymask` variable is assigned a value before it is used in the creation
of `textWindow`. This is due to the mask bits for creating a GC being different to
those used when creating a window. The background of the window is then assigned
to be black in colour.

5.4.1 Exercises

1. The text window in Fig. 5.6 is small in comparison with the base window. Is there
   any advantage in making the text window larger while continuing to use the same
   font?
2. What is the smallest height the text window can be made in the code of Fig. 5.7
   to display all characters of the selected font without truncation?
3. Write a program to display multiple lines of text contained in the program inside
   a text window. Colour the background of the text window red and that of the text
   blue. What is the optimal spacing of those lines of text using the font you use
   here? Why is it optimal?

5.5 Insertion Cursor

An *insertion cursor* is a marker placed on a line of text to indicate where the next
character from the keyboard will be placed. Xlib does not provide an insertion cursor.
The *cursor* provided in Xlib is a marker for the position of the mouse pointer on
screen. This is different from an insertion cursor. However, most toolkits provide an
insertion cursor for text input. So if an insertion pointer is required when using Xlib,
then it has to be constructed and its behaviour determined by program control.

The program listed in Fig. 5.8 is an example of code which implements keyboard text input while using an insertion cursor. Since no insertion cursor is provided, the cursor shape is created as a Pixmap using the utility program `bitmap`.

The shape of this insertion cursor is to be compatible with the text font with which it is used. Since the cursor is implemented by a constant dimension Pixmap, a text font in which all characters are of constant width, i.e. a *typewriter font*, is appropriate. The font used in the program of Fig. 5.8 is a `b&h-lucidatypewrite` at 18 pixel. This text was displayed/entered in a window 26 pixels in height. From the `width` element of the `XCharStruct` structure pointed by the `per_char` member of the structure of the `font1` variable linked to the `b&h-lucidatypewrite` font in the program of Fig. 5.8, the constant character width is 11 pixels. The width of the cursor was selected to be smaller than the character width, a value of 6 being used. So the dimensions of the insertion cursor Pixmap was set at 11×24. As a result, `bitmap` was executed by the command line:

```
bitmap  -size   6x24
```

The text input window was set to show 20 characters. So its dimensions were 220 pixels long by 24 high. The Pixmap created was copied into the programs source code with the associated variables (`width`, `height`, and `bits` having the prefix `cursoricon_`.

Because the cursor is constant in appearance, i.e. not blinking, another means needs to be found so it stands out from the text which it marks. In this example, this is done by colouring the foreground of the Pixmap red in colour, in contrast to the black of the text input.

The program of Fig. 5.8 has some, but limited, text-editing capacity. A `backspace` character from the keyboard deletes the character to the left of the insertion cursor, with all characters to the right of this deletion shifting to the left to fill the space created. A corresponding behaviour is implemented in the array `data[]` in which the keyboard entered characters are stored. The mouse pointer can be used to set the placement of the insertion cursor in the sequence of characters which have already been entered. If the pointer is beyond the length of the inserted text, then the cursor is set to the end of the text. The cursor can be placed in a position by moving the mouse pointer, then pressing any mouse button. The cursor then moves to this position. Actually, it is releasing the button which generates the event which results in the position being set.

Points to note with respect to the code of Fig. 5.8 are:

- In the program, the base window (`baseWindow`) was created with a standard white background. This was reset to the lightcyan colour by using the `XChangeWindowAttribute()` Xlib library call before the window was brought to the screen. This enables the base window to be created and be used before creating more application-specific colours.

```
/*   This  program  consists  of  a main window  and  a  single  text  entry
 *   window.   An insertion  cursor  is  created  using  a Pixmap.   With
 *   a  foreground  colour  of  red, this  Pixmap is  used  to  show  where
 *   the  next  character  entered  from  the  keyboard  will  be  placed.
 *   A 18 pixel  typewriter  text  font  is  used  to  show  the  keyboard
 *   characters  entered.   The  mouse  pointer, triggered  by  the
 *   release  of  any  mouse  button  can  be  used  to  position  this
 *   insertion  cursor.
 *
 *   Coded  by:   Ross  Maloney
 *   Date:       June 2011
 */

#include <X11/Xlib.h>
#include <X11/Xutil.h>

#define cursoricon_width 6
#define cursoricon_height 24
static unsigned char cursoricon_bits [] = {
    0x21, 0x1e, 0x0c, 0x0c, 0x0c, 0x0c, 0x0c, 0x0c, 0x0c, 0x0c,
    0x0c, 0x0c, 0x0c, 0x0c, 0x0c, 0x0c, 0x0c, 0x0c, 0x0c, 0x0c,
    0x0c, 0x0c, 0x1e, 0x21};

int main(int argc, char *argv)
{
    Display         *mydisplay;
    Window          baseWindow, textWindow;
    XSetWindowAttributes   myat;
    XSizeHints      wmsize;
    XWMHints        wmhints;
    XTextProperty   windowName, iconName;
    XEvent          baseEvent;
    GC              myGC;
    XGCValues       myGCvalues;
    XFontStruct     *font1;
    XColor          exact, closest;
    char *window_name = "Insertion_Cursor";
    char *icon_name = "IC";
    int             screen_num, done, lightcyan, red, count;
    int             charinc, position, end, current, i;
    unsigned long   mymask;
    char            data[20], bytes[3];
    KeySym          character;
    XComposeStatus  cs;
    Pixmap          cursor;

                    /* 1.  open connection to the server */
    mydisplay = XOpenDisplay("");

                    /* 2.  create a top-level window */
    screen_num = DefaultScreen(mydisplay);
    myat.border_pixel = BlackPixel(mydisplay, screen_num);
    myat.background_pixel = WhitePixel(mydisplay, screen_num);
```

Fig. 5.8 Text input assisted by an insertion cursor

```
myat.event_mask = ExposureMask;
mymask = CWBackPixel | CWBorderPixel | CWEventMask;
baseWindow = XCreateWindow(mydisplay,
                           RootWindow(mydisplay, screen_num),
                           100, 100, 300, 200, 2,
                           DefaultDepth(mydisplay, screen_num),
                           InputOutput,
                           DefaultVisual(mydisplay, screen_num),
                           mymask, &myat);
              /* 3.  give the Window Manager hints */
wmsize.flags = USPosition | USSize;
XSetWMNormalHints(mydisplay, baseWindow, &wmsize);
wmhints.initial_state = NormalState;
wmhints.flags = StateHint;
XSetWMHints(mydisplay, baseWindow, &wmhints);
XStringListToTextProperty(&window_name, 1, &windowName);
XSetWMName(mydisplay, baseWindow, &windowName);
XStringListToTextProperty(&icon_name, 1, &iconName);
XSetWMIconName(mydisplay, baseWindow, &iconName);

              /* 4.  establish window resources */
myGCvalues.background = WhitePixel(mydisplay, screen_num);
myGCvalues.foreground = BlackPixel(mydisplay, screen_num);
mymask = GCForeground | GCBackground;
myGC = XCreateGC(mydisplay, baseWindow, mymask, &myGCvalues);
font1 = XLoadQueryFont(mydisplay,
          "-b&h-lucidatypewriter-*-*-*-*-18-*-*-*-*-*-*");
XSetFont(mydisplay, myGC, font1->fid);
charinc = font1->per_char->width;
XAllocNamedColor(mydisplay,
                 XDefaultColormap(mydisplay, screen_num),
                 "LightCyan2", &exact, &closest);
lightcyan = closest.pixel;
myat.background_pixel = lightcyan;
XChangeWindowAttributes(mydisplay, baseWindow, CWBackPixel,
                        &myat);
XAllocNamedColor(mydisplay,
                 XDefaultColormap(mydisplay, screen_num),
                 "red", &exact, &closest);
red = closest.pixel;
cursor = XCreatePixmapFromBitmapData(mydisplay, baseWindow,
                          cursoricon_bits, cursoricon_width,
                          cursoricon_height,
                          red, WhitePixel(mydisplay, screen_num),
                          DefaultDepth(mydisplay, screen_num));

              /* 5.  create all the other windows needed */
mymask = CWBackPixel | CWBorderPixel | CWEventMask;
myat.event_mask = ButtonReleaseMask | KeyPressMask
                  | ExposureMask ;
myat.background_pixel = WhitePixel(mydisplay, screen_num);
textWindow = XCreateWindow(mydisplay, baseWindow,
```

Fig. 5.8 (continued)

```
                          60, 40, 220, 26, 2,
                          DefaultDepth(mydisplay, screen_num),
                          InputOutput,
                          DefaultVisual(mydisplay, screen_num),
                          mymask, &myat);

                 /* 6.  select events for each window */
                 /* 7.  map the windows */
XMapWindow(mydisplay, baseWindow);
XMapWindow(mydisplay, textWindow);

                 /* 8.  enter the event loop */
current = end = 0;
done = 0;
while ( done == 0 ) {
  XNextEvent(mydisplay, &baseEvent);
  switch ( baseEvent.type ) {
  case  Expose:
    break;
  case  ButtonRelease:
    position = baseEvent.xbutton.x/charinc;
    current = position;
    if ( position > end ) {
      position = end;
      current = end;
    }
    XClearWindow(mydisplay, textWindow);
    XCopyArea(mydisplay, cursor, textWindow, myGC, 0, 0, 6, 24,
        position * charinc, 2);
    XDrawString(mydisplay, textWindow, myGC, 0, 17,
                &data[0], end);
    break;
  case  KeyPress:
    count = XLookupString(&baseEvent.xkey, bytes, 3,
                          &character, &cs);
    switch ( count ) {
    case 0:       /* Control character */
      break;
    case 1:       /* Printable character */
      switch ( bytes[0] ) {
      case 8:     /* Backspace */
        current --;
        XClearWindow(mydisplay, textWindow);

        XCopyArea(mydisplay, cursor, textWindow, myGC,
                  0, 0, 6, 24,
            current * charinc, 2);
        for (i=current; i<end; i++)  data[i] = data[i+1];
        end--;
        XDrawString(mydisplay, textWindow, myGC, 0, 17,
                    &data[0], end);
        if ( current < 1 )  XBell(mydisplay, 50);
        break;
```

Fig. 5.8 (continued)

```
                   case 13:    /* Enter */
                     XBell(mydisplay, 50);
                     break;
                   default:
                     end++;
                     for (i=end; i>current; i--)  data[i] = data[i-1];
                     data[current] = bytes[0];
                     current++;
                     XClearWindow(mydisplay, textWindow);
                     XCopyArea(mydisplay, cursor, textWindow, myGC,
                               0, 0, 6, 24,
                         current * charinc, 2);
                     XDrawString(mydisplay, textWindow, myGC, 0, 17,
                               &data[0], end);
                 }
                 break;
             }
             break;
         }
     }

                 /* 9.  clean up before exiting */
         XUnmapWindow(mydisplay, baseWindow);
         XDestroyWindow(mydisplay, baseWindow);
         XCloseDisplay(mydisplay);
     }
```

Fig. 5.8 (continued)

- The keyboard key which generates each keypress event is translated by the XLookupString() library function call. The count of the number of bytes returned is used to determine if the key corresponded to a *standard* character, or a special(control) type character. Different processing followed from such determination.
- The same event structure linked to the variable baseEvent is processed as a button press using the xbutton member, and as a key press using the xkey member.
- The variables current and end are, respectively, the current position for inserting a character and the position of the last character. Both are indices of the storage array data. From these variables, the position of a character in the input window in pixels can be calculated by multiplying by the fixed size of each character (the variable charinc).
- The call to XCopyArea() to show the insertion cursor (cursor) uses myGC which has its foreground and background set to black and white, respectively. However when put on the window, the insertion cursor has a red foreground and a white background. These colours are set up in the XCreatePixmapFromBitmap Data() call which creates the cursor Pixmap. In effect, the myGC is a dummy (in the instance of copying a Pixmap).

Fig. 5.9 Inputting text with
an insertion cursor

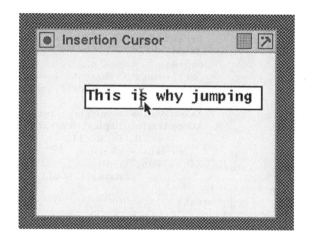

- When the cursor Pixmap is copied to, or cleared from, the window, the action partially obliterates the image of the character at that spot on the window. It is necessary to redraw the character in this position.
- The 0 case in the switch statement of the `count` variable is meant to process *non-printable* keyboard characters, for example, the arrow keys.
- The *string* passed over as the sixth parameter in the `XDrawString()` Xlib function call is not null terminated—the seventh (final) parameter is the number of characters being passed.

Figure 5.9 shows a screenshot of the program of Fig. 5.8 in operation. Shown are the base window and the single text window. Into the text window a single line of text with up to 20 characters can be entered from the keyboard. The mouse pointer has just been used to position the insertion cursor to be before the 7th character in the input character stream.

5.5.1 Exercises

1. Modify the program of Fig. 5.8 so the insertion cursor blinks.
2. Change the code of Fig. 5.8 so as to label the text input window `Text input:`. Use two different techniques to achieve this ends.
3. Increase the editing functionality of the program of Fig. 5.8. Such functionality could be by the use of the keyboard arrow keys to position the insertion cursor.
4. The program of Fig. 5.8 uses a technique of clear window, edits stored characters, and then redraws of all characters and cursor for showing the character input. Implement a different technique which achieves the same goal. Is this technique more efficient than the one used in Fig. 5.8? More efficient in what way?

5.6 Moving Between Text Input Windows Using Keys

Text entered from the keyboard is identified by the X server as belonging to the window on which the pointer currently sits when the text was received. This enables the client program to link the input received with where in the program it wishes the input to be processed. Since most X Window (client) programs are composed of multiple windows, this linkage is to be expected. However, when keyboard entering into a succession of windows, one after the other, physically moving the mouse pointer over the next keyboard entry window can be irritating. Setting up a program so the user can use the keyboard, in addition or as a substitute to moving the mouse pointer, is addressed in this section.

The fundamental is the mouse pointer must be over the window for it to receive the keyboard entry. Physically moving the pointer by hand is the standard technique use to achieve this ends. But this method is slow. A faster method is to do it under program control by using the `XWarpPointer()` Xlib call. This function relocates the pointer and its indicator (cursor) to the location specified by the parameters passed in the call. The `XWarpPointer()` library function has a number of *modes* by which it can relocate the pointer, and these are governed by the parameters passed when the function is called.

As a demonstration of how to create such a situation, consider a background window on which there is four text entry windows. Each entry window can store/display a single line of 20 characters. Successive windows contain the date, time, subject, and message. These windows are arranged in a ring so the top window is followed by the second from the top, the second by the third, and so on. The bottom window then is succeeded by the top window. Each text input window has no editing capability, not even a `backspace` will delete an input error. This is done to simplify the program. Further, pressing any mouse button has no effect on the behaviour of the program. However, positioning the mouse pointer on one of the four text entry windows will result in the next characters appearing at the end of the character sequence previously entered into that window. Pressing an *up arrow* key will move subsequent keyboard characters to go to the next input window above the current. A *down arrow* key will shift the keyboard input to be directed to the window below the current window. The up and down arrow keys in the primary and supplementary keyboard areas are treated the same within this program.

Figure 5.10 is a screenshot of the program listed in Fig. 5.11 in use. The pointer can be moved manually using the mouse and by the up and down arrow keyboard keys. If the mouse pointer is not located in one of the four text boxes, the program ignores the characters typed on the keyboard.

Note the following in the code of Fig. 5.11:

- The array `ring` via its structural components contains all information related to the four text input windows. This information is the ID number of the window in which the text is input and displayed, the array which stores the character input through the window, and the index of the first free storage location in that array.
- The same font, and GC in particular, is used with each text input window.

- The pointer is moved to indicate the last character in the window as indicated by the value of the variable `index` used in conjunction with the `ring` array.
- Aside from the `XWarpPointer()` call, there is no explicit reference to the pointer.
- To assist with clarity, only `KeyPress` events are used, and no error checking following Xlib calls is performed.
- The variable `mymask` is reused and assigned different values for both creating the windows and the GC.
- The identification number of the window in which the pointer is located when a character receives event occurs is found in the `window` member of the key press event type `xkey` of the `XEvent` structure to which the variable `baseEvent` is assigned (i.e. `baseEvent.xkey.window`).
- The characters typed in are accumulated, but nothing is done with them, so when the program is terminated the input is lost.
- The header file `X11/keysymdef.h` defines the constants `XK_Up`, `XK_KP_Up`, `XK_Down`, `XK_KP_Down`, etc., associated with the representation of the arrow keys.

Fig. 5.10 Four text windows arranged in an input ring

```
/*   This program consists of a main window on which is placed four
 *   text input windows.  These windows are to hold the date, name
 *   of the receiver, subject, and the message.  Each window
 *   contains a single line of text 20 characters in length.
 *   There is no editing facilities nor insertion cursor on any of
 *   these * windows.  However, the up arrow and down arrow
 *   keyboard keys move the keyboard focus the next window above or
 *   below, respectively, for receiving the next character from the
 *   keyboard.  These four windows are connected to form a ring.
 *
 *   Coded by:   Ross Maloney
 *   Date:       June 2011
 */

#include <X11/Xlib.h>
#include <X11/Xutil.h>
#include <X11/keysymdef.h>

int main(int argc, char *argv)
{
   Display            *mydisplay;
   Window             baseWindow;
   XSetWindowAttributes   myat;
   XSizeHints         wmsize;
   XWMHints           wmhints;
   XTextProperty      windowName, iconName;
   XEvent             baseEvent;
   GC                 mygc;
   XGCValues          myGCvalues;
   XFontStruct        *font1;
   char *window_name = "Text_window_switching";
   char *icon_name = "Swt";
   int                screen_num, done, y, i, index, charinc, count;
   unsigned long      mymask;
   char               bytes[3];
   KeySym             character;
   XComposeStatus cs;
   struct {                          /* Input window ring structure */
      Window   id;
      int      last;
      char     array[20];
   } ring[4];

                  /* 1.  open connection to the server */
   mydisplay = XOpenDisplay("");

                  /* 2.  create a top-level window */
   screen_num = DefaultScreen(mydisplay);
   myat.border_pixel = BlackPixel(mydisplay, screen_num);
   myat.background_pixel = WhitePixel(mydisplay, screen_num);
   myat.event_mask = ExposureMask;
```

Fig. 5.11 Window switching using up and down arrow keys

```
mymask = CWBackPixel | CWBorderPixel | CWEventMask;
baseWindow = XCreateWindow(mydisplay,
                      RootWindow(mydisplay, screen_num),
                      100, 100, 250, 270, 2,
                      DefaultDepth(mydisplay, screen_num),
                      InputOutput,
                      DefaultVisual(mydisplay, screen_num),
                      mymask, &myat);

                  /* 3.  give the Window Manager hints */
wmsize.flags = USPosition | USSize;
XSetWMNormalHints(mydisplay, baseWindow, &wmsize);
wmhints.initial_state = NormalState;
wmhints.flags = StateHint;
XSetWMHints(mydisplay, baseWindow, &wmhints);
XStringListToTextProperty(&window_name, 1, &windowName);
XSetWMName(mydisplay, baseWindow, &windowName);
XStringListToTextProperty(&icon_name, 1, &iconName);
XSetWMIconName(mydisplay, baseWindow, &iconName);

                  /* 4.  establish window resources */
myGCvalues.background = WhitePixel(mydisplay, screen_num);
myGCvalues.foreground = BlackPixel(mydisplay, screen_num);
mymask = GCForeground | GCBackground;
mygc = XCreateGC(mydisplay, baseWindow, mymask, &myGCvalues);
font1 = XLoadQueryFont(mydisplay,
            "-b&h-lucidatypewriter-*-*-*-*-14-*-*-*-*-*-*-*");
XSetFont(mydisplay, mygc, font1->fid);
charinc = font1->per_char->width;

                  /* 5.  create all the other windows needed */
y = 30;
mymask = CWBackPixel | CWBorderPixel | CWEventMask;
myat.event_mask = KeyPressMask;
for (i=0; i<4; i++) {
  ring[i].id = XCreateWindow(mydisplay, baseWindow, 70,
                      y, 20*charinc, 20, 2,
                      DefaultDepth(mydisplay, screen_num),
                      InputOutput,
                      DefaultVisual(mydisplay, screen_num),
                      mymask, &myat);
  ring[i].last = 0;
  y += 60;
}

                  /* 6.  select events for each window */
                  /* 7.  map the windows */
XMapWindow(mydisplay, baseWindow);
for (i=0; i<4; i++) XMapWindow(mydisplay, ring[i].id);
                  /* 8.  enter the event loop */
index = 0;
```

Fig. 5.11 (continued)

```
  done = 0;
  while ( done == 0 )  {
    XNextEvent(mydisplay , &baseEvent );
    switch ( baseEvent.type )  {
    case  Expose :
      break;
    case  KeyPress :
      count = XLookupString(&baseEvent.xkey , bytes , 3,
                            &character , &cs );
      index = 0;
      for  ( i =0;  i <4;  i++)
        if ( ring[i].id == baseEvent.xkey.window ) index = i;
      switch ( count )  {
      case  0:          /* Control character */
        switch ( character )  {
        case XK_Up:              /* Up arrow key */
        case XK_KP_Up:
          index --;
          if (index < 0 )  index = 3;
          XWarpPointer(mydisplay , None, ring[index].id ,
                       0, 0, 0, 0, ring[index].last*charinc , 10);
          break;
        case XK_Down:            /* Down arrow key */
        case XK_KP_Down:
          index++;
          if (index > 3 )  index = 0;
          XWarpPointer(mydisplay , None, ring[index].id ,
                       0, 0, 0, 0, ring[index].last*charinc , 10);
          break;
        }
        break;
      case  1:         /* Printable character */
        ring[index].array[ring[index].last] = bytes[0];
        XDrawString(mydisplay , ring[index].id , mygc,
                    ring[index].last*charinc , 15, bytes , 1);
        ring[index].last++;
        break;
      }
      break;
    }
  }

            /* 9.  clean up before exiting */
  XUnmapWindow(mydisplay , baseWindow );
}
```

Fig. 5.11 (continued)

5.6.1 Exercises

1. Modify the program of Fig. 5.11 so the *Enter* key on the keyboard is used to advance to the next text window.
2. When the window of Fig. 5.10 undergoes an exposure, the display of the contents of each text window is lost. Modify the code of Fig. 5.11 so the contents of each window are restored to the way it was before the window was covered over.

5.7 A Slider Bar

A slider bar is a means of interacting with a graphics program. It consists of a slide whose position on the slider guide can be changed using the mouse. The position of the slide on the guide is read by the program, and the interpretation of the meaning of the position is up to the program. This mechanism is also known as a *scroll bar*. A slider bar operates through the use of events. Slider bars are often used in association with text as is the subject of Sect. 5.8, but they are a general element applicable to wider usage.

The slider bar is composed of:

- a *slider bed*, which is usually a narrow window, in which the long dimension is taken as corresponding to the range of values which can be produced by the slider bar; and
- a *slider* which is an indicator, adjustable in location by the mouse, which marks the value obtained for the slider bar.

Calibrations marks could be added along the length of the slider bed if warranted to assist the user of the slider bar.

Potentially a slider can be implemented as either a cursor or a window. A pattern, possibly in the form of a bitmap (discussed in Sect. 4.3), can be used on each as decoration. For implementation of the slider bar, the following are needed:

- efficient drawing the slider in its transient positions;
- efficient redrawing of the screen the slider vacates;
- generation of coordinates for the position of the slide on the slider bed; and
- the slider remains attached to the slider bed.

A cursor and window are possible implementation components for a slider bar. A cursor is implemented as a lightweight process by the X Window System, and this suggests use as a slider. A cursor follows the position of the mouse across the screen. By using a `MotionNotify` event, the position of the cursor is available. The handling of drawing and redrawing of screen positions touched by the transient placement of the cursor on the screen is done automatically by the X11 server. This satisfies the first three of the above implementation needs. However, it is difficult to constrain a mouse pointer to follow the slider bed, thus satisfying the fourth need. Such a constraint would introduce loss of utility of the mouse.

By contrast, a window can be constructed to move only within another window. In this case, the window implementing the slider is constrained under program control to remain inside the window which implements the slider bed. The XMoveWindow() call provides a positioning mechanism for moving the slider window to the position in the slider window indicated by the mouse pointer.

On the slider bar and slider windows, three actions of the mouse are used. The slider is *picked up* by clicking a button on the mouse and released by ceasing to depress the button. These two actions are on the window which implements the slider. Thus, this window in its implementation is linked to ButtonPress and ButtonRelease events. The third action is the movement of the mouse, relative to the slider bed. The coordinates of the mouse pointer on this window are where the slider window is to be located. The movement of the mouse on the slider bed is obtained by linking it to a MotionNotify event. The coordinates provided when a MotionNotify event is sent by the X11 server contain the coordinate of the mouse pointer when the event was sent, relative to the window linked to the event. This window is the of the slider bed. Those coordinates then can be used in a XMoveWindow() call to re-position the window which represents the slider. But this is only to occur as long as the mouse button is depressed. Thus, pressing and releasing of the mouse button needs to be stored and this store checked by the program before re-positioning of the slider window.

The code of Fig. 5.12 is built around three windows; the background window baseWindow, the slider bed window sliderbedWindow, and the slider window sliderWindow. Each of these windows has a different colour. The backgrounds of the baseWindow are constructed to be white that of the sliderbedWindow window is pale grey, and that of the sliderWindow window is black. The way the mouse interacts with these windows, and thus how the slider bar works, is determined by linking the mouse events to those three windows. This again supports the claim on page xxii of Scheifler et al. (1988) that the X Window System *provides mechanism rather than policy*.

Figure 5.13 shows the slider generated by the code of Fig. 5.12 as consisting of a vertical slider bar contained in a window. Background colour of the three windows is chosen to give contrast. White is used for the base window, pale grey for the slider window, and black for the window representing the slider. No other decoration is used on any window so as not to obscure the major elements of the code.

To operate the slider, the left-hand mouse button is pressed when the mouse pointer is over the slider. This mouse button is held depressed while moving the mouse which drags the slider to the required position on the slider bed. The mouse button is released when the required slider position is obtained. While the mouse drags the slider, the coordinates of the slider relative to the slider bed, are printed on the terminal such as:

```
/*  A program which produces a window containing a vertical slider
 *  bar.  The slider is picked up by clicking the left-hand mouse
 *  button over the slider.  While that button is depressed the
 *  slider can be moved along the slider bed with the end of the
 *  motion indicated by releasing that mouse button.  The
 *  coordinates of the slider are printed on the terminal screen
 *  as the slider is moved.
 *
 *  Coded by:  Ross Maloney
 *  Date:      February 2009
 */

#include <X11/Xlib.h>
#include <X11/Xutil.h>
#include <string.h>
#include <stdio.h>


int main(int argc, char *argv)
{
    Display           *mydisplay;
    Window             baseWindow, sliderWindow, sliderbedWindow;
    XSetWindowAttributes   myat;
    XSizeHints         wmsize;
    XWMHints           wmhints;
    XTextProperty      windowName, iconName;
    XEvent             baseEvent;
    GC                 mygc;
    XGCValues          myGCvalues;
    XFontStruct        *font1;
    char *window_name = "Slider";
    char *icon_name   = "Sb";
    int                screen_num, done;
    unsigned long      mymask;

                    /* 1.  open connection to the server */
    mydisplay = XOpenDisplay("");

                    /* 2.  create a top-level window */
    screen_num = DefaultScreen(mydisplay);
    myat.border_pixel = BlackPixel(mydisplay, screen_num);
    myat.background_pixel = WhitePixel(mydisplay, screen_num);
    myat.event_mask = ExposureMask;
    mymask = CWBackPixel | CWBorderPixel | CWEventMask;
    baseWindow = XCreateWindow(mydisplay,
                               RootWindow(mydisplay, screen_num),
                               100, 100, 200, 200, 2,
                               DefaultDepth(mydisplay, screen_num),
                               InputOutput,
                               DefaultVisual(mydisplay, screen_num),
                               mymask, &myat);
```

Fig. 5.12 A program that produces and uses a slider bar

```
                    /* 3.   give the Window Manager hints */
wmsize.flags = USPosition | USSize;
XSetWMNormalHints(mydisplay, baseWindow, &wmsize);
wmhints.initial_state = NormalState;
wmhints.flags = StateHint;
XSetWMHints(mydisplay, baseWindow, &wmhints);
XStringListToTextProperty(&window_name, 1, &windowName);
XSetWMName(mydisplay, baseWindow, &windowName);
XStringListToTextProperty(&icon_name, 1, &iconName);
XSetWMIconName(mydisplay, baseWindow, &iconName);

                    /* 4.   establish window resources */
                    /* 5.   create all the other windows needed */
myat.background_pixel = 0xd3d3d3;
myat.event_mask = ExposureMask | Button1MotionMask;
mymask = CWBackPixel | CWBorderPixel | CWEventMask;
sliderbedWindow = XCreateWindow(mydisplay, baseWindow,
                          90, 30, 11, 140, 2,
                          DefaultDepth(mydisplay, screen_num),
                          InputOutput,
                          DefaultVisual(mydisplay, screen_num),
                          mymask, &myat);
myat.background_pixel = BlackPixel(mydisplay, screen_num);
myat.event_mask = ExposureMask;
mymask = CWBackPixel | CWBorderPixel | CWEventMask;
sliderWindow = XCreateWindow(mydisplay, sliderbedWindow,
                          1, 0, 7, 14, 1,
                          DefaultDepth(mydisplay, screen_num),
                          InputOutput,
                          DefaultVisual(mydisplay, screen_num),
                          mymask, &myat);

                    /* 6.   select events for each window */
                    /* 7.   map the windows */
XMapWindow(mydisplay, baseWindow);
XMapWindow(mydisplay, sliderbedWindow);
XMapWindow(mydisplay, sliderWindow);

                    /* 8.   enter the event loop */
done = 0;
while ( done == 0 ) {
  XNextEvent(mydisplay, &baseEvent);
  switch ( baseEvent.type ) {
  case  Expose:
    break;
  case  ButtonPress:
    break;
  case  ButtonRelease:
    break;
  case  MotionNotify:
    printf("Moving to: x = %d    y = %d \n",
```

Fig. 5.12 (continued)

```
                         baseEvent.xmotion.x,  baseEvent.xmotion.y);
            XMoveWindow(mydisplay,  sliderWindow,  1,
                         baseEvent.xmotion.y − 7);
          break;
        }
      }

                    /* 9.   clean up before exiting */
    XUnmapWindow(mydisplay,  baseWindow);
    XUnmapWindow(mydisplay,  sliderbedWindow);
    XUnmapWindow(mydisplay,  sliderWindow);
  }
```

Fig. 5.12 (continued)

Fig. 5.13 A window
containing a slider bar

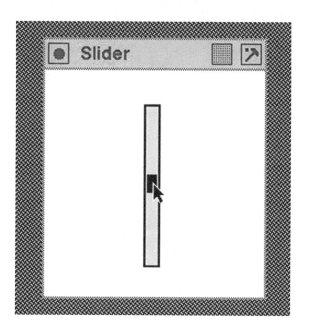

```
Moving to: x = 4   y = 12
Moving to: x = 4   y = 13
Moving to: x = 4   y = 14
Moving to: x = 4   y = 15
Moving to: x = 4   y = 16
Moving to: x = 4   y = 17
Moving to: x = 4   y = 18
Moving to: x = 5   y = 19
Moving to: x = 6   y = 20
```

When the program starts, the slider is positioned at the top extremity of the slider
bed.

The `ButtonPress` and `ButtonRelease` event types are not used to implement the chosen operating policy for the slider bar. The `MotionNotify` event type alone is used in the form of a `Button1MotionMask` event member which is linked to the `sliderbedWindow` window which implements the slider bed in the code of Fig. 5.12. This event occurs when the mouse pointer is moved, while the left-hand mouse button is depressed. This event is not linked to the `slider` window. So, if the mouse is clicked and move while above the slider, the `Button1MotionMask` event propagates to the `sliderbedWindow`. Thus, although the mouse is positioned over the slider, the event is received by the slider bed window, not the slider, and is thus ignored. The coordinates which accompany such event messages are relative to the `sliderbedWindow`. A `XMoveWindow()` call is then used to move the `slider` window to those coordinates, using the vertical coordinate alone.

The mode of operation of the slider bar is a property of how it is coded. For example, the centre of the slider window is used as the alignment point and this results in half of it disappearing at the extremity of the slide bar. This behaviour is different to what is obtained using, at least some, slider bars available in X11 toolkits. Another mode might be if the mouse pointer were depressed while over the slider bar not covered by the slider, the slider bar could be aligned to this location. Again a different mode then implemented in the code of Fig. 5.12.

5.7.1 Exercises

1. Modify the program of Fig. 5.12 so the slider operates vertically but the top-left-hand corner of the slider bed is at pixel coordinate (10, 20) of the base window.
2. Change the alignment point of the slider bar from its centre to other points. What is the result of this change?
3. The slider in Fig. 5.13 could be made to be wider than the slider bed. Would this cause complication in the code of Fig. 5.12? Prove your answer with working code.
4. Modify the program of Fig. 5.12 so the slider operates horizontally.
5. Change the mode of operation of the slider bar in Fig. 5.12 code so clicking the mouse on the slider bed above or below the slider moves the slider to the mouse pointer by a set movement increment.
6. When the slider in Fig. 5.13 is moved, its new position no longer appears on the display. What causes this to occur?

5.8 Scrolling Text

The term *scrolling* is used to describe the process of moving a window over an object larger than the window so the full capacity of the window is used to view a portion of the object. Since only a portion of the object is visible through the window at any one time, natural questions about what such a window needs include:

- what proportion of the object is visible in the window;
- how far from the start of the object is the window positioned; and
- how far from the end of the object is the window positioned.

A visual answer to these questions is provided by a *scroll bar*. Such a scroll bar is located adjacent to the window which shows the visible part of the object. The scroll bar itself is a slider bar as described in Sect. 5.7 but with its coordinate output applied to adjustment of the positioning of a window for viewing an object which is too large to fit into the window. In this section, object of interest is text.

The problem is how to align the viewing window with the object. This situation occurs in standard text output programs. Say a text window 10 characters wide is to be used to move across a single line of text such that only the characters under the window are visible. The line of text is held in a single-dimensional array. Showing the text which appears in the window is by printing 10 characters from the array holding the text starting from an offset. Positioning of the window on the text corresponds to changing the value of the offset. Everything in this situation is centred around the character, which is the unit of alignment.

In pixel-map graphics as used by X11, the pixel is the alignment unit. From Sect. 5.7, the output from a slider bar is coordinates, in units of pixels. To use the slider bar, the positioning of the window should be done in units of pixels. However, when X11 draws a string of text displayed using a font the result is a pixel map that represents the drawing. This pattern is created on a *drawable*, which can be either a screen window or an off-screen Pixmap. This off-screen Pixmap is measured and accessed in units of pixels and can be moved to a screen, in whole or part, as required. So a XDrawString() call can be used to create the Pixmap of the text of interest in an off-screen Pixmap, and a XCopyArea() call used to move to the screen the part corresponding to under the viewing window. In this arrangement, the creation of the off-screen Pixmap occurs once for all scrolled viewings. The positioning of the viewing window uses the coordinates coming from the slider bar.

Most, but not all, Xlib drawing calls can write into either a window or a Pixmap. These items are called **drawables**. A drawing operation on a window only appears on the screen after using a XMapWindow() call to send it to the screen. Further drawing on this window requires further sending of the window to the screen. Drawing into a Pixmap is not visible. It can be made visible by copying the contents of the Pixmap, or part of it, to a window. A nominated rectangle of the Pixmap can be copied to the desired position in a window.

The Pixmap, which is of type Pixmap, is created using a XCreatePixmap() call. This Pixmap is created in the X11 server's memory. Before it is used, it is recommended to clear this memory of residual content by using a XFillRectangle() call (a XClearArea() call only clears areas of a window, not a Pixmap). This Pixmap can then be used for drawing operations, for example to draw text using a XDrawImageString(). A portion of the Pixmap can then be copied to a window using a XCopyArea() call. In the context of scrolling, the size of the area copied from the Pixmap corresponds to the size of the viewing window. The starting location is adjusted by using the coordinates from the slider (scroll) bar.

The XCopyArea() call is applied as a result of an exposure event. When the slider is moved, the exposure of part of the slider bed window changes, and this generates an exposure event. The XCopyArea() requires the coordinate of the Pixmap to move to the viewing window. The raw coordinate values from which this is obtained is part of the Button1MotionMask event component. This value (or the appropriate value computed from it) is used in the XCopyArea() call.

5.8.1 Scrolling Horizontally

If a line of text is too long to be displayed in a window, the text can be moved, or scrolled, through the viewing window under the control of the program's user. This is not directly supported by Xlib although all X11 toolkits do provide this support. However, it can be achieved using what Xlib does provide and those components can be used to implement scrolling of more general graphic objects. Scrolling of text can be more difficult than such general objects since knowledge of fonts used in the text is required. Horizontal scrolling of text is simpler than vertical scrolling of text.

A program which implements horizontal scrolling of text is given in Fig. 5.14. This program builds upon the code of Fig. 5.7. Differences introduced into this code include the following:

- A more general means of handling colour via the XColor structure is used;
- A slide bar, similar to that of Fig. 5.13, is positioned horizontally below the text window;
- In the Fig. 5.7 code, the font-encoded text string is written into the textWindow *drawable*, which is of type Window. In the code of Fig. 5.14, the string is written into the buffer variable, which is a *drawable* of type Pixmap. The contents of buffer do not appear on the screen. In addition:
- The Pixmap buffer is created in the same part of the program to the text window, slider, and slider bed windows occurs;
- The contents of the Pixmap buffer are set to an initial condition using a XFillRectangle() call;
- Scrolling of the text results from processing exposure events;
- The starting position of the text string in the textWindow is done by assigning a value to the positioning variable x.

Coupling of the scroll bar and the scrolling occurs through the processing of events; the Exposure part handles the scrolling, while the MotionNotify handles changes to the position of the scroll bar. No attempt is made in the code of Fig. 5.14 to ensure the scroll bar is able to address all characters of the text so that all can pass through the viewing window.

```
/*   A program to scroll a line of text horizontally.  This is
 *   done to view portions of the line which is too long to fit
 *   into the viewing window.  A slider is used to move the
 *   viewing window along the line of text to bring the required
 *   continuous section of text into view.
 *
 *   Coded by:   Ross Maloney
 *   Date:       February 2009
 */

#include <X11/Xlib.h>
#include <X11/Xutil.h>
#include <string.h>


int main(int argc, char *argv)
{
   Display              *mydisplay;
   Window               baseWindow, textWindow, sliderWindow,
                           sliderbedWindow;
   XSetWindowAttributes myat;
   XSizeHints           wmsize;
   XWMHints             wmhints;
   XTextProperty        windowName, iconName;
   XEvent               baseEvent;
   GC                   mygc;
   XGCValues            myGCvalues;
   XFontStruct          *font1;
   XColor               white, black, grey;
   Pixmap               buffer;
   char *window_name = "Hscroll";
   char *icon_name   = "Hs";
   char *textline =
          "ABCDEFGHIJKLMNOPQRSTUVWXYZabcdefghijklmnopqrstuvwxyz";
   int                  screen_num, done, x;
   unsigned long        mymask;

                     /* 1.  open connection to the server */
   mydisplay = XOpenDisplay("");

                     /* 2.  create a top-level window */
   screen_num = DefaultScreen(mydisplay);
   black.pixel = BlackPixel(mydisplay, screen_num);
   white.pixel = WhitePixel(mydisplay, screen_num);
   grey.pixel = 0xd3d3d3;
   myat.border_pixel = black.pixel;
   myat.background_pixel = white.pixel;
   myat.event_mask = ExposureMask;
   mymask = CWBackPixel | CWBorderPixel | CWEventMask;
   baseWindow = XCreateWindow(mydisplay,
                              RootWindow(mydisplay, screen_num),
                              100, 100, 200, 200, 2,
```

Fig. 5.14 A program to scroll a line of text horizontally

```
                              DefaultDepth(mydisplay, screen_num),
                              InputOutput,
                              DefaultVisual(mydisplay, screen_num),
                              mymask, &myat);

        /* 3.  give the Window Manager hints */
wmsize.flags = USPosition | USSize;
XSetWMNormalHints(mydisplay, baseWindow, &wmsize);
wmhints.initial_state = NormalState;
wmhints.flags = StateHint;
XSetWMHints(mydisplay, baseWindow, &wmhints);
XStringListToTextProperty(&window_name, 1, &windowName);
XSetWMName(mydisplay, baseWindow, &windowName);
XStringListToTextProperty(&icon_name, 1, &iconName);
XSetWMIconName(mydisplay, baseWindow, &iconName);

        /* 4.  establish window resources */
myGCvalues.background = white.pixel;
myGCvalues.foreground = black.pixel;
mymask = GCForeground | GCBackground;
mygc = XCreateGC(mydisplay, baseWindow, mymask, &myGCvalues);
font1 = XLoadQueryFont(mydisplay,
        "-adobe-times-bold-r-normal--0-0-0-0-p-0-iso8859-1");

        /* 5.  create all the other windows needed */
mymask = CWBackPixel | CWBorderPixel | CWEventMask;
myat.background_pixel = black.pixel;
textWindow = XCreateWindow(mydisplay, baseWindow,
                              30, 40, 140, 26, 2,
                              DefaultDepth(mydisplay, screen_num),
                              InputOutput,
                              DefaultVisual(mydisplay, screen_num),
                              mymask, &myat);
myat.background_pixel = grey.pixel;
myat.event_mask = ExposureMask | Button1MotionMask;
mymask = CWBackPixel | CWBorderPixel | CWEventMask;
sliderbedWindow = XCreateWindow(mydisplay, baseWindow,
                              30, 80, 140, 11, 2,
                              DefaultDepth(mydisplay, screen_num),
                              InputOutput,
                              DefaultVisual(mydisplay, screen_num),
                              mymask, &myat);
myat.background_pixel = black.pixel;
myat.event_mask = ExposureMask;
mymask = CWBackPixel | CWBorderPixel | CWEventMask;
sliderWindow = XCreateWindow(mydisplay, sliderbedWindow,
                              0, 1, 14, 7, 1,
                              DefaultDepth(mydisplay, screen_num),
                              InputOutput,
                              DefaultVisual(mydisplay, screen_num),
                              mymask, &myat);
buffer = XCreatePixmap(mydisplay, baseWindow, 1000, 26,
```

Fig. 5.14 (continued)

```
                                    DefaultDepth(mydisplay, screen_num));
     XFillRectangle(mydisplay, buffer, mygc,
                         0, 0, 1000, 26);
     XDrawImageString(mydisplay, buffer, mygc,
                         0, 20, textline, strlen(textline));

                    /* 6.   select events for each window */
                    /* 7.   map the windows */
     XMapWindow(mydisplay, baseWindow);
     XMapWindow(mydisplay, textWindow);
     XMapWindow(mydisplay, sliderbedWindow);
     XMapWindow(mydisplay, sliderWindow);

                    /* 8.   enter the event loop */
     done = 0;
     while ( done == 0 ) {
       XNextEvent(mydisplay, &baseEvent);
       switch ( baseEvent.type ) {
       case   Expose:
         XCopyArea(mydisplay, buffer, textWindow, mygc, x, 0,
                 140, 20, 0, 0);
         break;
       case   ButtonPress:
         break;
       case   ButtonRelease:
         break;
       case   MotionNotify:
         XMoveWindow(mydisplay, sliderWindow,
                     baseEvent.xmotion.x−7, 1);
         x = baseEvent.xmotion.x;
         break;
       }
     }

                    /* 9.   clean up before exiting */
       XUnmapWindow(mydisplay, baseWindow);
     }
```

Fig. 5.14 (continued)

Figure 5.15 shows a screenshot of the code of Fig. 5.14 in use. Notice the two characters shown in the text window can be cut vertically through the character, this depending on the position of the scroll bar. Also all characters contained in the text cannot be scrolled through the viewing window.

Fig. 5.15 Horizontal
scrolling a line of text with a
scroll bar

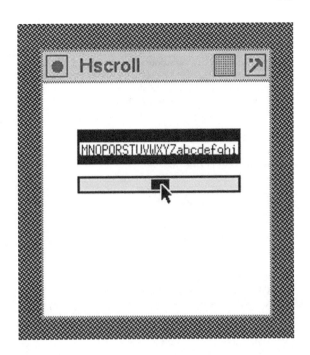

5.8.2 Scrolling Vertically

Two forms of vertical scrolling of text can be used: one in which *the pixels forming the text's characters* are moved vertically through the viewing window, and the other where *the lines of text* are moved vertically through the window. The first of these forms is similar to that shown above for scrolling a horizontal line of text. This is characterised by the chance of a partially complete line of text appearing in the viewing window. In the second form, a full line of text is added and removed from opposite ends of the viewing window. This technique is characterised by the scrolling by full lines of text. It is the technique used here.

Code to implement vertical text scrolling is shown in Fig. 5.16. It uses a vertical slider bar similar to that in the code of Fig. 5.12, laid on the right of the text viewing window `textWindow`. The font used to draw the text was known when the dimensions of the viewing window were selected. The height of the window was selected to accommodate five lines of text, but a 140 pixel width selected was too small to view the whole of each line of text which is held in the program in the array `lines`. Figure 5.17 shows the truncation of those longer lines and the appearance in the window of lines shorter than the window's width. The text viewing window background is in black, and the background of each text line is drawn with a white background. If there be unequal amount of black background at the top and bottom of the viewing window this indicates an error in the selection of the window's height for containing five lines of text.

```
/*   This program scrolls vertically through a passage of text.  A
 *   vertical scroll bar is used to control the position of the
 *   viewing window, bringing in and removing a line of text as
 *   the viewing window is scrolled past each line of text.
 *
 *   Coded by:    Ross  Maloney
 *   Date:        February  2009
 */

#include <X11/Xlib.h>
#include <X11/Xutil.h>
#include <string.h>


int main(int argc, char *argv)
{
  Display         *mydisplay;
  Window          baseWindow, textWindow, sliderWindow,
                     sliderbedWindow;
  XSetWindowAttributes  myat;
  XSizeHints      wmsize;
  XWMHints        wmhints;
  XTextProperty   windowName, iconName;
  XEvent          baseEvent;
  GC              mygc;
  XGCValues       myGCvalues;
  XFontStruct     *font1;
  XColor          white, black, grey;
  Pixmap          buffer;
  char *window_name = "Vscroll";
  char *icon_name   = "Vs";
  static char *lines[9] = {"Mary had a little lamb",
                           "Her father shot it dead",
                           "Now Mary takes the lamb to school",
                           "Between two hunks of bread",
                           "Now Mary is a very wise girl"
                           "And keeps her own counsel well",
                           "She never tells",
                           "That at home there is lamb stew",
                           "And fleece on the floor as well"};
  int             screen_num, done, i, y, newEnd, oldEnd;
  unsigned long   mymask;

                /* 1.  open connection to the server */
  mydisplay = XOpenDisplay("");

                /* 2.  create a top-level window */
  screen_num = DefaultScreen(mydisplay);
  black.pixel = BlackPixel(mydisplay, screen_num);
  white.pixel = WhitePixel(mydisplay, screen_num);
  grey.pixel = 0xd3d3d3;
  myat.border_pixel = black.pixel;
```

Fig. 5.16 A program to vertically scroll a piece of text

```
myat.background_pixel = white.pixel;
myat.event_mask = ExposureMask;
mymask = CWBackPixel | CWBorderPixel | CWEventMask;
baseWindow = XCreateWindow(mydisplay,
                           RootWindow(mydisplay, screen_num),
                           100, 100, 200, 200, 2,
                           DefaultDepth(mydisplay, screen_num),
                           InputOutput,
                           DefaultVisual(mydisplay, screen_num),
                           mymask, &myat);
```

```
                    /* 3.  give the Window Manager hints */
wmsize.flags = USPosition | USSize;
XSetWMNormalHints(mydisplay, baseWindow, &wmsize);
wmhints.initial_state = NormalState;
wmhints.flags = StateHint;
XSetWMHints(mydisplay, baseWindow, &wmhints);
XStringListToTextProperty(&window_name, 1, &windowName);
XSetWMName(mydisplay, baseWindow, &windowName);
XStringListToTextProperty(&icon_name, 1, &iconName);
XSetWMIconName(mydisplay, baseWindow, &iconName);
```

```
                    /* 4.  establish window resources */
myGCvalues.background = white.pixel;
myGCvalues.foreground = black.pixel;
mymask = GCForeground | GCBackground;
mygc = XCreateGC(mydisplay, baseWindow, mymask, &myGCvalues);
font1 = XLoadQueryFont(mydisplay,
          "-adobe-times-bold-r-normal--0-0-0-0-p-0-iso8859-1");
```

```
                    /* 5.  create all the other windows needed */
mymask = CWBackPixel | CWBorderPixel | CWEventMask;
myat.background_pixel = black.pixel;
textWindow = XCreateWindow(mydisplay, baseWindow,
                           10, 20, 140, 100, 2,
                           DefaultDepth(mydisplay, screen_num),
                           InputOutput,
                           DefaultVisual(mydisplay, screen_num),
                           mymask, &myat);
myat.background_pixel = grey.pixel;
myat.event_mask = ExposureMask | Button1MotionMask;
mymask = CWBackPixel | CWBorderPixel | CWEventMask;
sliderbedWindow = XCreateWindow(mydisplay, baseWindow,
                           160, 20, 11, 130, 2,
                           DefaultDepth(mydisplay, screen_num),
                           InputOutput,
                           DefaultVisual(mydisplay, screen_num),
                           mymask, &myat);
myat.background_pixel = black.pixel;
myat.event_mask = ExposureMask;
mymask = CWBackPixel | CWBorderPixel | CWEventMask;
sliderWindow = XCreateWindow(mydisplay, sliderbedWindow,
```

Fig. 5.16 (continued)

```
                                1,  0,  7,  14,  1,
                                DefaultDepth(mydisplay, screen_num),
                                InputOutput,
                                DefaultVisual(mydisplay, screen_num),
                                mymask, &myat);
buffer = XCreatePixmap(mydisplay, baseWindow, 2000, 100,
                        DefaultDepth(mydisplay, screen_num));
XFillRectangle(mydisplay, buffer, mygc, 0, 0, 2000, 100);
XDrawImageString(mydisplay, buffer, mygc, 0, 14, lines[0],
                    strlen(lines[0]));
for (i=1; i<5; i++) {
  XDrawImageString(mydisplay, buffer, mygc,
                    0, 14 + 20*i, lines[i], strlen(lines[i]));
}
oldEnd = 4;
newEnd = 4;

                    /* 6.  select events for each window */
                    /* 7.  map the windows */
XMapWindow(mydisplay, baseWindow);
XMapWindow(mydisplay, textWindow);
XMapWindow(mydisplay, sliderbedWindow);
XMapWindow(mydisplay, sliderWindow);

                    /* 8.  enter the event loop */
done = 0;
while ( done == 0 )  {
  XNextEvent(mydisplay, &baseEvent);
  switch ( baseEvent.type )  {
  case  Expose:
    if (newEnd == oldEnd )  {
      XCopyArea(mydisplay, buffer, textWindow, mygc, 0, 0,
              2000, 110, 0, 0);
    }
    if (newEnd > oldEnd)  {
      for (i=0; i<5; i++)  {
        XCopyArea(mydisplay, buffer, buffer, mygc, 0, 20*(i+1),
              2000, 20, 0, 20*i);
      }
      XFillRectangle(mydisplay, buffer, mygc, 0, 80, 2000, 20);
      XDrawImageString(mydisplay, buffer, mygc,
              0, 94, lines[newEnd], strlen(lines[newEnd]));
      XCopyArea(mydisplay, buffer, textWindow, mygc, 0, 80,
              2000, 20, 0, 80);
      oldEnd = newEnd;
    }
    if (newEnd < oldEnd)  {
      for (i=4; i>0; i--)  {
        XCopyArea(mydisplay, buffer, buffer, mygc, 0, 20*(i-1),
              2000, 20, 0, 20*i);
      }
      XFillRectangle(mydisplay, buffer, mygc, 0, 0, 2000, 20);
```

Fig. 5.16 (continued)

```
            XDrawImageString(mydisplay, buffer, mygc,
                     0, 14, lines[newEnd−4], strlen(lines[newEnd−4]));
            XCopyArea(mydisplay, buffer, textWindow, mygc, 0, 0,
                     2000, 20, 0, 0);
            oldEnd = newEnd;
        }
        break;
    case ButtonPress:
        break;
    case ButtonRelease:
        break;
    case MotionNotify:
        XMoveWindow(mydisplay, sliderWindow, 1,
                     baseEvent.xmotion.y−7);
        y = baseEvent.xmotion.y;
        newEnd = 4 + (y + 7)/40;
        break;
    }
}

              /* 9.  clean up before exiting */
  XUnmapWindow(mydisplay, baseWindow);
}
```

Fig. 5.16 (continued)

Fig. 5.17 Vertical scrolling
lines of text

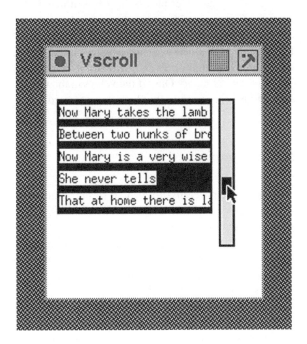

Figure 5.17 shows a result of executing the code of Fig. 5.16. As in the code of Fig. 5.14, the font used has an ascent of 14, and a descent 6, giving a line height of 20 pixels. The height of the text viewing window `textWindow` was assigned a value of 100 pixels so as to accommodate five lines of such text. The height of the slider bed window `sliderbedWindow` was set at 130 pixels. The nine lines of text processed by the program are set in the array `lines`, one line per array entry. Each of those lines of text is displayed in the text viewing window through the Pixmap `buffer`.

The code of Fig. 5.16 fills the viewing window with the first five lines of text available for viewing. After that, all scroll processing is triggered by the `Exposure` event generated by moving the scroll bar.

Scrolling is implemented by positioning of the slider in the scroll bar. In contrast to the code of Fig. 5.14 where the position of the slider could be used directly, here the position value needs to be transformed. When the program starts, the viewing window shows the text stored in elements 0 to 4 of array `lines[]` and the scroll bar is at the top of the scroll bar. When the slider is moved, its position (y) is converted to a text line index and that index is used to move one line of text from the top and bottom of the `buffer` Pixmap. When the slider is moved to a position that the next line should be displayed, text lines 1 to 5 of array `lines[]` are mapped into `buffer`. Here, the scroll bar bed of 130 pixels length is meant to enable movement of 4 lines of text. When the slider moves 30 pixels, a new line of text is moved into, and out from the Pixmap `buffer` and then onto the text viewing window `textWindow`. This scroll bar movement increments the index `newEnd` recording the last line of text contained in `lines[]` now shown on the viewing window. Handling of lines of text in the Pixmap `buffer` is done by comparing the `newEnd` to its previous value held in `oldEnd`. Only if the values in the variables `newEnd` and `oldEnd` are different is processing of the Pixmap performed.

5.8.3 Exercises

1. Modify the program of Fig. 5.16 so the scroll bar prints on the terminal the percentage position of the slider along the slide bed. Remove the link with the text string used in the program.
2. Describe three techniques for implementing vertical scrolling of text from the standpoint of the Pixmap (or Pixmaps) which would be involved in each.
3. Implement horizontal scrolling in the program of Fig. 5.16 so the end of the longer lines of text becomes visible.
4. In the code of Fig. 5.16, explain the choice of values which are used in transforming the coordinate values obtained from the slider.
5. The manner of moving lines of text in and out of the Pixmap in the code of Fig. 5.16 is limited. What is this limitation? Modify the code so multiple lines of text move in and out of the Pixmap.
6. Modify the program of Fig. 5.16 to use a different font.

5.9 Summary

Text remains an important source of input and output in modern computer programs. A graphical system such as X11 supports such operations. Text characters entered from a keyboard or taken from a disc file are drawn on the display by the X server. By choosing different font styles and sizes, the same characters can be made to appear differently in windows on a screen. How to achieve this using the services provided by Xlib has been the underlying theme of this chapter.

This chapter assumes creating windows, and the handling of events linked to such windows, is known. These are topic covered in previous chapters. Handling of keyboard input is here shown to be two separate processes. One of those processes is to get and interpret the meaning of a key pressed. The other is to provide a visual feedback of the keystroke on to the screen. It has been demonstrated here how to control this visual feedback by choosing a font to use, and finding which font styles and in what sizes they are available on a particular X11 server by using a user program. Finally, scroll bars were introduced and built up from windows and events as component parts. They are shown as both a general means of interacting with a program and also as a means for controlling the scrolling of text.

Chapter 6
Classic Drawing

Drawing pictures is arguably one of the most important application of computer graphics. A graph shows data in a pictorial manner. Computers can be used both to produce data and generate a pictorial representation – a visualisation – of this data, and a graph is a relatively simple pictorial representation. A graph is a simple graphic. But Xlib does not even support the drawing of graphs. However it does have facility to put on the screen lines of different types, and fill areas with colour, together with means supporting interaction between the computer user and those lines and areas. Although such components are simple they can lead to complex results. An outcome can be they provide flexibility for creating pictures but at the cost of more programming effort and required knowledge. In this chapter illustrations of those aspects of Xlib will be given by simple examples.

The drawing done here uses the concepts and handling methods of a window, Pixmap, graphics context (GC), and colour which have been used in other chapters of this book. Display of text is also drawing and it uses those same elements.

Because data is central to drawing, a different means of approach is warranted. Drawings should be done on a Pixmap and the Pixmap mapped to a window. Drawing done in a Pixmap remains while that on a window can be transient. If a window becomes hidden and then is exposed, the window needs to be redrawn by the program. This may not be possible when a drawing is built up incremental on a window and the data discarded. In this case re-running of the program would be required, if it was possible to obtain the data again. The difficulty is a Pixmap is not visible until it is mapped with it's drawing to a window. By contrast, when drawing directly on a window the drawing becomes visible immediately.

Electronic supplementary material The online version of this chapter
(https://doi.org/10.1007/978-3-319-74250-2_6) contains supplementary material, which is
available to authorized users.

If possible drawing should be done in colours with different elements done in different colour for emphasis. Both a window and a Pixmap have a foreground and background colour. Particularly in the case of Pixmaps they produce decorations in their foreground and background colours. As is shown in this chapter, more than those two colours can be used in drawing on a Pixmap. This is also the case for a window.

Drawing on a window by going through a Pixmap is less intuitive than by direct use of a window. This is the reason for positioning the contents of this chapter at this position in the book. Drawing is not simple.

6.1 Limit on Multiple Objects in a Request

A single graphic drawing call requests the creation of single or multiple visual objects on the screen. In X, those objects can be a point, a line, a polygon, and an arc. For example, a XDrawRectangle() call requests the drawing of a single object, in this case a rectangle defined by the height and width supplied with the call. But a XDrawRectangles() call requests drawing of multiple rectangles whose heights and widths are defined in an array which is passed to the call. The server used to perform those drawings limits the number of objects which can be drawn using one call.

If the client server knows the limitation of the drawing server, it can divide a user's program request for drawing multiple visual objects into multiple X protocol requests which together have the same result as the user program's request. However, in the case of the XDrawArcs() and XDrawLines() calls, breaking of the request would influence how the line segments are joined together, and with a XFillPolygon() call the inside of the polygon would become ill-defined. If the user program knows the limitation of the drawing server being used then steps can be taken to avoid the use of multiple protocol requests. The program of Fig. 6.1 illustrates obtaining the server protocol request limitation.

The maximum size of a server request is obtained by the XMapRequestSize() call and the value obtained is in units of four bytes. The X protocol guarantees this value will be greater than 4096 units. From this request maximum, the maximum number of points, lines, arcs, and polygons which can be include in a single request can be calculated. Running of the program code in Fig. 6.1 gave the results:

```
Single protocol size limit = 65535
Upper drawing limits:
  points    < 65532
  lines     < 32766
  arcs      < 21844
  polygons  < 65533
```

```
/*   This program prints the display request limitation of the
 *   current X server.
 *
 *   Coded by:   Ross Maloney
 *   Date:       March 2009
 */

#include <X11/Xlib.h>
#include <X11/Xutil.h>
#include <stdio.h>

int main(int argc, char *carv)
{
  Display         *mydisplay;
  long             size;

                  /* 1.  open connection to the server */
  mydisplay = XOpenDisplay("");

                  /* 2.  create a top-level window */
                  /* 3.  give the Window Manager hints */
                  /* 4.  establish window resources */
                  /* 5.  create all the other windows needed */
                  /* 6.  select events for each window */
                  /* 7.  map the windows */
                  /* 8.  enter the event loop */
  size = XMaxRequestSize(mydisplay);
  printf("Single protocol size limit = %d\n", size);
  size -= 3;
  printf("Upper limits:\n");
  printf("  points   < %d\n", size);
  printf("  lines    < %d\n", size/2);
  printf("  arcs     < %d\n", size/3);
  printf("  polygons < %d\n", size+1);

                  /* 9.  clean up before exiting */
  XCloseDisplay(mydisplay);
}
```

Fig. 6.1 A program to print drawing limits of display server

None of these values appear to be a high limitation. Similar limits also apply to text strings which can be drawn using the one call, with this limit determined by the length of the string.

6.2   Drawing Lines, Circles, and a Coloured-In Square

Xlib includes calls to draw points, straight lines, rectangles, polygons, and arcs. There are also calls which draw rectangles, closed polygons and arcs as outlines in colour and those figures a colour filled objects. There are no calls to draw spline lines as in Postscript. With the available calls, complex pictures can be built on a window with enhancements of those component parts by setting properties in the graphics context (GC) used with each component. Circles and ellipse are drawn as specific cases of arcs. A square is a particular case of a rectangle, but the rectangle itself is a particular case of a polygon. However, rectangles occur so frequently in drawing and their definition is simpler than that of a polygon to warrant separate rectangle specific calls.

Figure 6.2 is an example of creating a compound picture from parts. It is composed of two squares, two lines, and a circle. The resulting picture represents a *target plate* for drawing attention towards it's centre as opposed to the centre of the background window. One square is drawn in blue with the other in pink. Two different styles of lines are used; solid for the circle and the vertical line, and a dashed line for the horizontal. Those lines are drawn in black and red. The assemblage is drawn on a background window having a white background. Figure 6.3 contains the code used to produce the picture of Fig. 6.2.

Aspects of the code in Fig. 6.3 are worth noting. It is necessary to draw the pink square as a polygon for the XFillRectangle() call only draws a rectangle horizontally and there is no means of rotating the resulting object. Only one GC (baseGC) is used and the colour of the foreground, the line thickness, and line style are changed before it is used to draw each object. The XSetForeground() and XSetLineAttributes() calls are used to achieve those respective changes. A line thickness of 0 is used in the final XSetLineAttributes() call so to use the fastest line drawing algorithm available in the server which is to draw a line one pixel in thickness. The absolute technique of specifying coordinates of the square drawn with the XFillPolygon() is used as opposed to the relative addressing technique. Also the automatic polygon closure feature of that call is used. All drawing is done in the exposure clause of the event loop.

Note the order in which the components are drawn because overlapping components overwrite and thus hide what they overlay. Since the drawing is done on a background window, the window is created first. The blue square needs to be drawn first, after the background window has been created. Then the pink square is drawn before the straight lines and the circle.

Figure 6.2b also shows the original picture in Fig. 6.2a after it had being covered by another window on the screen and then re-exposed. The picture is both constructed and reconstructed in the expose clause of the event loop. However changes which are introduced into the GC during the construction are retained across exposure events. Thus the initial condition of the GC which produced the original picture is different in the subsequent exposure clause. A way around this problem is to set the GC to a know configuration within the expose clause before any drawing is performed. In

Fig. 6.2 A target plate in a window

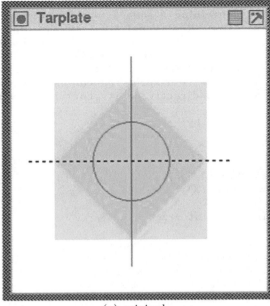

(a) original

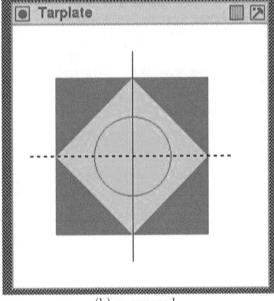

(b) re-exposed

```
/*   This program draws a target plate consisting of a square
 *   containing a square which is standing on its corners,
 *   extended diagonal lines of the inner square, and a circle
 *   centred at the intersection of those diagonal lines.  The
 *   squares are filled in pink and pale blue colour, one
 *   diagonal line is solid while the other is dotted, and the
 *   circle is a solid red coloured line.  This picture is
 *   drawn directly on its containing white coloured window.
 *
 *   Coded by:   Ross Maloney
 *   Date:       March 2009
 */

#include <X11/Xlib.h>
#include <X11/Xutil.h>

int main(int argc, char *argv)
{
  Display            *mydisplay;
  XSetWindowAttributes   baseat;
  Window             baseW;
  XSizeHints         wmsize;
  XWMHints           wmhints;
  XTextProperty      windowName, iconName;
  XEvent             myevent;
  GC                 baseGC;
  XGCValues          myGCValues;
  XColor             pink, blue, red, black, white;
  XPoint             corners[] = {{140,60},{230,150},{140,240},
                                  {50,150}};
  char *window_name = "Tarplate";
  char *icon_name   = "Tp";
  int                screen_num, done;
  unsigned long      valuemask;

                /* 1.  open connection to the server */
  mydisplay = XOpenDisplay("");

                /* 2.  create a top-level window */
  screen_num = DefaultScreen(mydisplay);
  black.pixel = BlackPixel(mydisplay, screen_num);
  white.pixel = WhitePixel(mydisplay, screen_num);
  red.pixel = 0xff0000;
  pink.pixel = 0xffb6c1;
  blue.pixel = 0xacc8e6;
  baseat.background_pixel = white.pixel;
  baseat.border_pixel = black.pixel;
  baseat.event_mask = ExposureMask;
  valuemask = CWBackPixel | CWBorderPixel | CWEventMask;
```

Fig. 6.3 A program to draw a target plate

```
baseW  =  XCreateWindow(mydisplay,
                        RootWindow(mydisplay, screen_num),
                        100, 100, 300, 300, 2,
                        DefaultDepth(mydisplay, screen_num),
                        InputOutput,
                        DefaultVisual(mydisplay, screen_num),
                        valuemask, &baseat);

                /* 3.   give the Window Manager hints */
wmsize.flags = USPosition | USSize;
XSetWMNormalHints(mydisplay, baseW, &wmsize);
wmhints.initial_state = NormalState;
wmhints.flags = StateHint;
XSetWMHints(mydisplay, baseW, &wmhints);
XStringListToTextProperty(&window_name, 1, &windowName);
XSetWMName(mydisplay, baseW, &windowName);
XStringListToTextProperty(&icon_name, 1, &iconName);
XSetWMIconName(mydisplay, baseW, &iconName);

                /* 4.   establish window resources */
valuemask = GCForeground | GCBackground;
myGCValues.background = white.pixel;
myGCValues.foreground = blue.pixel;
baseGC = XCreateGC(mydisplay, baseW, valuemask, &myGCValues);

                /* 5.   create all the other windows needed */
                /* 6.   select events for each window */
                /* 7.   map the windows */
XMapWindow(mydisplay, baseW);

                /* 8.   enter the event loop */
done = 0;
while ( done == 0 )  {
  XNextEvent(mydisplay, &myevent);
  switch(myevent.type)  {
  case  Expose:
     XFillRectangle(mydisplay, baseW, baseGC,
                 50, 60, 180, 180);
     XSetForeground(mydisplay, baseGC, pink.pixel);
     XFillPolygon(mydisplay, baseW, baseGC,
                 corners, 4, Convex, CoordModeOrigin);
     XSetForeground(mydisplay, baseGC, black.pixel);
     XDrawLine(mydisplay, baseW, baseGC, 140, 30, 140, 270);
     XSetLineAttributes(mydisplay, baseGC,
                     2, LineOnOffDash, CapButt, JoinMiter);
     XDrawLine(mydisplay, baseW, baseGC, 20, 150, 260, 150);
     XSetForeground(mydisplay, baseGC, red.pixel);
```

Fig. 6.3 (continued)

```
XSetLineAttributes(mydisplay, baseGC,
                   0, LineSolid, CapButt, JoinMiter);
    XDrawArc(mydisplay, baseW, baseGC,
             95, 105, 90, 90, 0, 360*64);
        break;
      }
   }


                   /* 9.  clean up before exiting */
   XUnmapWindow(mydisplay, baseW);
   XDestroyWindow(mydisplay, baseW);
   XCloseDisplay(mydisplay);
 }
```

Fig. 6.3 (continued)

the situation of this code this is possible but in other situations it may be impossible
or inappropriate for this to be done. This shows the wisdom in using a Pixmap for
creating a drawing and then placing the Pixmap onto a window as the result of an
exposure event.

6.2.1 Exercises

1. Change the code of Fig. 6.3 so it uses a triangle in place of the square.
2. Modify the code of Fig. 6.3 so the exposure event problem depicted in Fig. 6.2
   does not occur. There are at least two approaches to arriving at a solution.
3. As noted above, the manner of specifying colour in the code of Fig. 6.3 is not
   robust. Modify the code to improve the robustness of colour assignment.

6.3 A Symbol Composed from Circle Parts

On page 5–6 of Smith (1990) it is claimed the drawing of the Tao (or Tai-Chi) symbol
provides a good example to demonstrate the versatility of Postscript. Experience
has shown drawing this symbol also provides a good test for a X Window System
implementation and the screen being used.

The Tao symbol show in Fig. 6.4 is produced from the code contained in Fig. 6.5.
It is built up from five colour filled semi-circles and one full circle outline. Here the
symbol is drawn in black on a white base window.

The setup for drawing used here is the most appropriate to use in general. The
program of Fig. 6.5 consists of a base window baseW and a Pixmap pad. All drawing
is done in the Pixmap and its contents are made visible by moving those contents to

Fig. 6.4 A window
containing the tao symbol

the base window by using a XCopyArea() call when an Expose event occurs. The Pixmap is created using a XCreatePixmap() call specifying the window to which it is to be linked. The window to which it links has to have been created and have the InputOutput property configured into it. In this program this Pixmap is pad and the linked window is the base window baseW. This setup of using a Pixmap and window combination results in complete recovery of the screen image if either partial or whole covering of the baseW window occurs by another window on the screen being used.

When the Pixmap is created its contents are unpredictable and need to be put into a know state. The XFillRectangle() call is used for this purpose. This technique was also used in creating the buffer used in scrolling text both horizontally and vertically in Sects. 5.8.1 and 5.8.2.

For convenience the program uses two GCs, one (gc1) in which the foreground and background colours are respectively black and white, and in the other (gc2) those colours have the reverse rolls. The shapes (circles) from which the total drawing is formed use the foreground colour. Circles coloured in black and white are thus used.

The XCopyArea() call which transfers the drawing in the Pixmap to the window does not use the foreground and background members of the GC supplied in the call. It does, however, use other members of the GC specified. The colouring of the displayed drawing is determined by the colours contained in the GCs when drawing on the Pixmap. In the program of Fig. 6.5, use of gc1 in the XFillRectangle() call results in a black background in the window no matter what gc1 or gc2 used in the XCopyArea() call executed in the Expose clause. Correspondingly, using gc2 in the XFillRectangle() call changes that window's background to white.

```
/*   This program draws the Tao (or Tai-Chi) symbol in black on a
 *   300 by 300 white window.   The symbol is composed of 3
 *   semicircles, and 3 full circles.
 *
 *   Coded by:   Ross Maloney
 *   Date:       March 2009
 */

#include <X11/Xlib.h>
#include <X11/Xutil.h>

int main(int argc, char *argv)
{
    Display            *mydisplay;
    XSetWindowAttributes   baseat;
    Window             baseW;
    XSizeHints         wmsize;
    XWMHints           wmhints;
    XTextProperty      windowName, iconName;
    XEvent             myevent;
    GC                 gc1, gc2;
    XGCValues          myGCValues;
    XColor             black, white;
    Pixmap             pad;
    char *window_name = "Tao";
    char *icon_name   = "Ta";
    int                screen_num, done;
    unsigned long      valuemask;

                    /* 1.   open connection to the server */
    mydisplay = XOpenDisplay("");

                    /* 2.   create a top-level window */
    screen_num = DefaultScreen(mydisplay);
    black.pixel = BlackPixel(mydisplay, screen_num);
    white.pixel = WhitePixel(mydisplay, screen_num);
    baseat.background_pixel = white.pixel;
    baseat.border_pixel = black.pixel;
    baseat.event_mask = ExposureMask;
    valuemask = CWBackPixel | CWBorderPixel | CWEventMask;
    baseW = XCreateWindow(mydisplay,
                        RootWindow(mydisplay, screen_num),
                        100, 100, 300, 300, 2,
                        DefaultDepth(mydisplay, screen_num),
                        InputOutput,
                        DefaultVisual(mydisplay, screen_num),
                        valuemask, &baseat);

                    /* 3.   give the Window Manager hints */
    wmsize.flags = USPosition | USSize;
    XSetWMNormalHints(mydisplay, baseW, &wmsize);
```

Fig. 6.5 A program which draws the tao symbol

```
wmhints.initial_state = NormalState;
wmhints.flags = StateHint;
XSetWMHints(mydisplay, baseW, &wmhints);
XStringListToTextProperty(&window_name, 1, &windowName);
XSetWMName(mydisplay, baseW, &windowName);
XStringListToTextProperty(&icon_name, 1, &iconName);
XSetWMIconName(mydisplay, baseW, &iconName);

             /* 4.  establish window resources*/
valuemask = GCForeground | GCBackground;
myGCValues.background = white.pixel;
myGCValues.foreground = black.pixel;
gc1 = XCreateGC(mydisplay, baseW, valuemask, &myGCValues);
myGCValues.background = black.pixel;
myGCValues.foreground = white.pixel;
gc2 = XCreateGC(mydisplay, baseW, valuemask, &myGCValues);

             /* 5.  create all the other windows needed*/
pad = XCreatePixmap(mydisplay, baseW, 300, 300,
                    DefaultDepth(mydisplay, screen_num));
XFillRectangle(mydisplay, pad, gc2, 0, 0, 300, 300),
XFillArc(mydisplay, pad, gc1, 30, 30, 240, 240, 90*64, 180*64);
XFillArc(mydisplay, pad, gc1, 90, 150, 120, 120, 270*64, 180*64);
XFillArc(mydisplay, pad, gc2, 90, 30, 120, 120, 90*64, 180*64);
XFillArc(mydisplay, pad, gc2, 140, 200, 20, 20, 0, 360*64);
XFillArc(mydisplay, pad, gc1, 140, 80, 20, 20, 0, 360*64);
XDrawArc(mydisplay, pad, gc1, 30, 30, 240, 240, 0, 360*64);

             /* 6.  select events for each window */
             /* 7.  map the windows*/
XMapWindow(mydisplay, baseW);

             /* 8.  enter the event loop */
done = 0;
while ( done == 0 )  {
  XNextEvent(mydisplay, &myevent);
  switch(myevent.type)  {
  case  Expose:
    XCopyArea(mydisplay, pad, baseW, gc1, 0, 0, 300, 300, 0, 0);
    break;
  }
}

             /* 9.  clean up before exiting*/
XUnmapWindow(mydisplay, baseW);
XDestroyWindow(mydisplay, baseW);
XCloseDisplay(mydisplay);
}
```

Fig. 6.5 (continued)

All drawing in the code of Fig. 6.5 is done outside of the event loop by positioning arc segments within the Pixmap pad. Only the transfer of the Pixmap to the screen is inside the event loop.

6.3.1 Exercises

1. Modify the program in Fig. 6.5 so the white portions within the tao symbol are coloured yellow.
2. Modify the program in Fig. 6.5 so all black and white colouring's are exchanged.
3. What other means apart from the event mechanism in the X Window System are available to transfer the contents of the Pixmap used for drawing to a screen?
4. With respect to data transfer, and thus network traffic between the client and the server, what are the advantages of using a Pixmap for drawing? Justify your answer. Contrast this situation to when using an image structure for storing graphics information. Hint: This question is concerned with where data is stored and when data is transferred between the client and server.
5. Compare and contrast the program in Fig. 6.5 with code having the same functionality and the drawing using the Win32 API (Applications Programming Interface) of Microsoft Windows.
6. What are the aspects of a screen and the X Window system which are highlighted by drawing the Tao symbol as in the code of Fig. 6.5?

6.4 A Circle Bouncing off Plain Edges

If a series of pictures of an object are displayed on the screen they can give the impression the object in the picture is moving. One application to which this technique could be applied is in simulation.

A simple demonstration of a moving object in continuous motion is considered here and is shown in Fig. 6.6. The motion is in the plane of the viewing surface and resembles a billiard ball bouncing off the cushions which run along the boundaries of the viewing surface. The code in Fig. 6.7 draws such a ball as a circle filled in white on a black Pixmap. The Pixmap pad is used for creating the drawings. Its colour black results from the black foreground colour of gc1 GC used in the XFillRectangle() call which initialises the viewing plane. The circle is drawn in white by using the white foreground colour of gc2 GC supplied in the XFillArc() call used in drawing it. The simplicity in the demonstration is apparent from Fig. 6.6 while Fig. 6.6a attempts to show free movement of the ball (circle) while striking of the bounding cushions. Figure 6.6b also shows the problem in the code of Fig. 6.7 in that the circle appears to penetrate the cushion – before rebounding.

Fig. 6.6 A moving circle

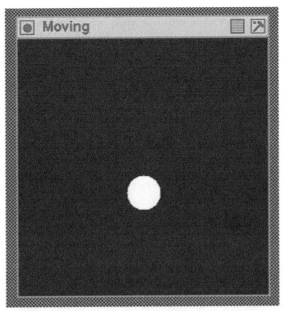

(a) free motion

(b) rebounding

```
/*   This program draws a continuously bouncing ball that canons
 *   off the cushions that surround the viewing screen.   All
 *   drawing is done in a Pixmap that is moved to the screen at
 *   intervals of time to give the ball movement.
 *
 *   Coded by:   Ross Maloney
 *   Date:       March 2009
 */

#include <X11/Xlib.h>
#include <X11/Xutil.h>
#include <unistd.h>

int main(int argc, char *argv)
{
   Display          *mydisplay;
   XSetWindowAttributes   baseat;
   Window           baseW;
   XSizeHints       wmsize;
   XWMHints         wmhints;
   XTextProperty    windowName, iconName;
   XEvent           myevent;
   GC               gc1, gc2;
   XGCValues        myGCValues;
   XColor           black, white;
   Pixmap           pad;
   char *window_name = "Moving";
   char *icon_name   = "Mo";
   int              screen_num, done;
   unsigned long    valuemask;
   int              x, y, dx, dy;
   float            ratio;

                    /* 1.   open connection to the server */
   mydisplay = XOpenDisplay("");

                    /* 2.   create a top-level window */
   screen_num = DefaultScreen(mydisplay);
   black.pixel = BlackPixel(mydisplay, screen_num);
   white.pixel = WhitePixel(mydisplay, screen_num);
   baseat.background_pixel = white.pixel;
   baseat.border_pixel = black.pixel;
   baseat.event_mask = ExposureMask;
   valuemask = CWBackPixel | CWBorderPixel | CWEventMask;
   baseW = XCreateWindow(mydisplay,
                         RootWindow(mydisplay, screen_num),
                         100, 100, 300, 300, 2,
                         DefaultDepth(mydisplay, screen_num),
                         InputOutput,
                         DefaultVisual(mydisplay, screen_num),
                         valuemask, &baseat);
```

Fig. 6.7 A program which bounces a circle off plain edges

```
                    /* 3.   give the Window Manager hints */
wmsize.flags = USPosition | USSize;
XSetWMNormalHints(mydisplay, baseW, &wmsize);
wmhints.initial_state = NormalState;
wmhints.flags = StateHint;
XSetWMHints(mydisplay, baseW, &wmhints);
XStringListToTextProperty(&window_name, 1, &windowName);
XSetWMName(mydisplay, baseW, &windowName);
XStringListToTextProperty(&icon_name, 1, &iconName);
XSetWMIconName(mydisplay, baseW, &iconName);

                    /* 4.   establish window resources */
valuemask = GCForeground | GCBackground;
myGCValues.background = white.pixel;
myGCValues.foreground = black.pixel;
gc1 = XCreateGC(mydisplay, baseW, valuemask, &myGCValues);
myGCValues.background = black.pixel;
myGCValues.foreground = white.pixel;
gc2 = XCreateGC(mydisplay, baseW, valuemask, &myGCValues);

                    /* 5.   create all the other windows needed */
pad = XCreatePixmap(mydisplay, baseW, 300, 300,
                    DefaultDepth(mydisplay, screen_num));
XFillRectangle(mydisplay, pad, gc1, 0, 0, 300, 300);
x = 100;
y = 100;
dx = 10;
ratio = 2.0;
XFillArc(mydisplay, pad, gc1, x, y, 40, 40, 0, 360*64);

                    /* 6.   select events for each window */
                    /* 7.   map the windows */
XMapWindow(mydisplay, baseW);

                    /* 8.   enter the event loop */
done = 0;
while ( done == 0 ) {
  XNextEvent(mydisplay, &myevent);
  switch(myevent.type) {
  case Expose:
    XCopyArea(mydisplay, pad, baseW, gc1,
              0, 0, 300, 300, 0, 0);
    XFillArc(mydisplay, pad, gc1, x, y, 40, 40, 0, 360*64);
    x += dx;
    if ( x < 0 )   { x = 0; dx = 10; ratio = -ratio;}
    if ( x > 300 ) { x = 300; dx = -10; ratio = -ratio;}
```

Fig. 6.7 (continued)

```
    if  ( y > 300 ) { y = 300; ratio = −ratio;}
    if  ( y < 0 )   { y = 0; ratio = −ratio;}
    y += dx*ratio;
    XFillArc(mydisplay, pad, gc2, x, y, 40, 40, 0, 360*64);
    sleep(1);
    XSendEvent(mydisplay, baseW, 0, ExposureMask, &myevent);
    break;
  }
}


                    /* 9.   clean up before exiting */
  XUnmapWindow(mydisplay, baseW);
  XDestroyWindow(mydisplay, baseW);
   XCloseDisplay(mydisplay);
}
```

Fig. 6.7 (continued)

The object is shown on the screen by sending the contents of the Pixmap to the screen. This occurs by executing a XCopyArea() call when an Expose event is received in the event loop. Once that call has been executed, the next position of the ball in the Pixmap is computed and re-positioned in the Pixmap. This display-compute process can be repeated by sending an Expose event after the new position of the call is calculated. This event is created by a XSendEvent() call. The initial conditions of the placement of the ball in the Pixmap and the parameters which are to be used to compute the motion are set before the event loop of the program in Fig. 6.7 is entered.

The XSendEvent() is a general method of performing inter-process communication between X11 client processes offered by Xlib. In this particular instance the communication is withing the one process, the process which contains this program. This simplifies the XSendEvent() call used since the ID of the window being sent to receive the message is know within the code (baseW in this case). This also enables the third parameter of the XSendEvent() call (the *propagation*) to be set as FALSE (or 0).

The motion simulated is by drawing a white circle on a Pixmap. A new position of the circle is calculated taking into consideration any collision with the boundary cushions which may occur. In the code of Fig. 6.7 those collisions are handled by four if statements. Before the circle can be drawn in a new position on the Pixmap, the circle is erased from its current position by redrawing it in the colour of the Pixmap (using GC gc1). Then the process is paused using a sleep() call before the next Expose event is given by the XSendEvent() call. There needs to be a time delay between the drawing of the circle and erasing it. In this program the standard system sleep() call was used but this has the problem that the time delay specified in the parameter to the call is measured in seconds. Even one second is too long for the motion being simulated here.

An alternate approach is to draw the object as a window. The window would be created once. The XCreateWindow() (or XCreateSimpleWindow()) which forms the window sets the position on the screen where the window is to be displayed. Those coordinates are used when the XMapWindow() call is used to show the window on the screen. The window is removed from the screen using a XUnmapWindow() call. The position can be changed using a XMoveWindow() call between the map and unmap calls.

6.4.1 Exercises

1. Does the initial position of the ball appear in the screen output generated by the program code in Fig. 6.7? Give reasoning for your answer.
2. Modify the code in Fig. 6.7 so the circle bounces off the correct face of the boundary cushions without penetrating them.
3. In the code in Fig. 6.7, the current position of the circle is erased by overwriting it with the (black) colour of the Pixmap on which it is drawn. What other technique, based around a single Xlib call, could be used? In what situations would the proposed technique be advantageous when compared with the overwrite technique?
4. What happens if the sleep() call is removed from the code in Fig. 6.7? What other methods could be used to introduce a delay in the displaying process used there?
5. Rewrite the program of Fig. 6.7 using a window which shows the movement instead of a Pixmap. For this use a sequence of XMoveWindow() and XUnmapWindow() calls. Using this technique, how is the circle of the moving object created?

6.5 Displaying the Multi Colours of a Photograph

A common application of computer graphics is to show on the screen photographic quality pictures generated externally from the program. The aim here is to map the photographic data to visible pixels on the screen without loss of information contained in the original photographic data. The graphics data is generally a collection of many colour values over the range of all the individual pixels which make up the total picture, together with the position each of those pixels occupies in the two-dimensional matrix of pixels which form the total picture. Placing those colours in the correct order is the mapping process considered here. This process is more complex than using bitmaps and Pixmaps considered in Sects. 4.3 and 4.7. In those respective cases, two and several colours were involved which contrast to the many colours involved here. However, the X11 image format used in those Sections, and also in Sect. 4.5, is also able to handle the multi-colour data required here.

A two step process is generally used in displaying a photographic picture. The pictures of interest are generally stored in a format such as JPEG, PNG, TIFF, etc.

Fig. 6.8 A view of a
simulated photograph

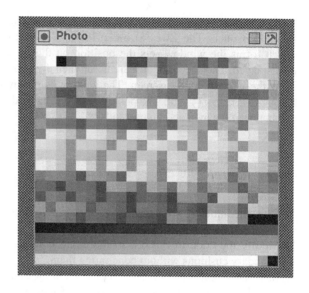

which minimises the amount of storage required. The first step in displaying the
required picture is to recover the matrix of pixel colour values which form the picture.
Each picture format is supported by a library of manipulation functions and their use
is a specialised topic which will not be considered further here. Here those functions
will be assumed to have been applied and their output of a two-dimensional array of
pixel values will be assumed to be available. The following step, which is considered
here, is to transfer this matrix of colour values to the display window. In the code of
Fig. 6.9 this matrix of photographic data is generated by a simple numerical algorithm.
The resulting output is shown in Fig. 6.8.

A simulated picture is used in the code of Fig. 6.9 it having been derived from the
753 colours defined in the standard /etc/X11/rgb.txt file available on Unix
and Unix-like computer systems. This file lists the names of colours defined by their
8-bit red, green, and blue components. Each of those colours is a 24-bit TrueColor.
However, only 503 of those colour values are unique. The names of the colours where
filtered out and the unique hexadecimal 24-bit value of each unique colour was used.
The sequential order of the first occurrence of each colour value found in the file was
retained in making this colour data. In the code of Fig. 6.9, these values are set in the
array colours, with an additional values of 0x0 added to enable this array to be
2-dimensional complete with dimensions of 24x21.

Since the colour values of the image data used are 24 bit values, it is natural to set
the containing array imagedata to be of type integer. However, this necessitates a
type conversion to be made before it is used with the XCreateImage() call which
allocates the memory used by Xlib as the image structure in the client program.
In using the X11 image technique to display a photograph, the colours and their
arrangement which make up the photograph, are stored in this array. This is linked
into the XImage structure which is then used in the XPutImage() call. Notice
this picture array is a one-dimensional vector. The height and width interpretation

```
/*   The X11 image format is used to create and then display
 *   multi-coloured picture derived from the   rgb.txt   file
 *   included with X11.   All 503 unique colours in that file
 *   are displayed in a 15x15 colour swatch each.
 *
 *   Coded by:   Ross Maloney
 *   Date:       March 2009
 */

#include <X11/Xlib.h>
#include <X11/Xutil.h>

static unsigned int colours[] = {
   0xfffafa ,   0xf8f8ff ,   0xf5f5f5 ,   0xdcdcdc ,   0xfffaf0 ,
   0xfdf5e6 ,   0xfaf0e6 ,   0xfaebd7 ,   0xffefd5 ,   0xffebcd ,
   0xffe4c4 ,   0xffdab9 ,   0xffdead ,   0xffe4b5 ,   0xfff8dc ,
   0xfffff0 ,   0xfffacd ,   0xfff5ee ,   0xf0fff0 ,   0xf5fffa ,

       .
       .
       .

   0xc4c4c4 ,   0xc7c7c7 ,   0xc9c9c9 ,   0xcccccc ,   0xcfcfcf ,
   0xd1d1d1 ,   0xd4d4d4 ,   0xd6d6d6 ,   0xd9d9d9 ,   0xdbdbdb ,
   0xdedede ,   0xe0e0e0 ,   0xe3e3e3 ,   0xe5e5e5 ,   0xe8e8e8 ,
   0xebebeb ,   0xededed ,   0xf0f0f0 ,   0xf2f2f2 ,   0xf7f7f7 ,
   0xfafafa ,   0xfcfcfc ,   0xa9a9a9 ,   0x0 };

int main(int argc , char *argv )
{
   Display              *mydisplay ;
   Window               baseW ;
   XSetWindowAttributes    baseat ;
   XSizeHints           wmsize ;
   XWMHints             wmhints ;
   XTextProperty        windowName , iconName ;
   XEvent               myevent ;
   GC                   GC1 ;
   XImage               *photo ;
   int                  imagedata[225];
   char *window_name = "Photo";
   char *icon_name    = "Ph";
   int                  screen_num , done , i , j , k , kk ;
   unsigned long        valuemask ;

                  /* 1.   open connection to the server */
   mydisplay = XOpenDisplay("" );

                  /* 2.   create a top-level window */
   screen_num = DefaultScreen(mydisplay );
```

Fig. 6.9 A program to display a simulated photograph

```
baseat.background_pixel = WhitePixel(mydisplay, screen_num);
baseat.border_pixel = BlackPixel(mydisplay, screen_num);
baseat.event_mask = ExposureMask;
valuemask = CWBackPixel | CWBorderPixel | CWEventMask;
baseW = XCreateWindow(mydisplay,
                      RootWindow(mydisplay, screen_num),
                      300, 300, 360, 315, 2,
                      DefaultDepth(mydisplay, screen_num),
                      InputOutput,
                      DefaultVisual(mydisplay, screen_num),
                      valuemask, &baseat);

                /* 3.  give the Window Manager hints */
wmsize.flags = USPosition | USSize;
XSetWMNormalHints(mydisplay, baseW, &wmsize);
wmhints.initial_state = NormalState;
wmhints.flags = StateHint;
XSetWMHints(mydisplay, baseW, &wmhints);
XStringListToTextProperty(&window_name, 1, &windowName);
XSetWMName(mydisplay, baseW, &windowName);
XStringListToTextProperty(&icon_name, 1, &iconName);
XSetWMIconName(mydisplay, baseW, &iconName);

                /* 4.  establish window resources */
GC1 = XCreateGC(mydisplay, baseW, 0, NULL);
XSetForeground(mydisplay, GC1,
               BlackPixel(mydisplay, screen_num));
XSetBackground(mydisplay, GC1,
               WhitePixel(mydisplay, screen_num));
photo = XCreateImage(mydisplay,
                     DefaultVisual(mydisplay, screen_num),
                     DefaultDepth(mydisplay, screen_num),
                     ZPixmap, 0, (char *)imagedata,
                     15, 15, 32, 0);

                /* 5.  create all the other windows needed */
                /* 6.  select events for each window */
                /* 7.  map the windows */
XMapWindow(mydisplay, baseW);

                /* 8.  enter the event loop */
done = 0;
while ( done == 0 )  {
  XNextEvent(mydisplay, &myevent);
  switch (myevent.type)  {
  case Expose:
    for (j=0; j<504; j++)  {
      for (i=0; i<225; i++) imagedata[i] = colours[j];
```

Fig. 6.9 (continued)

```
        k = (j%24)*15;
        kk = (j/24)*15;
        XPutImage(mydisplay, baseW, GC1, photo,
                        0, 0, k, kk, 15, 15);
    }

        break;
    }
}

                /* 9.   clean up before exiting */
    XUnmapWindow(mydisplay, baseW);
    XDestroyWindow(mydisplay, baseW);
    XCloseDisplay(mydisplay);
}
```

Fig. 6.9 (continued)

necessary to convert it into the photograph displayed on the screen is stored in the XImage structure when that structure is created by the XCreateImage() call.

The graphics context GC1 which is part of the XPutImage() call used to move the image to the server, and thus onto the display (through the window baseW), does not play an active part in process in this instance. However, there are special instances where the GC does play a role.

In the code of Fig. 6.9, the array colours was initially linked to the data of the photo structure, assigning it the dimensions of 24x21 in the XCreateImage() call. The whole picture was output to the baseW using a XPutImage() call. Figure 6.8 shows the resulting screen picture.

In the initial screen picture produced it was difficult to see individual pixel colours. This was resolved by magnifying the screen view of the colour data in the colours array. This is show in the code of Fig. 6.9. Each of the colour values in the colours array is displayed on the screen in a 15x15 colour patch, with each patch having the same neighbours on the screen as in the original 24x21 presentation of the visual data. The array imagedata is linked to the photo structure to have dimensions of 15x15. The formation of each colour patch in imagedata is done on the server and does not involve protocol exchanges between the client and the server which makes this technique attractive. Although this is done in the event loop of the code in Fig. 6.9, only the XPutImage() call involves protocol exchange between the client and the server. Figure 6.8 shows the screen output obtained.

6.5.1 Exercises

1. Modify the code in Fig. 6.9 so the pixel values of the array colours are shown on part of the screen, verifying the above statement that the colour content is difficult to fully appreciate.

2. Verify by the appropriate print statements inserted in the code shown in Fig. 6.9 that 4 bytes are there used to represent each pixel in the photograph, and the horizontal width of the photograph is 4 times the value specified in the XCreateImage() call. Why does this value 4 occur in each of these situations?

3. In the program of Fig. 6.9, indicate whether imagedata, colours, and photo are stored on the client or the server, and which of the Xlib calls used involve X11 protocol use.

4. Why are client-based techniques such as used with image structures attractive?

5. Describe advantages and disadvantages of using image structure based techniques such as used in the code of Fig. 6.9 for presentation of menus.

6.6 Summary

This chapter showed how to use Xlib to draw graphics with the X Window graphics system. The chapter assumes creation of a window which is to be drawn upon, and how to keep such a window visible on the screen, is known. Examples were given od a selection of the drawing primitives available through Xlib.

Such graphics are composed from straight lines, polygons and ellipses of different styles, both of themselves, and in closed figures formed from combining those elements. Colour can be specified for both the lines and the areas they enclose. By displaying, removing, re-positioning, and then re-displaying, the illusion of motion of objects so drawn can be produced. The examples given show how this is achieved.

Chapter 7
Extensions

Three extensions are considered in this chapter. Two are additions made to the original X Window system. One of those additions extents the Pixmap concept to enable use of more than two colours in a pattern which can be mapped onto a window. The other is the introduction of fonts which are scalable, i.e. can be changed to any size required. Both are now a part of standard X Window system. The remainder is an extension to the manner of executing a X Window program.

In all the examples given in this book, and in books generally relating to X Window programming, little mention is made of network connection. The programs given are client programs while the server is *somewhere* else. The client program sends messages via the X Window protocol to the server which performs the required graphic function such a drawing a window, accepting a mouse button click, or whatever. The client and server in those programs is assumed to be executing on the same computer. The protocol messages are passed internally on the computer between the client program and the X Window server process running on it. Alternately those messages can be passed across a network connecting the computer executing the client program and the server. This is stated in the literature as a big advantage of X Window. Although this advantage is mentioned, examples do not show it in operation.

In contrast to multiple colour Pixmaps and scalable fonts which are additions to X Window, including a network in an X Window program is nothing new; it has been there since X Window was first released. The extension is showing how to incorporate this in a X Window program and deploying of the program. Both these extensions are shown using Xlib programs.

Electronic supplementary material The online version of this chapter
(https://doi.org/10.1007/978-3-319-74250-2_7) contains supplementary material, which is available to authorized users.

7.1 Multi-colour XPM Pixmaps

Xlib provides bitmaps in support of its Pixmap facility, but this facility is capable of expanded use as proposed by Hors and Nahaboo (1991). This expansion enables the programmer to describe the placement of fixed colours in a fixed image. A bitmap provides a means of performing this operation only with two colours as is shown in Sect. 4.3. Those colours are the foreground and background colours. Changing the foreground and background colour assignment changes the colour in the bitmap, although their position in the bitmap remain fixed. Also, needing only to represent two colours enables a compact hexadecimal representation of these bitmaps. Such a representation makes manual creation of these images difficult.

By contrast, the layout of a XPM Pixmap makes manual creation of Pixmaps straight forward. This format is described in Hors and Nahaboo (1991) and now is part of the standard X Window System distribution. It offers fixed, multi-colour laying out of a fixed image in a manner which is visually straight forward to understand. To assists integration of these new Xlib function with more traditional bitmaps, they use similar names and parameters to those library functions for handling the more traditional Pixmaps. As a result, the XPM library is regarded as being at the same level as that of Xlib. Handling of XPM Pixmaps, however, contracts to the handling of multiple colours used in Sect. 6.5.

The overall parameters of the Pixmap need to be assigned. The height and width of the Pixmap needs to be specified. The other parameter is the number of characters in the Pixmap design which are used to specify all the colours present in the XPM Pixmap. In most cases, one character is used to indicate one colour. As each colour is introduced into the image portion of the Pixmap layout, the count of colour specifying characters contained in the colour index portion of the Pixmap must be incremented. Placement of the character in the image portion of the Pixmap directly corresponds to its position in the displayed Pixmap. The Pixmap data can be created using a text editor. Each pixel is described by a character. If the width of the Pixmap is greater than the line length of the editor a distortion of the Pixmap pattern will be seen on the editor screen.

As an illustration of this creation process a smiley face is used. It is to be a multi-coloured object, having six colours. Those colours are encoded into the Pixmap. The distribution of each colour is fixed by placed the character representing each colour in the image portion of the Pixmap. The image portion is an array of characters with its width and height corresponding to the width and height of the image on screen.

This smiley face Pixmap was formed using an editor starting from a binary coloured bitmap. The bitmap was used to overcome the difficulty of manually drawing circles. Using the `bitmap` program, a 51x51 bitmap was opened with the command:

bitmap −size 51x51

Into this array a filled circle was drawn using the circle drawing option of `bitmap` so it touched all sides of the grid. Then circles were drawn for the outlines of the two eyes. The mouth was drawn as a circle, and the part of the circle beyond the extent of the mouth was deleted. Once saved, this file was transformed into Pixmap format using the `convert` program which is part of the source distribution of the `ImageMagick` program.

An editor was used to colour this bitmap by positioning in the Pixmap a character which denoted a colour. The background colour was defined as `None` to indicate that it was to be transparent when the Pixmap was on the screen. The characters for the eyes, face, and mouth were assigned a colour and then inserted into the appropriate places in the bitmap template. The resulting Pixmap was used in the code contained in Fig. 7.1. This illustrated process is capable of generalisation, for example to generate Pixmaps with coloured, or multi-coloured lettering, for use in menus.

The program of Fig. 7.1 starts by displaying a 300x300 pixel window coloured purple. When the user clicks the left mouse button on this window, a smiley face Pixmap which is stored in the program is deposited on the purple window at the position of the pointer. It is similar in overall design to the program of Fig. 4.1 but the use of the Pixmap instead of a bitmap makes a difference. Those significant differences are:

- Include a <X11/xpm.h> header file ;
- The function `XpmCreatePixmapFromData()` replaces the standard Xlib function `XCreatePixmapFromBitmapData()`;
- The `XpmCreatePixmapFromData()` function returns the success or failure status of the call;
- Storage for the Pixmap to be created is passed as a parameter in the `XpmCreatePixmapFromData()` function;
- The XPM library needs to be included in the compile and link command by the addition of the `-lXmp` switch;
- The `XCopyArea()` function is used to display the Pixmap in contrast to a `XCopyPlane()` function;
- The foreground and background colours of the GC included in copying the XPM Pixmap to the screen are not used.

It is necessary to use the `XCopyArea()` function call for all eight colour planes of the Pixmap created from the XPM data need to be moved together to the window. In the case of a `XCopyPlane()` function call, only one plane is moved.

In the XPM data, the background colour of the smiley-face is set as *None* indicating a transparent colour. This tells the `XpmCreatePixmapFromData()` function call that a clipping-mask is to be generated together with the Pixmap. In the program of Fig. 7.1 this is stored in the variable `clipper`. This mask is then linked to the graphics context (`mygc`) that is used in the `XCopyArea()` function call that displays the Pixmap by the `XSetClipMask()` function. For this mask to work correctly, the origin for applying this clipping mask needs to be included in that graphics context as well. This is done using the `XSetClipOrigin()` function. If this mask was not used, then the portion of the smiley-face indicated to have a transparent colour would appear as black. If the colour `None` is not used in the XPM data, then no clipping-mask is generated by the `XpmCreatePixmapFromData()` function, then `NULL` can be used in the function parameters in place of storage for the clipping

```
/*   This program first displays a 300x300 pixel window coloured
 *   purple.  When the left-hand mouse button is clicked in this
 *   window, a 6 coloured smiley face appears on the screen to
 *   indicate when the mouse pointer was located when the button
 *   was pressed.  The smiley face is created using a XPM Pixmap.
 *
 *   Coded by:   Ross Maloney
 *   Date:       April 2009
 */

#include <X11/Xlib.h>
#include <X11/Xutil.h>
#include <X11/xpm.h>

/* XPM */
static char *smile[] = {
/* columns rows colors chars-per-pixel */
"51 51 6 1",
"  c None",
". c yellow",
"b c blue",
"x c black",
"w c white",
"r c red",
/* pixels */
```

Fig. 7.1 A XPM multi-colour pattern at a mouse click

```
"  ...............................................  ",
"  ...............................................  ",
"  ...............................................  ",
"  ...............................................  ",
"  ...............................................  ",
"  ...............................................  ",
"  ...............................................  ",
"  ...............................................  ",
"  ...............................................  ",
"  ...............................................  ",
"  ...............................................  ",
"  ...............................................  ",
"  ...............................................  ",
"  ...............................................  ",
"  ...............................................  ",
"  ......r.............................r......  ",
"  .......r...........................r.......  ",
"  ......rr.........................rr.......  ",
"  .......rrr.....................rrr........  ",
"  ..........rrrr..........rrrr...........  ",
"  ...............rrrrrrrrr..............  ",
"  .................................  ",
"  ...............................  ",
"  .............................  ",
"  ...........................  ",
"  .........................  ",
"  .......................  ",
"  ...................  ",
"  ...........  "
};
```

```c
int main(int argc, char *argv)
{
    Display             *mydisplay;
    Window              baseW;
    XSetWindowAttributes    myat;
    XSizeHints          wmsize;
    XWMHints            wmhints;
    XTextProperty       windowName, iconName;
    XEvent              baseEvent;
    GC                  mygc;
    Pixmap              pattern, clipper;
    char *window_name = "ColourClick";
    char *icon_name   = "CCl";
    int                 screen_num, done, status;
    unsigned long       mymask;
    int                 x, y;
    XpmAttributes       faceAt;

                /* 1.  open connection to the server */
    mydisplay = XOpenDisplay("");
```

Fig. 7.1 (continued)

```
                    /* 2.  create a top-level window*/
screen_num = DefaultScreen(mydisplay);
myat.border_pixel = 0x0;              /* black */
myat.background_pixel = 0xA020F0;     /* purple */
myat.event_mask = ButtonPressMask | ExposureMask;
mymask = CWBackPixel | CWBorderPixel | CWEventMask;
baseW = XCreateWindow(mydisplay,
                        RootWindow(mydisplay, screen_num),
                        350, 400, 300, 300, 2,
                        DefaultDepth(mydisplay, screen_num),
                        InputOutput,
                        DefaultVisual(mydisplay, screen_num),
                        mymask, &myat);

                    /* 3.  give the Window Manager hints*/
wmsize.flags = USPosition | USSize;
XSetWMNormalHints(mydisplay, baseW, &wmsize);
wmhints.initial_state = NormalState;
wmhints.flags = StateHint;
XSetWMHints(mydisplay, baseW, &wmhints);
XStringListToTextProperty(&window_name, 1, &windowName);
XSetWMName(mydisplay, baseW, &windowName);
XStringListToTextProperty(&icon_name, 1, &iconName);
XSetWMIconName(mydisplay, baseW, &iconName);

                    /* 4.  establish window resources */
faceAt.color_key = XPM_COLOR;
faceAt.valuemask = XpmColorKey | XpmColorTable;
status = XpmCreatePixmapFromData(mydisplay, baseW,
                        smile, &pattern, &clipper, &faceAt);
mygc = XCreateGC(mydisplay, baseW, 0, NULL);
XSetForeground(mydisplay, mygc,
                        WhitePixel(mydisplay, screen_num));
XSetBackground(mydisplay, mygc,
                        BlackPixel(mydisplay, screen_num));
XSetClipMask(mydisplay, mygc, clipper);
XSetClipOrigin(mydisplay, mygc, 0, 0);

                    /* 5.  create all the other windows needed*/
                    /* 6.  select events for each window */
                    /* 7.  map the windows */
XMapWindow(mydisplay, baseW);

                    /* 8.  enter the event loop */
done = 0;
while ( done == 0 ) {
  XNextEvent(mydisplay, &baseEvent);
  switch( baseEvent.type ) {
  case Expose:
    break;
```

Fig. 7.1 (continued)

```
case ButtonPress:
  if ( baseEvent.xbutton.button == Button1 )  {
    x = baseEvent.xbutton.x;
    y = baseEvent.xbutton.y;
    XSetClipOrigin(mydisplay, mygc, x, y);
    XCopyArea(mydisplay, pattern, baseW, mygc, 0, 0,
              51, 51, x, y);
    }
      break;
    }
  }

            /* 9.  clean up before exiting*/
  XUnmapWindow(mydisplay, baseW);
  XDestroyWindow(mydisplay, baseW);
  XCloseDisplay(mydisplay);
}
```

Fig. 7.1 (continued)

Fig. 7.2 Multi-coloured smiley faces deposited on a window

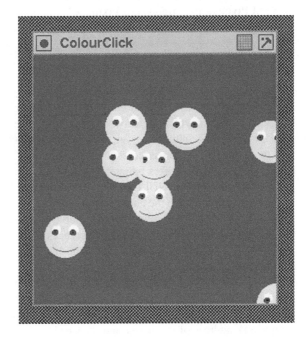

mask. The constant XPMk_COLOR is defined in the xpm.h header file indicating that the Pixmap is coloured, in contrast to being monochrome or grey scale.

Figure 7.2 shows the visual results of using the program of Fig. 7.1. Notice the overlaying of the Pixmaps achieved, and a Pixmap of circular shape is evident by the window's purple colour surrounding each of the circular faces.

7.1.1 Exercises

1. Change the background colour to the Pixmap in the program of Fig. 7.1 to be the purple colour of the background window. What effect does this change have on the visual affect of the Pixmap?
2. Make the colour of the left hand eye in the Pixmap different to that of the right hand eye in the smiley face.
3. Change the Pixmap used in the program of Fig. 7.1 so it uses the word "Click" to replace the smiley face. Use the technique of Sect. 4.6 to create the bitmap containing the letters. Then make each letter a different colour. The background of the Pixmap should be transparent.
4. Use the code of Fig. 7.1 to verify that the transparent colour if no mask is used with the XCopyArea() call is black, and this is independent of the foreground and background colours set in the graphics context used with that function call.
5. Rework the code of Fig. 7.1 so the smiley-face has a five star boundary as opposed to a circular boundary. Following from this exercise, what other advantage have XPM Pixmaps over traditional Pixmaps?

7.2 Network Connecting Client to Server

X Window enables the separation of the client program and the server onto two separate computers which are network connected. The client program specifies the network connection with the server, creates this connection, and maintains it.

A network connection is created by the familiar XOpenDisplay() library function. This function takes one parameter which is a NULL terminated character string. If the parameter is NULL then no network is involved and the server is located on the computer in which the client program will execute. More correctly, it uses the contents of the DISPLAY environment variable of the computer executing the client program and this variable, by default references, indicates no network connection. The XOpenDisplay() function returns the display structure if the call is successful in linking with the server, or a NULL if unsuccessful. With a request for a network connection it is appropriate to check the connection has been made by testing the return from the XOpenDisplay() function call.

For a network connection, the parameter string consists of two parts. There is the network address of the server and the display number to be used on the server. The two parts are separated by a colon (:) character. The server address part can be of two forms: server or server.display. In most instances the server and display values are 0 (zero). The network address, reflecting the history of X Window, can use DECnet or TCP/IP network protocol but IP addressing is the most common today. The format of the network connection parameter to the XOpenDisplay most commonly used is:

```
address:server.display
```

```
/*  This program creates and displays a basic window.  The window
 *  has a default white background.
 *
 *  Coded by:  Ross Maloney
 *  Date:      October 2017
 */

#include  <X11/Xlib.h>
#include  <X11/Xutil.h>
#include  <stdio.h>
#include  <stdlib.h>      /* for exit() */

int main(int argc, char *argv[])
{
    Display            *mydisplay;
    XSetWindowAttributes   myat;
    Window             mywindow;
    XSizeHints         wmsize;
    XWMHints           wmhints;
    XTextProperty      windowName, iconName;
    XEvent             myevent;
    char *window_name = "Netprog";
    char *icon_name   = "Net";
    int                screen_num, done;
    unsigned long      valuemask;


                    /* 1. open connection to the server */
    mydisplay = XOpenDisplay("192.168.14.9:0.0");
    if ( mydisplay == NULL )  {
        printf("Error: cannot open display\n");
        exit(1);
    }

                    /* 2. create a top-level window */
    screen_num = DefaultScreen(mydisplay);
    myat.background_pixel = WhitePixel(mydisplay, screen_num);
    myat.border_pixel = BlackPixel(mydisplay, screen_num);
    myat.event_mask = ButtonPressMask;
    valuemask = CWBackPixel | CWBorderPixel | CWEventMask;
    mywindow = XCreateWindow(mydisplay,
                             RootWindow(mydisplay, screen_num),
                             200, 200, 350, 250, 2,
                             DefaultDepth(mydisplay, screen_num),
                             InputOutput,
                             DefaultVisual(mydisplay, screen_num),
                             valuemask, &myat);

                    /* 3. give the Window Manager hints */
    wmsize.flags = USPosition | USSize;
    XSetWMNormalHints(mydisplay, mywindow, &wmsize);
```

Fig. 7.3 A basic window displayed on a networked screen

```
wmhints. initial_state = NormalState;
wmhints. flags = StateHint;
XSetWMHints(mydisplay, mywindow, &wmhints);
XStringListToTextProperty(&window_name, 1, &windowName);
XSetWMName(mydisplay, mywindow, &windowName);
XStringListToTextProperty(&icon_name, 1, &iconName);
XSetWMIconName(mydisplay, mywindow, &iconName);

                    /* 4. establish window resources */
                    /* 5. create all the other windows needed */
                    /* 6. select events for each window */
                    /* 7. map the windows */
XMapWindow(mydisplay, mywindow);

                    /* 8. enter the event loop */
done = 0;
while ( done == 0 ) {
  XNextEvent(mydisplay, &myevent);
  switch (myevent.type) {
  case ButtonPress:
    break;
  }
}

                    /* 9. clean up before exiting */
XUnmapWindow(mydisplay, mywindow);
XDestroyWindow(mydisplay, mywindow);
XCloseDisplay(mydisplay);
}
```

Fig. 7.3 (continued)

To use the server on the computer executing the client program, the network connection parameter :0 or :0.0 could be used. In both, server 0 is being called to use, using screen 0. A large number of computers acting as servers have one server and one screen: the counting of both starts at 0.

The program in Fig. 7.3 is a network connected version of the program in Fig. 2.2. It creates a window like that in Fig. 2.1 on the screen of the computer with network address 191.168.14.9. The only change between these programs is the parameter used in the XOpenDisplay() call and the associated error detecting clause in Fig. 7.3. If the connection cannot be made, a NULL is returned by the XOpenDisplay() call: if successful the structure of the variable mydisplay is filled in for use by following Xlib calls.

7.2.1 Exercises

1. Modify the program of Fig. 7.3 so the network connection to be used in entered from the command line which starts execution of the program.
2. What network configuration is required to enable such programs as in Fig. 7.3 to operate? What network configuration would prevent it from operating?
3. Does X Window need to be running on the computer used to execute correctly the program in Fig. 7.3? Explain your answer.

7.3 Scalable Fonts

Initially in X Window, fonts were bitmap patterns as discussed in Sect. 5.2. Such fonts were of fixed sizes. A number of sizes, say 10, 12, or 14 point high representations of Courier, Helvetica, Bookman, and others, all in different styles, were available. Each character of each font was formed in a box of screen pixels which were mapped to the screen to show text. They could be resized, however increasing their size results in jagged edges of the font due to their bitmap formulation. The bitmap font is defined on a grid with a grid cell inside, or not inside, a character. This is completely different to the way Postscript handles fonts as described in Smith (1990). X Window now has scalable fonts analogous to those of Postscript where the outline of a character is defined mathematically and the inside of the character is the space enclosed by the mathematically defined boundary. Postscript stores the basic font styles as outlines and then the Postscript program scales the font outlines to the size required.

Scalable fonts of X Window are formulated in the same manner. With increase in font size jagged edges do not appear because the mathematical formula defining the boundary remains smooth as it is transformed to the required size. However, in contrast to Postscript, the X Window program does not scale the font. When the scalable font is loaded using the Xlib function XLoadQueryFont() the font is scaled as required in the loading process. Fonts can be scaled to any size required, both standard sizes and non-standard.

Scalable fonts now make up a large portion of the fonts in a X Window distribution. Additional scalable fonts are available from both commercial and public sources.

Running the system program xlsfonts lists all fonts available on the computer system being used. In this listing the scalable fonts are identified by having the fields -0-0-0-0- in their name, i.e 4 zero hyphen fields after the double hyphen. Most font families, examples being Courier, Bookman, and Helvetica, are available in different weights and slope are available in both fixed and scalable varieties. In the fixed resolution fields they are defined as 75 or 100 bits per inch fonts: a font from the 100 size field is larger than one from the 75 collection. Fixed size fonts control the size of objects they are used in, for example as labels or menu items, so the combination looks correct. Scalable fonts remove this size limitation.

```
/*  A program to show lines of the same alphabetic character on a
 *  white window,  Each line of characters is drawn in the same
 *  font which is scaled larger with each successive line.
 *
 *  Coded by:   Ross Maloney
 *  Date:       October 2017
 */

#include <X11/Xlib.h>
#include <X11/Xutil.h>
#include <stdio.h>
#include <string.h>
#include <stdlib.h>       /* for exit() */

char    message[]  =  "AaBbCcDdEeFfGgHhIiJjKk";
char    fontName1[]  =
        "−adobe−courier−bold−i−normal−−0−120−75−75−p−0−iso8859−1";
char    fontName2[]  =
        "−adobe−courier−bold−i−normal−−*−240−75−75−p−0−iso8859−1";
char    fontName3[]  =
        "−adobe−courier−bold−i−normal−−*−420−75−75−p−0−iso8859−1";
char    fontName4[]  =
        "−adobe−courier−bold−i−normal−−*−720−75−75−p−0−iso8859−1";

main()
{
   Display          *mydisplay;
   XSetWindowAttributes    myat;
   Window             mywindow;
   XSizeHints         wmsize;
   XWMHints           wmhints;
   XTextProperty      windowName, iconName;
   XEvent             myevent;
   GC                 myGC1, myGC2, myGC3, myGC4;
   XGCValues          myGCvalues;
   XFontStruct        *fontDetail;
   char *window_name = "Scaling";
   char *icon_name    = "Sc";
   int                screen_num, done, i;
   unsigned long      valuemask;

                  /* 1.  open connection to the server */
   mydisplay = XOpenDisplay("");

                  /* 2.  create a top−level window */
   screen_num = DefaultScreen(mydisplay);
   myat.background_pixel = WhitePixel(mydisplay, screen_num);
   myat.border_pixel = BlackPixel(mydisplay, screen_num);
   myat.event_mask = ExposureMask;
   valuemask = CWBackPixel | CWBorderPixel | CWEventMask;
```

Fig. 7.4 Producing a window with text of different sizes

```
mywindow = XCreateWindow(mydisplay,
                         RootWindow(mydisplay, screen_num),
                         60, 70, 500, 300, 3,
                         DefaultDepth(mydisplay, screen_num),
                         InputOutput,
                         DefaultVisual(mydisplay, screen_num),
                         valuemask, &myat);

                  /* 3.  give the Window Manager hints */
wmsize.flags = USPosition | USSize;
XSetWMNormalHints(mydisplay, mywindow, &wmsize);
wmhints.initial_state = NormalState;
wmhints.flags = StateHint;
XSetWMHints(mydisplay, mywindow, &wmhints);
XStringListToTextProperty(&window_name, 1, &windowName);
XSetWMName(mydisplay, mywindow, &windowName);
XStringListToTextProperty(&icon_name, 1, &iconName);
XSetWMIconName(mydisplay, mywindow, &iconName);

                  /* 4.  establish window resources */
myGCvalues.foreground = BlackPixel(mydisplay, screen_num);
valuemask = GCForeground | GCFont;
if ( ( fontDetail = XLoadQueryFont(mydisplay, fontName1) )
                 == NULL )  {
  printf("Could not load font %s\n", fontName1);
  exit(1);
}
myGCvalues.font = fontDetail->fid;
myGC1 = XCreateGC(mydisplay, mywindow, valuemask, &myGCvalues);
if ( ( fontDetail = XLoadQueryFont(mydisplay, fontName2) )
                 == NULL )  {
  printf("Could not load font %s\n", fontName2);
  exit(1);
}
myGCvalues.font = fontDetail->fid;
myGC2 = XCreateGC(mydisplay, mywindow, valuemask, &myGCvalues);
if ( ( fontDetail = XLoadQueryFont(mydisplay, fontName3) )
                 == NULL )  {
  printf("Could not load font %s\n", fontName3);
  exit(1);
}
myGCvalues.font = fontDetail->fid;
myGC3 = XCreateGC(mydisplay, mywindow, valuemask, &myGCvalues);
if ( ( fontDetail = XLoadQueryFont(mydisplay, fontName4) )
                 == NULL )  {
  printf("Could not load font %s\n", fontName2);
  exit(1);
}
myGCvalues.font = fontDetail->fid;
myGC4 = XCreateGC(mydisplay, mywindow, valuemask, &myGCvalues);
```

Fig. 7.4 (continued)

```
                    /* 5.   create all the other windows needed*/
                    /* 6.   select events for each window */
                    /* 7.   map the windows*/
         XMapWindow( mydisplay ,  mywindow );

                    /* 8.   enter the event loop */
         done = 0;
         while ( done == 0 )   {
           XNextEvent( mydisplay ,  &myevent );
           switch ( myevent.type )   {
           case  Expose :
             XDrawString( mydisplay ,  mywindow,  myGC1,  10,  20,  message ,
                     strlen ( message ));
             XDrawString( mydisplay ,  mywindow,  myGC2,  10,  90,  message ,
                     strlen ( message ));
             XDrawString( mydisplay ,  mywindow,  myGC3,  10,  180,  message ,
                     strlen ( message ));
             XDrawString( mydisplay ,  mywindow,  myGC4,  10,  280,  message ,
                     strlen ( message ));
             break;
           }
         }
                    /* 9.   clean up before exiting */
         XUnmapWindow( mydisplay ,  mywindow );
         XDestroyWindow( mydisplay ,  mywindow );
         XCloseDisplay ( mydisplay );
       }
```

Fig. 7.4 (continued)

Figure 7.4 is an example Xlib program which uses scalable fonts to draw text on a window. The text is a alphabet of alternating upper and lower case characters. This sequence of characters is repeated four times using different size of the Courier bold font with each repeat. The point fields of 120, 240, 420, and 720 request 12 point, 24 point, 42 point, and 72 point characters. These request fields indicate the scaling required. Only the 12 point size is a standard character height. The characters are loaded with a XLoadQueryFont() call, checked for having been correctly loaded, and then incorporated into a GC which is then used to display the text at a specified starting position on the window. Figure 7.5 shows the result.

With respect to Fig. 7.5 note the following. The outline of all characters remain smooth as the font size increases from top to bottom of the window. The shape of corresponding characters is the same between lines, thus scaling preserves shape. This particular font, Courier, is proportional spacing. This is evident from the A character and the i character taking up different amounts of space on the line. This is corresponds to the −p− field in the name of the font assigned in the program of Fig. 7.4. If text extends beyond a window, characters are cut smoothly as see it the case of J and F in the last two lines of text, respectively.

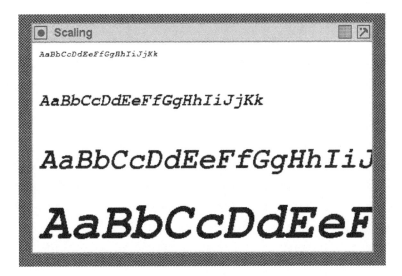

Fig. 7.5 A window with alphabet in different size Courier font

7.3.1 *Exercises*

1. Rework the program in Fig. 7.4 five times, using a different scalable font each time.
2. By changing the horizontal and vertical resolution of the font from 75 to 100 in the Fig. 7.4 program, what effect is observed in the screen image produced? Is this to be expected?
3. If the background of the GC containing the font was set to the colour green, what would be the result? What information would this give?
4. Write a Xlib program which displays a white coloured window on the screen. When the left-handle mouse button is clicked on this window a menu containing the items drink, fries, and burger appears on the screen written in a 15 point Helvetica font.

7.4 **Summary**

This chapter introduced three additions to the coverage of Xlib. Making a network connection between the client computer in which the Xlib program is executing and the server computer used to control the program has been part of X Window from it's first distribution. It needs to be mentioned. XPM and scalable fonts are additions to Xlib. XPM enables the creation of Pixmaps with more than the two colours initially available in X. Scalable fonts enable the display of text at any size thought appropriate for the program as opposed to the sizes fixed in the X Window system.

All three of these extensions are discussed and demonstrated by an example program to show their use and setting up.

Chapter 8
The Xcb Alternative

Xcb (for X-protocol C language Binding) is a recently introduced and ongoing project which is attempting to provide a more efficient programming interface to the X Window system than provided by Xlib. It is proposed by its developers to both be used with Xlib or in place of Xlib. The use of Xcb in client programming is in its infancy. It is, however, a standard part of modern X Window distributions. Despite this availability, there is minimal information available about the Xcb library interface and its use. One source of information and guidance on the use of Xcb can be obtained from the `<xcb/xproto.h>` file and the tutorial in the `doc/` directory of recent X Window System source distributions.

With respect to the treatment of Xcb given here, note the following. The programs here are cast into the same nine point division used throughout this book. The `parent` variable is a substitute for the `RootWindow()` macro of Xlib. Xcb unlocks the *request wait for reply* model of Xlib by the use of `cookies` which are only briefly mentioned.

All X Window programs whether they be written in Xlib, a toolkit, or Xcb use the same standard X Window system server. All use the same protocol exchange between the client application program and the standard X server. The writers of Xcb library functions claim to make more efficient use of this protocol.

Xcb is evolving. A problem with such evolution is a program which works on one distribution may not work the same on another. Version 1.11.1 of the Xcb distribution is considered here.

Electronic supplementary material The online version of this chapter (https://doi.org/10.1007/978-3-319-74250-2_8) contains supplementary material, which is available to authorized users.

R. J. Maloney, *Low Level X Window Programming*,
https://doi.org/10.1007/978-3-319-74250-2_8

8.1 Starting and Finishing with Xcb

An Xcb program is compiled and linked using the command:

gcc −o example −lXcb example.c

where `example.c` is the file of source code and `result` is the name to be given to the resultant file containing the executable code.

Like in a Xlib program, a Xcb client program first establishes a connection with the server. In Xlib, this is done using `XOpenDisplay()`. In Xcb, it is done using `xcb_connect()`. The form taken by the `xcb_connect()` function is:

xcb_connect(**char** *name, **int** number)

where `name` is a name to be assigned to the display, say from the system environment variable `DISPLAY`, and `number` contains the screen number to be used for the connection. Either, or both, of these parameters can be assigned to be NULL if standard values are to be used for each of these parameters. If successful, this function returns a structure of type `xbc_connection_t` which describes the connection. It cannot be freed while the connection exists.

As of version 1.11.1 of the Xcb library distribution, support is not provided for network connection between server and client which is considered in Sect. 7.2 with respect to Xlib.

This returned structure which operates the connection is opaque and not directly accessible. However, it is used as a parameter to other functions. For instance, the function `xcb_get_setup()` is available to access the members of the structure `xbc_connection_t` structure. Returned from this function is the structure `setup_t` describing the connection. The header file `<xcb/xproto.h>` contains members such as `protocol_major_version`, `image_byte_order`, and `bitmap_format_bit_order` to be part of this structure—all of which are generally of little interest to a client program. The major use of this `setup_t` structure is as the parameter to the `xcb_setup_roots_iterator()` function which is used to obtain screen information.

A single server–client connection can have multiple screens. The structure `xcb_setup_iterator_t` is defined as:

```
typedef  struct {
  xcb_screen_t    *data; /* screen pointer */
  int             rem;   /* number of screens in this connection */
  int             index;
} xcb_screen_iterator_t;
```

and is returned filled by calling the `xcb_setup_roots_iterator()` function. In this structure, the screen data structure pointed to is defined as:

```
typedef  struct {
  xcb_window_t      root;              /* root's ID number (a long) */
  xcb_colormap_t    default_colormap;
  long              white_pixel;
  long              black_pixel;
```

```
long              current_input_mask;
int               width_in_pixels;
int               height_in_pixels;
int               width_in_millimeters;
int               height_in_millimeters;
int               min_installed_maps;
int               max_installed_maps;
xcb_visualid_t    root_visual;
char              backing_store;
char              save_unders;
char              root_depth;
char              allowed_depths_len;
} xcb_screen_t;
```

Access to each screen is through the xcb_screen_t structure.

All screens and associated windows are related to the client–server connection. All are freed when this link is broken by using a xcb_disconnect() call with the connection structure returned by xcb_connect() as its parameter.

8.2   Creating and Using a Window

To produce visible output on the screen, Xlib requires the creation and use of a window, graphics context, and maybe a font. Xlib considers each of those to be a structure. Xcb also requires those same objects but considers each to be a 32-bit unsigned integer value. Subsequently, those objects are referred to by those integer value. The required value is obtained using the xcb_generate_id() function with the connection returned by xcb_connect() as its parameter.

Before it can be used, a window needs to be created. This is done using the call:

```
xcb_void_cookie_t
xcb_create_window(
       xcb_connection_t *;
       char           ; /* depth of screen */
       long           ; /* ID of window */
       long           ; /* ID of root window */
       int            ; /* x position of window's top–left point */
       int            ; /* y position of window's top–left point */
       int            ; /* width of window */
       int            ; /* height of window */
       int            ; /* width of border */
       int            ; /* class */
       xcb_visual_t   ; /* visual */
       long           ; /* value_mask */
       long *         ; /* value_list */
)
```

Note: The value_list is an array of integers. It is a parameter in a large number of Xcb function calls to provide further information to the call. There is no corresponding inclusion in the Xlib functions.

Most protocol request generating Xcb functions have this xcb_void _cookie_t return. It is available to the client program when the protocol packet is received back from the server. When the reply is received the same value is used for the duration of the connection. The function `xcb_request_check()` can be used to test whether the cookie value requested has been received. This testing enables the client program to avoid waiting for a reply. In the simplest case, this value is ignored.

In this `xcb_create_window()`, call the `value_mask` is a bit mask. It is created using one or more of the constants defined in the left-hand column of Table 8.1. Multiple constants are combined using the bitwise OR operator of the C language and the result stored in a 32-bit integer which is then included in the `xcb_create_window()` call in the `value_mask` position. The `value list` is an array where each integer element provides a value to be assigned to the constant in the `mask`, where necessary. Those values in the array must be in ascending order of the bits given in Table 8.1 for each constant used in the `value_mask`. The `class` is one of:

Window Class	Value
XCB_WINDOW_CLASS_COPY_FROM_PARENT	0
XCB_WINDOW_CLASS_INPUT_OUTPUT	1
XCB_WINDOW_CLASS_INPUT_ONLY	2

After the window is created by `xcb_create_window()`, it is know by the window ID value (an integer) which had been returned by the `xcb_generate_id()` call which was also used as a parameter in the `xcb_create_window()` call used in its creation. Having created the window is not on the screen. It is placed on the screen, and thus made visible, by the `xcb_map_window()` call.

Drawing on a window is done by using a graphics context. Like a window, a graphics context is identified by a number and this number, like in the case of a window, is obtained from the `xcb_generate_id()` function. With this identifier available, the graphics context is created by the function:

```
xcb_void_cookie_t
xcb_create_gc(
        xcb_connection_t  *;
        long              ; /* ID of GC */
        long              ; /* ID of drawable (window to draw upon) */
        long              ; /* value_mask */
        long *            ; /* value_list */
)
```

Construction of the `value_mask` and `value_list` is the same as in the window creation function but here the `value_mask` constants are from the right-hand column of Table 8.1.

With a window and a graphics context available, a drawing can be made on a window and then this window made visible on the screen. Table 8.2 lists the drawing functions available in Xcb. Each of those functions have the same parameters with exception of the last parameter which defines the data being displayed. As an example, to draw a sequence of connected straight lines, the function call is:

Table 8.1 Mask values for creating windows and graphics contexts

Window mask values	Bit	Graphics context mask values
XCB_CW_BACK_PIXMAP	0	XCB_GC_FUNCTION
XCB_CW_BACK_PIXEL	1	XCB_GC_PLANE_MASK
XCB_CW_BORDER_PIXMAP	2	XCB_GC_FOREGROUND
XCB_CW_BORDER_PIXEL	3	XCB_GC_BACKGROUND
XCB_CW_BIT_GRAVITY	4	XCB_GC_LINE_WIDTH
XCB_CW_WIN_GRAVITY	5	XCB_GC_LINE_STYLE
XCB_CW_BACKING_STORE	6	XCB_GC_CAP_STYLE
XCB_CW_BACK_PLANES	7	XCB_GC_JOIN_STYLE
XCB_CW_BACKING_PIXEL	8	XCB_GC_FILL_STYLE
XCB_CW_OVERRIDE_REDIRECT	9	XCB_GC_FILL_RULE
XCB_CW_SAVE_UNDER	10	XCB_GC_TILE
XCB_CW_EVENT_MASK	11	XCB_GC_STIPPLE
XCB_CW_DONT_PROPOGATE	12	XCB_GC_TILE_STIPPLE_ORIGIN_X
XCB_CW_COLORMAP	13	XCB_GC_TILE_STIPPLE_ORIGIN_Y
XCB_CW_CURSOR	14	XCB_GC_FONT
	15	XCB_CG_SUBWINDOW_MODE
	16	XCB_CG_GRAPHICS_EXPOSURES
	17	XCB_CG_CLIP_ORIGIN_X
	18	XCB_CG_CLIP_ORIGIN_Y
	19	XCB_CG_CLIP_MASK
	20	XCB_CG_DASH_OFFSET
	21	XCB_CG_DASH_LIST
	22	XCB_CG_ARC_MODE

Table 8.2 Xcb drawing functions

Function	Purpose
xcb_poly_point()	One or more points
xcb_poly_line()	One or more connected line segments
xcb_poly_segment()	One or more disconnected line segments
xcb_poly_arc()	A full or partial ellipse
xcb_poly_rectangle()	A box
xcb_poly_fill_poly()	Coloured in polygon
xcb_poly_fill_arc()	Coloured in full or partial ellipse
xcb_poly_fill_rectangle()	Coloured in rectangle

```
xcb_void_cookie_t
xcb_poly_line(
      xcb_connection_t    *;
      char                ; /* coordinate mode,
                              usually XCB_COORD_MODE_ORIGIN */
      long                ; /* ID of drawable */
      long                ; /* ID of GC */
      long                ; /* number of line segments */
      xcb_point_t *  ; /* drawing data */
)
```

with the drawing data given in an array like:

```
xcb_point_t {
      {int, int}, /* x and y coordinates of first point */
      {int, int), /* x and y coordinates of second point */
      {int, int} } /* x and y coordinates of third point */
```

where each pair of adjacent array entries describe a point, i.e. its coordinates. This function draws a straight line between the first and second point, the second and third point, etc. This particular array of values would correspond to drawing a set of two line segments.

An alternate manner of drawing on a window is to copy one or more bitmaps or Pixmaps to a window. These maps are fixed, prepared patterns which are identified by a value generated by the xcb_generate_id() function in the same way as for a window and a graphics context. A bitmap is a Pixmap with only two colours, black and white. Once the ID is available, the function xcb_create_Pixmap() forms the Pixmap itself. As with a window, the drawing functions of Table 8.2 can be used on bitmaps and Pixmaps which only become visible when copied to a visible window using the xcb_copy_area() function.

8.3   Communicating with the Window Manager

Xcb, like Xlib, enables a client program to communicate with the window manager of the X server. Xcb considers these as *properties* and uses the function:

```
xcb_void_cookie_t
xcb_change_property(
      xcb_connection_t    *;
      char                ; /* 8 bit mode type */
      long                ; /* ID of window */
      xcb_atom_t          ; /* property */
      xcb_atom_t          ; /* property type */
      char                ; /* format of the request */
      long                ; /* data length */
      long                ; /* pointer to the data */
)
```

to do this communication. In this call, the format is one of the value of 8, 16, or 32. The mode is one of:

Mode	Value
XCB_PROP_MODE_REPLACE	0
XCB_PROP_MODE_PREPEND	1
XCB_PROP_MODE_APPEND	2

The property and property type are both prefixed by XCB_ATOM_ which denote values from a list of pre-defined Xcb values. The property parameter is selected from:

Mode	Value
XCB_ATOM_WM_OMMAND	34
XCB_ATOM_WM_HINTS	35
XCB_ATOM_WM_CLIENT_MACHINE	36
XCB_ATOM_WM_ICON_NAME	37
XCB_ATOM_WM_ICON_SIZE	38
XCB_ATOM_WM_NAME	39
XCB_ATOM_WM_NORMAL_HINTS	40
XCB_ATOM_WM_SIZE_HINTS	41
XCB_ATOM_WM_ZOOM_HINTS	42
XCB_ATOM_WM_CLASS	67
XCB_ATOM_WM_TRANSIENT_FOR	68

while the property type is from the selection:

Mode	Value
XCB_ATOM_INTEGER	19
XCB_ATOM_PIXMAP	20
XCB_ATOM_STRING	31
XCB_ATOM_VISUALID	32
XCB_ATOM_	

In all these cases, the value is obtained from the <xcb/xcb.h> header file.

Of these available selections, the XCB_PROP_MODE_REPLACE, and XCB_ATOM_STRING are the most commonly used, particularly in giving hints for the property XCB_ATOM_WM_NAME for the name to be shown on the window title bar, and XCB_ATOM_WM_ICON_NAME for the title of the iconified window.

8.4 Events

A window can be created and made visible on the screen without events, but drawing on the window, or interacting with it through a keyboard or a mouse, uses events. The server creates events as a result of the behaviour of hardware connected to the

Table 8.3 Some of the event masks and tags for their processing

Event mask	Switch tag	Source
XCB_EVENT_MASK_EXPOSURE	XCB_EXPOSE	Window
XCB_EVENT_MASK_ENTER_WINDOW	XCB_ENTER_NOTIFY	Window
XCB_EVENT_MASK_LEAVE_WINDOW	XCB_LEAVE_NOTIFY	Window
XCB_EVENT_MASK_KEY_PRESS	XCB_KEY_PRESS	Keyboard
XCB_EVENT_MASK_KEY_RELEASE	XCB_KEY_RELEASE	Keyboard
XCB_EVENT_MASK_BUTTON_PRESS	XCB_BUTTON_PRESS	Mouse
XCB_EVENT_MASK_BUTTON_RELEASE	XCB_BUTTON_RELEASE	Mouse
XCB_EVENT_MASK_BUTTON_MOTION	XCB_MOTION_NOTIFY	Mouse
XCB_EVENT_MASK_POINTER_MOTION	xCB_MOTION_NOTIFY	Mouse
XCB_EVENT_MASK_FOCUS_CHANGE	XCB_FOCUS_CHANGE	Window
XCB_EVENT_MASK_PROPERTY_CHANGE	XCB_PROPERTY_CHANGE	Window
XCB_EVENT_MASK_BUTTON_1_MOTION	XCB_BUTTON_1_MOTION	Window
XCB_EVENT_MASK_VISIBILITY_CHANGE	XCB_VISIBILITY_CHANGE	Window

server. It then sends notification of such occurrences to the client program which has asked to be told of those specific occurrences. The client program is written to act upon each different type of events in the manner it sees as appropriate.

X Window is event driven. So like Xlib, Xcb is also event driven. Like Xlib, the events of interest to a Xcb program are specified in the attributes of a window to which the events apply. A XCB_CW_EVENT_MASK constant in the mask used in creating a window links the window to the event. When one or more of the event types in the left-hand column of Table 8.3 are included in the value_list array and also in the mask entry (logical ORed if there is more than one) when the window is created, the window is notified of the occurrence of the event.

Events are processed within an indefinite loop. In this loop, a function call to xcb_wait_for_event() is generally made to wait for notification of an event having occurred on the connection path. An alternative is a xcb_poll_for _event() call to check for an event but not to wait. Each event produces a different data structure specific to describing the circumstances of the event. However, each of those data structures contains a response_type member available from the data returned by the xcb_wait_for_event() call. Based on this, specific processing can occur at labels in the second column of Table 8.3. The final column of Table 8.3 indicates the part of the hardware which gives rise to each of the events.

Each of the events in Table 8.3 has a different structure although each has a response_type member. This common member enables quick identification of the event type received. To obtain the remaining information in the different event types, the correct type must be linked to the event received. This can be done by using the C language casting operation. Event-specific information might be in the case of a button press, the window in which the mouse pointer was located when the button creating the event, or the coordinates of the point where the mouse pointer

Table 8.4 Pattern of QWERTY keyboard key codes

Alphabetic		Non-alphabetic		
Key	Code	Key	Code	State
1	10	Left Ctrl	37	4
2	11	Right Ctrl	109	4
q	24	Left Shift	50	1
w	25	Tab	23	
e	26	Left Alt	64	8
r	27	Right Alt	113	8
a	38	PgUp	81	
s	39	PgDn	89	
z	52	Caps Lock	66	2
x	53	Esc	115	
BkSp	22	F1	67	
Space	65	Right Shift	62	1

was located (see Fig. 8.6). This information is also contained in a key press event structure, but in a different position than in the button press event.

The `reference_type` member may provide insufficient identification of the event. For example, Table 8.3 shows there is no separate event for the different buttons present on a mouse. Only button 1 motion event is shown although buttons 1 through 5 is available. However, the `detail` member of a button press (or button release) event contains the number of the button which produced the event.

When a key on the keyboard is pressed and/or released, an event is generated if the program requests this to happen using the event masks shown in Table 8.3. Included in the event message is the `key code` and `state` member, not the ASCII code for the character corresponding to the key. These two members are integer values. From these two members, the application program must construct the character. Table 8.4 indicates the pattern of the key codes. The key code of adjacent keys on a line of keys on the keyboard has adjacent integer values. For example, from Table 8.4, the `q, w` and `e` keyboard keys have integer representations of 24, 25, and 26 respectively.

On the right-hand half of Table 8.4, some of the non-alphabetic character keys on a Latin 1 keyboard are listed. Also listed with them is the value of the `state` member which accompanies the key code in a key press event structure. When a key is press alone on the keyboard, the state member is 0 (zero). This applies to all keys, both alphabetic and non-alphabetic. However, some of the non-alphabetic keys can be depressed while another key is pressed. Those non-alphabetic character keys which cannot be depressed simultaneously with another are shown with a blank in the associated *State* column entry. For the other keys, when they are depressed while another key is pressed, the key code listed in the *State* entry indicates the key's involvement. For example, typing shift q (to indicate Q), the key code would be 24 denoting the q key and the state member 1 indicating the shift key (left or right) was also depressed. The individual key state members are ORed together. For example, a control s would be indicated by a key code of 39 and a state of 4 but a control S would be indicated by a key code of 39 but with a state member of 5 (the result of 1 and 4 being logically ORed).

8.5   A Consolidation Program

Figure 8.2 is a Xcb program which creates a window and a graphics context and then draws a thick straight line coloured black across this window. The result produced on the screen is given in Fig. 8.1. Only an exposure event is used in this example.

Notice in the program of Fig. 8.2, the server/client connection is called `mypath` while in the Xlib programs `mydisplay` is used. This is to emphasise there is a difference in the way Xcb and Xlib handle this connection.

Also note the two `xcb_flush(c)` calls. These are to force the previously made requests (Xcb function calls) to be sent to the server. Also of note is the simplification which Xcb enables in sending hints to the window manager in comparison to Xlib.

Fig. 8.1 A straight line drawn by Xcb program

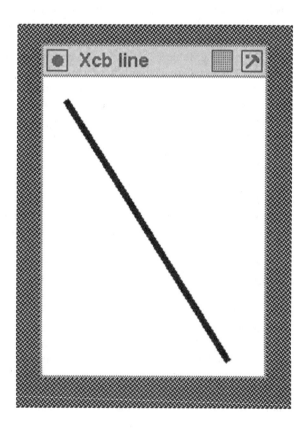

```
/*   A Xcb  program  which  draws  a  thick  black  line  across  a  window
 *   previously  created  using  a  created  GC.
 *
 *   Coded  by:    Ross  Maloney
 *   Date:         March  2016
 */

#include  <xcb/xcb.h>
#include  <string.h>

int  main(int  argc,  char  *argv)
{
  xcb_connection_t        *mypath;
  xcb_screen_t            *myscreen;
  xcb_generic_event_t     *myevents;
  xcb_screen_iterator_t   iter;
  int                     mywindow, mygc;
  int                     mask, values[3];
  char                    winName[] = "Xcb_line";
  char                    winIcon[] = "Li";
  xcb_point_t             data[] = { {20, 20}, {167, 247} };

                /* 1.  open connection to the server */
  mypath = xcb_connect(NULL, NULL);

                /* 2.  create a top-level window */
  iter = xcb_setup_roots_iterator( xcb_get_setup(mypath) );
  myscreen = iter.data;
  mywindow = xcb_generate_id(mypath);
  mask = XCB_CW_BACK_PIXEL | XCB_CW_EVENT_MASK;
  values[0] = myscreen->white_pixel;
  values[1] = XCB_EVENT_MASK_EXPOSURE;
  xcb_create_window(mypath, XCB_COPY_FROM_PARENT, mywindow,
                    myscreen->root,
                    100, 120, 200, 260, 2,
                    XCB_WINDOW_CLASS_INPUT_OUTPUT,
                    myscreen->root_visual,
                    mask, values);

                /* 3.  give the Window Manager hints */
  xcb_change_property(mypath, XCB_PROP_MODE_REPLACE, mywindow,
                      XCB_ATOM_WM_NAME, XCB_ATOM_STRING, 8,
                      strlen(winName), winName);
  xcb_change_property(mypath, XCB_PROP_MODE_REPLACE, mywindow,
                      XCB_ATOM_WM_ICON_NAME, XCB_ATOM_STRING, 8,
                      strlen(winIcon), winIcon);

                /* 4.  establish window resources */
  mygc = xcb_generate_id(mypath);
  mask = XCB_GC_FOREGROUND | XCB_GC_LINE_WIDTH;
  values[0] = myscreen->black_pixel;
  values[1] = 6;  /* line thickness */
```

Fig. 8.2 Drawing a thick black line on the screen

```
xcb_create_gc (mypath, mygc, mywindow, mask, values);

                    /* 5.  create all the other windows needed */
                    /* 6.  select events for each window */
                    /* 7.  map the windows */
xcb_map_window (mypath, mywindow);
xcb_flush (mypath);

                    /* 8.  enter the event loop */
while ( 1 ) {
  myevents = xcb_wait_for_event (mypath);
  switch ( myevents->response_type )  {
  case XCB_EXPOSE:
    xcb_poly_line (mypath, XCB_COORD_MODE_ORIGIN, mywindow,
                   mygc, 2, data);
    xcb_flush (mypath);
    break;
  }
}

                    /* 9.  clean up before exiting */
xcb_disconnect (mypath);
}
```

Fig. 8.2 (continued)

8.5.1 Exercises

1. How would the program of Fig. 8.2 behave if the mask and value array entries were not assigned values?
2. Modify the program of Fig. 8.2 so the line is drawn on a transparent background window.

8.6   Colour, Fonts, then Text

X Window uses the red, green, blue (RGB) true colour definition scheme. Each of those component primary colours can take on a value in the range 0–255 which is generally written as two hexadecimal digits. Any colour required is defined by specifying different amounts of those primary colours as a single hexadecimal RGB value.

A colour map is a table which converts a colour required by the program to that which the screen can show. Old screen controllers could only hold a limited number of RGB-defined colours. To overcome this problem, an application would fill this table with the colour RGB values it needed. However, the controllers of today's screens support all colours (although this is not completely true) so attention to the colour map is not so important. But colour map creation and filling is supported by Xcb although such functions are not commonly used on modern hardware. The colour map for the screen in use is found as the `default_colormap` field of the screen's `xcb_screen_t` structure (see Sect. 8.1).

Colour is applied in two ways: by the foreground or the background. Foreground and background colours can be defined for both a window and the graphics context which is used when drawing on the window. In this respect, defining the background colour of the window and the foreground colour of a graphics context is adequate for simple window drawing. Whereas previously, the `XCB_CW_BACK_PIXEL` and `XCB_GC_FOREGROUND` mask entries were set to white and black colours default by `white_pixel` and `black_pixel` respectively, colour as an RGB figure is through a `value_list` entry instead.

Using the foreground colour of a graphics context the functions of Table 8.2 could be used to draw on a window. Drawing text also uses a graphics context but needs both the foreground and background colours to be defined. In addition to a graphics context, drawing text also requires defining both the characters and the font with which to express them on the screen.

A font within Xcb is identified by an ID which, like in the case of a window, graphics context, and colour map is obtained from a `xcb_generate_id()` function call. This ID is linked to an available font by the call:

```
xcb_void_cookie_t
xcb_open_font(
      xcb_connection_t    * ;
      long                ; /* ID of font */
      int                 ; /* length of the font name */
      char *              ; /* name of the font */
)
```

The fonts available from a server can be found from the listing produced by running the `xlsfonts` utility program. Xcb currently cannot handle scalable fonts which is a sizeable portion of the fonts listed by `xlsfonts`. Also, the `XCB_GC_FONT` needs to be included in the `mask` when the graphics context to be used in drawing the fonts is created with the ID number of the font in the `value_list`.

A graphics context can only link with one font at a time. A general manner of changing the contents of an existing graphics context is by using the `xcb_change-_gc()` function with its `mask` and associated `value_list` to revise attributes. Only attributes given in the change call are altered. A font is one attribute.

Text is written to the window using the call:

```
xcb_void_cookie_t
xcb_image_text_8(
      xcb_connection_t   * ;
      int        ; /* length of text */
      long       ; /* ID of target drawable (window) */
      long       ; /* ID of GC */
      int        ; /* x coordinate to top–left of text on window */
      int        ; /* y coordinate to top–left of text on window */
      char *     ; /* text */
)
```

This call is best used to display one line of text with each call.

Fig. 8.3 Colour drawing by
a Xcb program

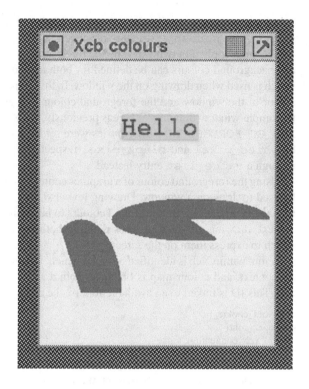

Figure 8.4 contains an example Xcb program which creates coloured text and elliptic arcs on a coloured window. Figure 8.3 shows the result produced on the screen. Notice the same foreground colour is used to draw the arcs and the text. Since the background of the graphics context used to draw the text is different than for the window, this is seen under the hello text. One difficulty of the standard available bitmap fonts is seen in Fig. 8.4. It is difficult to get large text. Although in Fig. 8.4 one of the larger fonts was used, the resulting text is small.

In programs which use a graphic content (GC) containing font information as in Fig. 8.4, it is important not to close the font, by calling `xcb_close_font()`, before creating the GC.

```
/*   This program creates of a main window on which is placed a
 *   coloured text and a partial ellipse
 *
 *   Coded by:    Ross Maloney
 *   Date:        March 2016
 */

#include <xcb/xcb.h>
#include <string.h>

int main(int argc, char *argv)
{
    xcb_connection_t      *mypath;
    xcb_screen_t          *myscreen;
    xcb_generic_event_t   *myevents;
    int                   mywindow, mygc, myfont;
    int                   mask, values[3];
    char                  winName[] = "Xcb_colours";
    char                  winIcon[] = "Col";
    xcb_arc_t         data[] = { {0, 150, 80, 140, 0, 120 << 6},
                                 {70, 130, 155, 40, 0, 290 << 6} };
    char fontname[]=
    "-adobe-courier-bold-r-normal--24-240-75-75-m-150-iso10646-1";
    char                      message[] = "Hello";


                    /* 1.  open connection to the server */
    mypath = xcb_connect(NULL, NULL);

                    /* 2.  create a top-level window */
    myscreen = xcb_setup_roots_iterator( xcb_get_setup(mypath) ).data;
    mywindow = xcb_generate_id(mypath);
    mask = XCB_CW_BACK_PIXEL | XCB_CW_EVENT_MASK;
    values[0] = 0xffff00;
    values[1] = XCB_EVENT_MASK_EXPOSURE;
    xcb_create_window(mypath, XCB_COPY_FROM_PARENT, mywindow,
                    myscreen->root,
                    300, 400, 230, 270, 2,
                    XCB_WINDOW_CLASS_INPUT_OUTPUT,
                    myscreen->root_visual, mask, values);

                    /* 3.  give the Window Manager hints */
    xcb_change_property(mypath, XCB_PROP_MODE_REPLACE, mywindow,
                    XCB_ATOM_WM_NAME, XCB_ATOM_STRING, 8,
                    strlen(winName), winName);
    xcb_change_property(mypath, XCB_PROP_MODE_REPLACE, mywindow,
                    XCB_ATOM_WM_ICON_NAME, XCB_ATOM_STRING, 8,
                    strlen(winIcon), winIcon);

                    /* 4.  establish window resources */
    mygc = xcb_generate_id(mypath);
    myfont = xcb_generate_id(mypath);
    xcb_open_font(mypath, myfont, strlen(fontname), fontname);
```

Fig. 8.4 Xcb drawing text and arcs in colour

```
mask = XCB_GC_FOREGROUND | XCB_GC_BACKGROUND | XCB_GC_FONT;
values [0] = 0xff0000;
values [1] = 0x00ffff;
values [2] = myfont;
xcb_create_gc (mypath, mygc, mywindow, mask, values );
xcb_close_font (mypath, myfont );

                    /* 5.  create all the other windows needed */
                    /* 6.  select events for each window */
                    /* 7.  map the windows */

xcb_map_window (mypath, mywindow );
xcb_flush (mypath );

                    /* 8.  enter the event loop */
while ( 1 ) {
  myevents = xcb_wait_for_event (mypath );
  switch ( myevents->response_type ) {
  case XCB_EXPOSE:
    xcb_poly_fill_arc (mypath, mywindow, mygc, 2, data );
    xcb_image_text_8 (mypath, strlen (message ), mywindow,
                      mygc, 80, 70, message );
    xcb_flush (mypath );
    break;
  }
}

                    /* 9.  clean up before exiting */
xcb_disconnect (mypath );
}
```

Fig. 8.4 (continued)

8.6.1 Exercises

1. What happens to the execution of the program in Fig. 8.4 if the `while` loop is removed from the program? Is there any advantage of having the `while` loop in place?
2. Modify the program of Fig. 8.4 so it produces jagged characters in the text string.
3. Modify the program of Fig. 8.4 so the string `Hello` is written is an ascending staircase with each stair composed on one letter from the string.
4. Why cannot a modern screen controller reproduce all colours? Is it the screen or controller hardware which is the problem?

8.7 A Classic Program Converted to Xcb

The Pountain (1998) article describes the X Window System. It includes a Xlib program which displays a white 350x250 pixel window on a screen. This window is to be located at 200 pixels to the right and 200 pixels down from the top left-hand

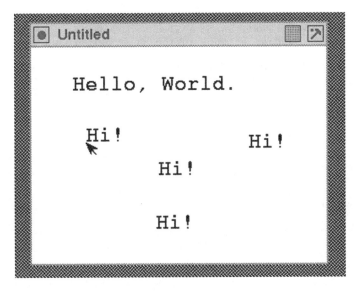

Fig. 8.5 Static text and text put in place

corner of the screen. When the window appears, the words `Hello, World` are
to be shown on it. Then as the mouse is moved over the window, pressing a mouse
button results in the word `Hi!` appearing on the window under the current position
of the mouse pointer. Typing a `q` character on the keyboard quits the program. The
character typed is not echoed onto the window.

Converting the program into Xcb produces a program which extends the examples
of Figs. 8.2 and 8.4. Neither of those examples gathered information from the mouse
regarding the position of its pointer and then uses this information to display a
string. It also receives keyboard character entry. As with those previous examples, it
needs to create a window and place it at a given position on the screen. Because the
Pountain (1998) example gave no hints to the window manager, the implementation
in Fig. 8.6 also does not. This results in the `Untitled` name across the window
header generated by the window manager, as shown in Fig. 8.5 as it shows the display
produced by the Fig. 8.6 program.

Currently, hint capability of Xcb is limited. It can indicate the name to be used
for the window and for an iconified version of the window. But it cannot instruct the
window manager as to where on the screen the window is to be shown. So the desired
initial location of (200, 200) on the screen could not be achieved in the Xcb version.

The window is created, so it can generate Xcb events when it is exposed on the
screen, when a keyboard key is pressed while the pointer is over the window, and
when a mouse button is pressed over the window. Each message resulting from
these events, like events in Xlib, is different in content, with the exception of the
`response_type` member, which is common to all event types. To enable correct
interpretation of the key press event, the event pointed to by the `myevent` variable is recast into the `xcb_key_press_event_t` structure for key press events.

```
/*    Program to create a window coloured white and print the
 *    phrase "Hello, World" on it.  Then as the mouse is moved
 *    around the window, pressing of the mouse button causes the
 *    phrase "Hi!" to be shown under the current mouse pointer
 *    position.  Typing the character 'q' on the keyboard quits
 *    the program.  The window is initially to be sited at the
 *    point (200,200) on the screen.
 *
 *    Coded by:    Ross Maloney
 *    Date:        October 2017
 */

#include <xcb/xcb.h>
#include <string.h>

int    main(int argc,    char *argv)
{

   xcb_connection_t         *mypath;
   xcb_screen_t             *myscreen;
   xcb_generic_event_t      *myevent;
   int                      mywindow, mygc, myfont, done;
   int                      mask, values[3];
   int                      x, y;
   int                      key, how;
   char   fontname[] =
      "-adobe-courier-bold-r-normal--24-240-75-75-m-150-iso10646-1";
   char   hello[] = "Hello, World.";
   char   hi[] = "Hi!";
   char   pountain[] = "Pountain";

                     /* 1.   open connection to the server */
   mypath = xcb_connect(NULL, NULL);

                     /* 2.   create a top-level window */
   myscreen = xcb_setup_roots_iterator( xcb_get_setup(mypath) ).data;
   mywindow = xcb_generate_id(mypath);
   mask = XCB_CW_BACK_PIXEL | XCB_CW_EVENT_MASK;
   values[0] = myscreen->white_pixel; /* white window background */
   values[1] = XCB_EVENT_MASK_EXPOSURE | XCB_EVENT_MASK_KEY_PRESS
               | XCB_EVENT_MASK_BUTTON_PRESS;
   xcb_create_window(mypath, XCB_COPY_FROM_PARENT, mywindow,
                     myscreen->root,
                     200, 200, 350, 250, 2,
                     XCB_WINDOW_CLASS_INPUT_OUTPUT,
                     myscreen->root_visual,
                     mask, values);

                     /* 3.   give the Window Manager hints */
                     /* 4.   establish window resources */
   mygc = xcb_generate_id(mypath);
   myfont = xcb_generate_id(mypath);
```

Fig. 8.6 Xcb drawing text and arcs in colour

```
xcb_open_font (mypath, myfont, strlen (fontname), fontname);
mask = XCB_GC_FOREGROUND | XCB_GC_BACKGROUND | XCB_GC_FONT;
values [0] = myscreen–>black_pixel; /* foreground colour */
values [1] = myscreen–>white_pixel; /* background colour */
values [2] = myfont;
xcb_create_gc (mypath, mygc, mywindow, mask, values);
xcb_close_font (mypath, myfont);

                    /* 5.   create all the other windows needed */
                    /* 6.   select events for each window */
                    /* 7.   map the windows */
xcb_map_window (mypath, mywindow);
xcb_flush (mypath);

                    /* 8.   enter the even loop */
done = 1;
while (done) {
  myevent = xcb_wait_for_event (mypath);
  switch ( myevent –>response_type )  {
  case XCB_EXPOSE:
    xcb_image_text_8 (mypath, strlen (hello), mywindow,
                      mygc, 50, 50, hello);
    xcb_flush (mypath);
    break;
  case XCB_MAPPING_NOTIFY:
    break;
  case XCB_KEY_PRESS:
    key = (( xcb_key_press_event_t *) myevent)->detail;
    how = (( xcb_key_press_event_t *) myevent)->state;
    if ( key == 24 && how == 0 )   done = 0;
    break;
  case XCB_BUTTON_PRESS:
    x = (( xcb_button_press_event_t *) myevent)->event_x;
    y = (( xcb_button_press_event_t *) myevent)->event_y;
    xcb_image_text_8 (mypath, strlen (hi), mywindow,
                      mygc, x, y, hi);
    xcb_flush (mypath);
    break;
  }
}

                    /* 9.   clean up before exiting */
xcb_disconnect (mypath);
}
```

Fig. 8.6 (continued)

Similarly, button press events are recasted using the xcb_button_press_event_t structure.

The original program received characters typed from the keyboard and tested for it being a q character. This character was interpreted as a request to terminate the program. The Xcb program checks for the key stroke corresponding to the keyboard's q key which from Table 8.4 is an integer value of 24. Any key combination containing the q key would satisfy this condition. To ensure only a lower case q character terminates the program the `state` member of the key press event must be checked for being 0 (zero). This ensures no other keys on the keyboard were depressed when the `q` character was typed.

Notice all buttons on a mouse activate the `XCB_BUTTON_PRESS` event processing in both the original Xlib and also the Xcb version of the program. Both programs do not discrimination as to which mouse button was pressed.

There are two other difference between the original and Xcb version of this program. In the original, a `MappingNotify` event was processed using a `XRefresh KeyboardMapping()` function. The event `XCB_MAPPING_NOTIFY` exists in Xcb, but the corresponding `xcb_refresh_keyboard_mapping()` function is not in the Xcb library. Also, Xcb requires the font to use in displaying text needs to be defined otherwise no text is displayed.

8.7.1 Exercises

1. Modify the original Xlib version of this program so it compiles and runs. Compare this program with the Xcb version.
2. What is the underlying reason why the original program did not compile?
3. Modify the program of Fig. 8.6 so as to use a different fonts for the hello string and the hi string.
4. Modify the program of Fig. 8.6 so instead of printing `Hi!` on the window, it draws a small checker-box pattern. The checker-box is to be of alternating red- and blue-coloured cells 10 pixels on each side with three such cells in height and width across the pattern.
5. Extend the program of Fig. 8.6 so the character typed on the keyboard is displayed on the window at the point where the mouse pointer is currently located. Consider under- and lower-case alphabetic characters only.

8.8 Summary

An overview of implementing X Window programs using Xcb is given. A lot of work has been done in creating Xcb as a recently introduced alternative to Xlib. Changes can be expected as Xcb is brought to maturity. One aim of Xcb is to enable writing programs using fewer instructions than with Xlib while retaining close correspondence with the underlying X protocol. This chapter suggests this aim is being achieved.

A coverage of window creation, creation and use of events for a mouse and keyboard, together with placing text on the window is outlined. Three full example programs are used to demonstrate the discussion. Application of colour to windows, window objects, and text is included. This is done using the same nine section approach used throughout the examples in this book.

Chapter 9
Closer to the X Protocol

Up to this point in this book, all graphics handling has been done by calls to library functions provided in the X Window System. This is a practical approach when writing programs. But X Window is a client–server relationship. Those programs are client programs. The graphic behaviour which appears is a result of the server. Graphics are produced by the client program sending particular message types to the server. If input is received by the server from a keyboard or mouse, the server sends this data as messages to the client program for its interpretation and use. There is only a finite number of such messages which the client and server can understand. Data, which do change, are embedded in such messages. Such messages are the building blocks of X Window. Every graphical interaction, whether it be drawing a window in various configurations, taking characters from a keyboard and displaying them in a window, or whatever, must be expressed in such messages. As an analogue, such messages are the machine language of X Window.

Xlib is a higher level language than such protocol messages. It is loosely analogous to assembly language. In some instances, an Xlib function will generate, or handle, a single protocol message but in most instances, the one Xlib function is associated with two, or maybe three, protocol messages. Toolkits are even higher level libraries. Their functions generally map down onto a greater number protocol messages. The progression of Xlib to toolkits makes writing of graphics program easier by increasingly embody the `glue` the designer of such toolkit libraries has used to link messages to library functions. With Xlib, such glue is at a minimum.

This chapter is concerned with what goes on *under the covers* of the X Window system. The approach is an analogue of using *assembler language* to understand the make-up of computer hardware. Here the machine language is the protocol which Xlib functions produce and their movement for creation of the operation of

---

Electronic supplementary material The online version of this chapter
(https://doi.org/10.1007/978-3-319-74250-2_9) contains supplementary material, which is available to authorized users.

245

X Window. There is little reason to write practical graphics programs in the manner shown. However, a deeper understanding of Xlib and the internal operation of X Window itself should follow.

9.1   The X Window Environment

To get close to the X Protocol, some knowledge of the composition of X Window is an advantage. The X Protocol is embedded in this system.

Since 2004 the standard distribution of X Window has been from the X.Org Foundation, which has taken over the development and distribution of X from XFree86. X Window is available for use when the X server is running on the computer. In the X.Org distributions, this server executable for Unix/Linux computers is `Xorg`.[1]

The standard manner of starting X is to use `startx` which is a front-end for `xinit`. `startx` is a shell script which in turn calls the C program `xinit` to load the server and start it executing as a daemon process. The server daemon process then runs continuously in the background without a control terminal linked to it.

When X is started for the first time on a computer, it needs to be configured for this computer. Configuration involves finding the screen size, keyboard available, mouse available, and other details. These parameters can be manually set or left to the configuration script which generally does a good job.

Following the configuration script approach. First, to generate a configuration file for the hardware on which it is to run, the command:

```
Xorg -configure
```

is issued by the `root` user. This produces the file `xorg.conf.new` in the `/root` directory. This configuration file can be edited to further tailor it to the hardware being used. However, such editing is generally not needed for modern releases of X Window.

The next step is to run the server using the configuration now available. Since there can be only one X server on a computer, any currently running X server must be terminated. Form the resulting shell terminal, the command:

```
Xorg -config /root/xorg.conf.new
```

will start the `Xorg` server. A window with black–grey–white texture pattern should appear covering the screen with a `X` marking the position of the mouse pointer. Moving the mouse about should move this indicator. This pattern indicates x Window is running but without a window manager. Using a standard keyboard, the key combination `Ctrl+Alt+backspace` will terminate the server with the window disappearing.

---

[1]From comments in the source code of `xinit` the executable of which is a means of starting X Window, the server `Xquartz` is used by Mac OS X and `XWin` for Cygwin.

The command:

```
Xorg -config /root/xorg.conf.new -terminate & \
sleep 2 ; DISPLAY=:0 xterm
```

also starts `Xorg` server but this time the terminal emulator program `xterm` also is started and appears on the screen. The screen background now is black. The command runs the `Xorg` server in the background and `xterm` in the foreground. The `-terminate` parameter tells `Xorg` to shutdown when it no longer has client programs. Before the `xterm` client is started, a delay of 2 s is requested to occur. This is to allow `Xorg` to commence running. `xterm` is to use display 0 of the computer. Any commands can be typed into `xterm`. Typing the command `exit` in the `xterm` window terminates `xterm`, and its window disappears from the screen. But from this starting technique, `xterm` is the only `Xorg` client, so this termination stops `Xorg` as well.

The Unix command `ps -aux` typed in the `xterm` window resulting from the previous initiation technique will list all processes running on the system including `Xorg`, `xterm`, and `ps` itself. The numbers in the second from the left column are the process ID of the process shown on the right-hand column of the corresponding line. It is these numbers assigned by the operating system to the processes which are used to communicate with that process.

Using the above `Xorg` starting technique is for initial configuration and trial of x Window. Every day loading of the server is done using the command:

```
startx
```

where `startx` is a standard script supplied with each X Window distribution. Notice it is run in the foreground. This script loads the `.xinitrc` file from the user's home directory. This file can be used to name a window manager which should be run to control the X Window environment which has been loaded. For example, the contents of `.xinitrc` could be:

/usr/local/bin/vtwm

to indicate the `vtwm` window manager in directory `/usr/local/bin` is to be used. Notice also this window manager is to be run in the foreground, displacing the `startx` script.

9.1.1 Exercises

1. The description above gives one method of terminating the `Xorg` server. Give two other techniques. Compare and contrast each of these three techniques?
2. Change the starting position on the screen and the foreground and background colours of the `xterm` in the above command line. How do they affect the processes indicated by `ps -aux`?

3. Verify the Xorg environment started with the above command line including xterm is an X Window environment by executing one of the previous examples of xlib programs. Are there any differences in behaviour of those program now compared with before?

4. Use startx to initiate an X Window environment containing only xterm. By using xterm or otherwise, determine the differences between this processing environment and that created via the command in the description above.

9.2 Client/Server Interaction

An X Window program does not produce graphical results itself, and it sends requests for the graphic to be produced. The X Window program is a *client* of the *server*, it is the server which produces the graphics. The server is a program which runs on the computing hardware attached to a screen, on which the graphic is to appear. Also attached to this computer hardware would be the keyboard and mouse to interact with the graphic. This hardware would have one such server program running which could interact with one or more X Window client programs. The window manager mentioned in the previous section also runs on this computer hardware. The window manager and client programs exchange packets of data with the server to obtain the services of the server which is responsible for producing the requested outcome. In this regard, the window manager is a special class of client program enabling it to make *super user* type requests of the server which are beyond those permitted by general client programs.

The operating system is required to maintain a reliable byte stream between the client program and the server. With the client and server being separate program, in Unix/Linux this implies separate processes to be maintained by the Unix/Linux operating system together with interprocess communications between those processes. There are a number of interprocess communication techniques available in such an environment as detailed in Gray (1998). Of these, X Window uses the socket mechanism to provide both communications between client and server processes whether they be on one computer or between two computers connected by a network. The client program requests connection to the server by an XOpenDisplay() call. The local or remote connection required is contained in the parameters passed in this call. The code implementing the call interacts with the operating system to use its appropriate socket connection between this client's process and the server process before passing X Window specific data across this link to synchronize the client to the server. Once established, the connection between client and server remains open until called, mainly by the client, to close.

The file x11protocol.pdf available from the X.Org web site for X11 release 7.7 describes the X Window protocol as consisting of four packet types. Those four types are Request, Reply, Error, and Event. Table 9.1 provides a summary of those packet types using the data from Appendix B of that x11protocol.pdf file. Each Request contains a single byte Op Code. Only 120 of those are implemented,

Table 9.1 Overview of X Window's protocol packets

Type	Number	Size
Request	120	4 bytes +
Reply	41	32 bytes +
Error	17	32 bytes
Event	33	32 bytes

with those between 128 and 255 meant for extensions of this standard code. Such requests also contain additional data which refines the Op Code, the window or windows involved in the request, etc. The smallest Request packet is a request to sound the bell and is 4 bytes in length. Of those 120 Request packets, 41 can result in a Reply packet being sent back from the server to the client program. The minimum size of such a Reply packet is 32 bytes. A Request can also result in an Error packet, and there are 17 different types of them, each 32 bytes in length. The 33 event packets are generally generated by the client program resulting from actions of the program user. These Event packets are a constant length of 32 bytes, but all bytes may not be used by a particular event. The format of each member of the four packet types is detailed in the `x11protocol.pdf` file from the `X.Org` web site.

Table 9.2 shows the Xlib functions used in this book and their X protocol implementations as given in Appendix A of Gettys and Scheifler (2002). Although this table is not a complete picture of the Xlib function-to-protocol relationships, it shows important features. In most case, there is a one-to-one correspondence between the Xlib function and the protocol. In a number of cases, there is no protocol implementation. Code to service such calls and the data required are part of the client program itself. Those with and without protocol relations are listed together.

Of particular note is the functions listed in Table 9.2 which have no associated protocol request. These play a central roll in writing Xlib programs. The `XCloseDisplay()` function enables the client to open the client/server connection. Colour management via the CMS Color Management System is performed with the `XCmsLookupColor()` function. Data such as defining the root window, the screen white and black pixel values, text properties, and the availability of screen backing store have no protocol request. The `XFlush()` function which enables the client to force all events which have been queued to be sent immediately to the server is in this grouping. With no protocol request, there is no way the client can request the service corresponding to the function call from the server. Implementation of these non-protocol generating functions are implemented as code which is part of the client's code. This positioning is taken advantage of by the `Default` attribute calls such as colourmap, depth, screen, and visual which are implemented as C language macro calls.

The Xlib function `XNextEvent()` is interesting. It has no associated protocol but has a central roll in the execution of a X client program. It is a client function which blocks its own execution until an event message is received from the server.

In operation, the Xlib protocol locks a reply to a request. After a request is sent by the client to the server, the client program pauses execution while it waits for the reply

Table 9.2 Linking Xlib functions used in examples to their protocol request

Xlib function	Protocol request	Op Code
XAllocNamedColor()	AllocNamedColor	85
XBell()	Bell	105
XChangeWindowAttributes()	ChangeWindowAttributes	2
XCleanWindow()	ClearArea	61
XConfigureWindow()	ConfigureWindow	12
XCopyArea()	CopyArea	62
XCopyPlane()	CopyPlane	63
XCreateBitmapFromData()	CreateGC	55
	CreatePixmap	53
	FreeGC	60
	PutImage	72
XCreateGC()	CreateGC	55
XCreatePixmap()	CreatePixmap	53
XCreateBitmapFromBitmapData()	CreateGC	55
	CreatePixmap	53
	FreeGC	60
	PutImage	72
XCreateSimpleWindow()	CreateWindow	1
XCreateWindow()	CreateWindow	1
XDestroyWindow()	DestroyWindow	4
XDrawArc()	PolyArc	68
XDrawImageString()	ImageText8	76
XDrawLine()	PolySegment	66
XDrawString()	PolyText8	74
XDrawText()	PolyText8	74
XFillArc()	PolyFillArc	71
XFillPolygon()	FillPoly	69
XFillRectangle()	PolyFillRectangle	70
XGetImage()	GetImage	73
XLoadQueryFont()	OpenFont	45
	QueryFont	47
XMapWindow()	MapWindow	8
XMoveWindow()	ConfigureWindow	12
XPutImage()	PutImage	72
XSelectInput()	ChangeWindowAttributes	2
XSendEvent()	SendEvent	25
XSetBackground()	ChangeGC	56
XSetClipMask()	ChangeGC	56
XSetClipOrigin()	ChangeGC	56

(continued)

Table 9.2 (continued)

Xlib function	Protocol request	Op Code
XSetFont()	ChangeGC	56
XSetForeground()	ChangeGC	56
XSetLineAttributes()	ChangeGC	56
XSetWindowBackground()	ChangeWindowAttributes	2
XSetWindowBackgroundPixmap()	ChangeWindowAttributes	2
XSetWMHints()	ChangeProperty	18
XSetWMIconName()	ChangeProperty	18
XSetWMName()	ChangeProperty	18
XSetWMNormalHints()	ChangeProperty	18
XUngrabPointer()	UngrabPointer	27
XUnmapWindow()	UnmapWindow	10
XWarpPointer()	WarpPointer	41
XOpenDisplay()		
XCloseDisplay()		
XCmsLookupColor()		
XDefaultColormap()		
XFlush()		
XKeycodeToKeysym()		
XLookupString()		
XMaxRequestSize()		
XNextEvent()		
XRebindKeysym()		
XStringListToTextProperty()		
XTextWidth()		
BlackPixel()		
DefaultDepth()		
DefaultScreen()		
DefaultVisual()		
DoesBackingStore()		
DoesSaveUnders()		
RootWindow()		
WhitePixel()		

or error message from the server to be received. There is a one-to-one correspondence between a request and what is returned for a specific request. In execution, when a Xlib function is encountered, the execution of the client program is paused (locked) after the protocol is sent to the server, it then waits for the reply to occur. When the reply is received, the program is unlocked and execution continues beyond the Xlib function. Although the server can stack a number of requests from any one server, in Xlib this is not the case. So a delay will occur if a number of requests are required to be sent by the client. From a protocol perspective, Xlib is more restricted than the general capacity of the X Window system. This behaviour of Xlib may or may not be significant to the overall required performance of the client application.

9.2.1 Exercises

1. Use the Xlib functions listed in Table 9.2 as a revision of their operational relation shown in the programs of this book.
2. Would there be an advantage in implementing some of the functions listed in Table 9.2 on the server? This would require an extension to the protocol. Which of those functions could be moved and discuss the advantage and disadvantage of each move.
3. It is often stated X Window via its protocol presents a low load on a network. Discuss this statement with respect to an appropriate selection of Xlib functions listed in Table 9.2 which would produce a functional X client program.
4. Review the example programs of this book for the effect the locking behaviour of Xlib would have on the performance of each program and the significance of such locking.

9.3   More than a Protocol is Required

The underlying protocol implementing Xlib functions leads to the communications efficiency of programs in which they are a part. Without the protocol, a client program could not request services from the server. The server handles all input and output related to the graphical interface of the client program. With no server, then interacting using the graphical interface would not be available or the code to do it would need to be in the client itself. Also, one server can serve more than one client which reduces the memory footprint of implementing graphics programming in the practical situation of many concurrent program running. By using the protocol, a client can communicate with a server either on the same computer using interprocess communications or between computers connected by a network employing enhanced interprocess communications. So the protocol is central to the character of Xlib and X Window in general.

Consider a basic program to obtain some appreciation of efficiency and operation of the protocol involved with a Xlib program. This program operated correctly but with minimum complexity such as error checking. It is not meant as a practical program, but one constructed for purpose demonstrating the protocol requests sent by a X client program and the X server.

Figure 9.1 is this basic Xlib program. It displays a 350x250 pixel window with a white background on the screen. It then draws a straight line, black in colour, on this window. A number of simplifications have been made in this program including:

1. Hints to the window manager were removed. This includes those which enabled the program to control how the program first appears on the screen. But there are defaults for such behaviours which are used here. The structures for such *hints* to the window manager are contained in the Xutil.h header file. With no hints, this file was also not needed.

2. The XNextEvent(mydisplay, &myevent) call inside the infinite while loop was necessary for the window to appear on the screen with the only event being an exposure.

3. The valuemask variable was required for the call to XCreateWindow() to be successful by indicating background colour, border colour, and an exposure mask was required were set for the window being formed.

4. No cleaning up prior to program termination was to be performed.

5. The call to DefaultScreen() to define screen_num was replaced by the default value 1 which the call generally returns.

6. The myat.background_pixel variable was assigned the value 0xffffff instead of calling WhitePixel() to define this value.

7. The myat.border_pixel variable was assigned the value 0 instead of calling BlackPixel() to set this value.

8. Screen depth was assigned the value 24 instead of calling DefaultDepth().

9. The value 28 was used to indicate foreground and background colours which were defined for the GC together with the width of a line.

The resulting program after such simplifications works but with lost utility and generality. It also violates a number of the programming model conditions which were the foundation of previous chapters.

A client initially sends bytes specifying whether little- or big-ended data transmission is to be used and an identification of the protocol version proposed for use. This agreement must be made for each client and server combination. The XOpenDisplay() initiates this interaction. The argument of this call determines whether the server is local or remote from the computer on which the client is running. In the case of the program in Fig. 9.1, it is local.

The program of Fig. 9.1 contains four Xlib functions which generate protocol requests which are passed to the server by the client across the established link. The minimum content of a protocol request is the operations code (Op code) and a request length. The request length is the total length of the request packet expressed in units of 32-bit words (4-byte units).

With respect to the program of Fig. 9.1, the contents of the protocol packets would be the following. In this formulation, decimal numbers are used except when prefixed by 0x. The XCreateWindow() call uses the CreateWindow protocol packet which would be formed as:

Note the following with respect to this packet. The value-mask is the value of valuemask which is computed by OR operation on the values CWBackPixel (hex constant 2) and CWBorderPixel (hex constant 8). The screen is assumed to be of depth 24 and the window to be of class InputOutput (represented as 1) in the CreateWindow packet. It has been assumed the value returned from the

```
/* Creating of a window using the minimum of xlib calls.
 *
 * Coded by:   Ross Maloney
 * Date:       March 2016
 */

#include  <X11/Xlib.h>

int   main(int argc , char *argv [])
{
  Display                *mydisplay;
  XSetWindowAttributes   myat;
  Window                 mywindow;
  XEvent                 myevent;
  GC                     gc;
  XGCValues              values;
  unsigned long          valuemask;
  int                    screen_num , done;

                    /* 1. open connection to the server */
  mydisplay = XOpenDisplay ("");

                    /* 2. create a top-level window */
  screen_num = 0;
  myat.background_pixel = 0xffffff;
  myat.border_pixel = 0;
  myat.event_mask = ExposureMask;
  valuemask = CWBackPixel | CWBorderPixel | CWEventMask;
  mywindow = XCreateWindow(mydisplay ,
                           RootWindow(mydisplay , screen_num),
                           200,  440,  350,  250,  2,
                           24,  InputOutput ,
                           DefaultVisual(mydisplay , screen_num),
                           valuemask , &myat);

                    /* 3. give the Window Manager hints */
                    /* 4. establish window resources */
  values.foreground = 0;
  values.background = 0xffffff;
  values.line_width = 6;
  gc = XCreateGC(mydisplay , mywindow, 28, &values);

                    /* 5. create all the other windows needed */
                    /* 6. select events for each window */
                    /* 7. map the windows */
  XMapWindow(mydisplay , mywindow);

                    /* 8. enter the event loop */
```

Fig. 9.1 Simple Xlib program to draw a single window

```
while ( 1 ) {
  XNextEvent(mydisplay , &myevent );
  switch ( myevent.type )  {
  case Expose:
    XDrawLine(mydisplay ,  mywindow ,  gc ,  20 ,  30 ,  80 ,  200);
    break ;
  }
}
}

                      /* 9. clean up before exiting*/
}
```

Fig. 9.1 (continued)

Field size [bytes]	Field content description	Content for program
1	opcode	1
1	depth	24
2	request length	11
4	window ID	
4	parent ID	10003
2	x	200
2	y	440
2	height	350
2	width	250
2	border-width	2
2	class	1
4	visual	1
4	value-mask	0x8a
4	background-pixel	0xffffff
4	border-pixel	0
4	event-mask	0x8000

RootWindow() call is 10003, and 0 (representing CopyFromParent from the DefaultVisual()) call. The place for the window ID number this is not set. This value is returned to the client from the server and in this case (say) this value is 10444. The value-mask indicates only the background-pixel, border-pixel event mask follow the value-mask field of the protocol packet.

The second Xlib call protocol packet generated would be:

Field size [bytes]	Field content description	Content for program
1	opcode	55
1	unused	
2	request length	7
4	cid	
4	drawable	10444
4	value-mask	0x1c
4	foreground	0
4	background	0xffffff
2	line-width	6

This results from the XCreateGC() call which uses the CreateGC packet encoding. It also uses the ID number returned from the previous XCreateWindow() call. This packet requests a graphics context (GC) to be created having foreground and background colour defined and the line drawing width set to 6 pixels. The packet is padded by two extra bytes after the line-width field. In the following packet formulations, it is assumed the ID of the gc returned by the server is 34.

The window which has been created is made visible on the screen by the XMapWindow() call which uses the MapWindow protocol encoding. For this program, this encoding is:

Field size [bytes]	Field content description	Content for program
1	opcode	8
1	unused	
2	request length	2
4	window	10444

Finally, the required line is drawn on the window by the XDrawLine() Xlib call using the PolyLine protocol encoding:

Field size [bytes]	Field content description	Content for program
1	opcode	65
1	coordinate-mode	0
2	request length	7
4	drawable	10444
4	gc	34
4	x1	20
4	y1	30
4	x2	80
4	y2	200

Assuming big-ended data transmission is agreed upon, the request hexadecimal byte stream for the program of Fig. 9.1 becomes:

```
01 18 00 0b xx xx xx xx 00 00 27 13 00 c8 01 b8 01 5e 00 fa
00 02 00 01 00 00 00 01 00 00 00 8a ff ff ff ff 00 00 00 00
00 00 80 00
37 xx 00 07 xx xx xx xx 00 00 28 cc 00 00 00 1c 00 00 00 00
ff ff ff ff 00 06 xx xx
08 00 00 02 00 00 28 cc
41 00 00 07 00 00 28 cc 00 00 00 22 00 00 00 14 00 00 00 1e
00 00 00 50 00 00 00 c8
```

where the horizontal line divides one request from the next. In this sequence, an xx is used to indicate what the client's Xlib call inserts are undefined.

No matter whether the server is local or remote to the client, the byte stream exchanged is the same. The X Window system provides the interface to the process communications available on the computers.

From this example program, the communications overhead using Xlib can be seen. This example indicates 44 bytes are needed to create a window, 28 bytes to create a drawing palette, 8 bytes to make the window visible on the screen, and 28 bytes to draw a line. Each is a separate packet. Each would fit into a single Ethernet type packet for network cartage.

There is more to the X Window system than the underlying protocol. As shown in Table 9.2, Xlib has a number of functions which do not have protocol counterparts. Instead, those functions manipulate data structures which the library embodies into the code of the client when it is compiled and linked. Also there is more to using the protocol than creating it. The Xlib contains constants (e.g. CWBackPixel used in creating the window mask) which assist writing client code in a portable fashion. There is also more involved in creating a link between a client and server than finding their process identifications and then establishing a (say) socket link between them. The XOpenDisplay() Xlib function hides those complexities and does the processing—silently.

This simple example demonstrates the mapping involved in converting Xlib calls and the data in their parameters into protocol messages for passing from client to server. Most Xlib programs contain more than four Xlib calls and thus the packets for passing become more numerous. The availability of macros in Xlib such as DefaultVisual(), DefaultDepth(), WhitePixel(), and others make coding simpler. Then there are the packets passed back from the server to the client which may contain data or error indicators. The unpacking of these, as is the packing of, protocol packets are most productively handled by the Xlib function library.

9.3.1 Exercises

1. With the simplifications introduced in arriving at the coding in Fig. 9.1, what are the consequences to the operation of the program?
2. How does the code of Fig. 9.1 behave if the values assigned to screen_num and my.border_pixel are incorrect for the computer set-up used for its execution?
3. Modify the code of Fig. 9.1 to produce a yellow-coloured window.
4. Modify the code of Fig. 9.1 so the code generates the window on another computer connected across a TCP/IP network. How does such a change affect the protocol packets which implement the program's graphical behaviour?
5. How does the availability of macros in Xlib assists Xlib programming?
6. Start a X server and then pass the example protocol messages through to it. Is the required result produced on the screen? If not, what is missing?

7. Compare the efficiency of the protocol exchange of this example with a program to perform the same operation of creating a window on the screen using Windows Application Programming Interface (API).

9.4 Summary

X Window is a client–server graphics system. In this system, only the server does the interaction with the computer hardware to generate graphics. The client program needs to ask the server to perform the graphics operations it wants.

This chapter has looked at X Window from the layers of its formation. If the server is to operate on the hardware, then it needs to be configured. The techniques of doing this have been shown. First the server was shown to be an executable process installed on the computer when then X Window system is loaded. This process is different from the window manager which the user of the system most often sees. The functions of Xlib were then related to the protocol encodings available by using a purpose-written client program. Some detail has been given of the protocol which is exchanged between the server and the client for this specific example. Through the encoding of those Xlib functions into their corresponding protocols, the communications overhead imposed were indicated as being low.

References

Champine GA (1991) MIT Project Athena: a model for distributed campus computing. Digital Press, Massachusetts, USA

Gettys J, Scheifler RW (2002) Xlib - c language x interface: X consortium standard. Technical report, The Open Group, ftp://mirror.csclub.uwaterloo.ca/x.org/X11R7.7/doc/libX11/libX11/libX11.pdf

Gray JS (1998) Interprocess communications in Unix: The Nooks & Crannies, 2nd edn. Prentice Hall, Upper Saddle River

Hors AL, Nahaboo C (1991) XPM: the x Pixmap format. http://koala.ilog.fr/ftp/pub/xpm/xpm-2-paper.ps.gz. Accessed 1 Dec 2007

Mansfield N (1993) The joy of X: an overview of the X window system. Addison-Wesley, Wokingham, England

Nye A (ed) (1993) Xlib Reference manual for version 11, vol 2, 3rd edn for x11, release 4 and release 5 edn. O'Reilly & Associates, Inc., Sebastopol, California

Nye A (1995) Xlib Programming manual for version 11, vol 1, 3rd edn for version 11 of the x window system edn. O'Reilly & Associates, Inc., Sebastopol, California

Pountain D (1998) The x window system. Byte 14(1):353–4–356–60

Scheifler RW, Gettys J, Newman R (1988) X window system: C library and protocol reference. Digital Press, Bedford, Massachusetts

Smith R (1990) Learning postscript: a visual approach. Peachpit Press, Berkeley, California

© Springer International Publishing AG, part of Springer Nature 2017
R. J. Maloney, *Low Level X Window Programming*,
https://doi.org/10.1007/978-3-319-74250-2

Index

© Springer International Publishing AG, part of Springer Nature 2017
R. J. Maloney, *Low Level X Window Programming*,
https://doi.org/10.1007/978-3-319-74250-2

Printed in the United States
By Bookmasters